Covenant of Grace Renewed

Covenant of Grace Renewed

A Vision of the Eucharist in the Seventeenth Century

KENNETH STEVENSON

Foreword by Richard Holloway

DARTON·LONGMAN + TODD

First published in 1994 by
Darton, Longman and Todd Ltd
1 Spencer Court
140–142 Wandsworth High Street
London SW18 4JJ

ISBN 0–232–52061–5

A catalogue record of this book is available
from the British Library

Phototypeset in 10/12½pt Goudy by Intype, London
Printed and bound in Great Britain
at the University Press, Cambridge

For Sarah

CONTENTS

FOREWORD

I read the typescript of Kenneth Stevenson's magisterial and affectionate study of Anglican eucharistic thought in the Seventeenth Century
while I was leading a mission in a British university. We didn't push
the word mission, describing it rather as a presentation of Christian
faith in the university. The enterprise engaged the support and participation of every Christian group in the university except one. All the
main chaplains were involved, including the Roman Catholic. Christian members of staff were particularly prominent, not only in attendance at the various events, but in leading seminars on science and
religion, the role of art, and so on. The students involved came from
most of the churches in this country and it was easy to see the whole
enterprise as a prophetic foretaste of what a united Christian movement
could achieve. The mission was itself an act of unity and an expression
of our one-ness in Christ.

Except, of course, for the one group that not only held itself aloof
but uttered imprecations against us. This group was of no single
denomination, but it could accurately be described as the fundamental-
ist tendency in Christianty. This tendency is dominant and assertive
in university circles and appropriates exclusive rights on the word
Christian. I found myself at several points during the two weeks of the
mission engaging not in debate, because no debate was possible, but
in a frustrating encounter with exponents of this position. Productive
dialogue on any topic has to take place close to the frontiers where
ideas collide or share a common boundary. There has to be continuity
as well as discontinuity. Above all, there has to be an attempt to

understand the other and a desire to respect the integrity of ideas one
does not share. In my encounter with these young fundamentalists
there was none of that. There was absolute assurance on their part
that they were right about everything and that no other way of holding
the Christian faith was possible and, indeed, that only theirs was the
way to salvation.

We have been here before in Christian history, particularly in the
seventeenth century. This is why I found Kenneth Stevenson's book
something of an anti-depressant. It is easy to become obsessed by our
own problems and to see the difficulties of our own day as uniquely
intractable. That's why it is wise to read history, to identify the ways
in which we go on repeating it. Kenneth Stevenson's affectionate
portrait of the seventeenth century concentrates on the evolution of
a particularly Anglican eucharistic theology. Almost any theological
topic could have been used to demonstrate what we might call the
Anglican Method in Theology, but the eucharist is probably the best
model, because it touches on all the great Christian mysteries and
gathers them into a single vision.

Behind this attractive study of Richard Hooker and Lancelot
Andrewes, William Laud and William Forbes, John Cosin and Daniel
Brevint, Jeremy Taylor and Richard Baxter, Herbert Thorndike and
Simon Patrick, we certainly hear the sounds of battles long ago. We
revisit the great Puritan controversies as they touched, not only on
the nature of the eucharist but on the nature of Christian ministry, the
doctrine of salvation and the status of holy scripture. And glowering
in the background is the great Roman Catholic theory of transubstantiation, which has mesmerised and distorted eucharistic thought for
centuries. At first Anglican theology appears to be reactive, the exas-
perated response of easygoing, good-natured men to the crazy prejudices
of neighbours who insist on disturbing their peace. But increasingly,
as these pages show, there emerges in Anglican thought and experience
a positive and integrating vision that, at its best, still exemplifies
Anglican theological method.

In this scholarly but accessible study of seventeenth-century writing
on the eucharist, Kenneth Stevenson has sketched a portrait of a
theological method that can be applied to every Christian controversy
and not just to the eucharist. First of all, he identifies it as a genuinely
ecumenical theology that integrates insights from other traditions,
which were often seen in opposition, into fruitful new paradoxes.

Related to this is the emergence of what he calls 'a synthesis of continuity and discontinuity'. Valid theological method is always a conversation between the past, the present and what we can discern of the future. This means that theology is a living reality that changes and develops, not a sort of pass-the-parcel game in which each generation hands on the same tattered object to the next.

Another crucial element in the Anglican theological method, which is particularly appropriate to this study, is the relationship between theology and prayer. Each of the subjects in this book was a man of prayer in whom theology constantly merged into devotion and back again. It is this almost erotic element in theological study that saves it from the chilly neutrality of the modern techno-theological method, which engages only the mind and rarely touches the heart. Kenneth Stevenson adduces other aspects of the seventeenth century eucharistic vision, but these, it seems to me, are the main enduring characteristics from which we have still much to learn.

In commending this study, however, I wish to end on a cautionary note. Britain in the seventeenth century was technically a Christian nation. It was certainly a disputatious nation with no settled understanding of the word Christian, and the Caroline Divines sought to place the eucharist at its heart. They wanted to gather the people of God round the table of the Lord. In that they have largely succeeded. The eucharist is the normative act of worship for Anglicans today in a way that it wasn't in the seventeenth century. However, we now face a profounder problem. For them, the people of God were already gathered together and the question was what to do with them. In our day, the people of God are scattered abroad. We are no longer gathered as a nation, but only as tiny groups within the nation. Were Hooker and Andrewes and Taylor alive today they would, I am sure, be struggling with the challenge of how to be a gathering people sent into the world, not only to set the table and make it glorious, but to call people to share in it.

Richard Holloway
*Bishop of Edinburgh and Primus
of the Scottish Episcopal Church*

PREFACE

The idea for writing this book really started when it began to dawn on me how central the seventeenth-century divines are for their own time and for ours, and how inaccessible their works are to most people today. The nineteenth-century editions of their writings are only available in libraries. C. W. Dugmore's book on their eucharistic theology was published in 1942 and is long since out of print. There seemed to be a case for a study that would be more focused than his. I decided to write on a smaller selection of people, which would enable me to concentrate on the circumstances under which they wrote (hence the biographical sketches), the different kinds of works they produced, and – where appropriate – special features in their use of language.

In offering the following pages to the reader, I do not lay claim to any originality, nor indeed to have said it all. But I hope I have brought alive to a fresh generation how significant is the tradition represented by these divines, not only for the Church of England and for Anglicanism in general, but also for the whole Church Catholic. While the spotlight has generally – and rightly – fallen on Richard Hooker and Lancelot Andrewes, I have supported and amplified more recent studies of Jeremy Taylor and Richard Baxter in underlining their prominence too. William Laud and John Cosin have reputations primarily in the crucial area of liturgical presentation, which has tended to underplay their gifts as theologians. Above all, however, I have set out to demonstrate the importance of four neglected writers, William Forbes and Daniel Brevint, and Herbert Thorndike and Simon Patrick. Far more work needs to be done on each one of them. Indeed, it is something of an embarrassment that only one – Taylor – should have elicited a special study of his eucharistic theology, and that is the recent distinguished work by Henry McAdoo.

In recent months, I sense that I have got to know them all personally, as I have read – and re-read – much of their work, which has often felt like coming home. In many cases, I have used their prayers for the eucharist myself, which has at least helped me to experience part of their work in context. There have been many moments when I have wondered which century I was living in, because – with the notable exception of the Civil War! – a series of interesting parallels stands between our own time and theirs. Several questions emerge, such as authority, an inclusive or exclusive Church, imaginative and resonant imagery in preaching and liturgy, and also the sense of awe and wonder before the intimate and apparently familiar words, actions and symbolism of the eucharist.

Many people deserve my thanks for the formation of the ideas contained in these pages. Over the years, Geoffrey Cuming and Richard Buxton began to fire my enthusiasm for the seventeenth century. More recently, however, I owe a great debt to Donald Allchin, Henry McAdoo, and Christopher Cocksworth. Each one of them read the first draft of this book and made many shrewd and helpful comments. They have influenced me far more than they perhaps realise. On more specific issues, Nicholas Lossky, Gordon Wakefield, Bryan Spinks, David Stancliffe, Colin James, Paul Avis, Stephen Sykes, Geoffrey Rowell, Roger Greenacre, and Charles Miller have all given me assistance and encouragement in one way or another. David Scott kindly agreed to make his own fresh translation of Andrewes' eucharistic devotions which is reproduced in full in the course of the Andrewes chapter. My father, Eric Stevenson, offered much wisdom on the connections between liturgy and architecture, and my only sadness is that he died before I started writing this book.

I have to thank, too, the Parish of Holy Trinity and St Mary's, Guildford, for allowing me leave of absence over the summer of 1993 to read, think, and write – a venture in which Frank Telfer gave much encouragement and assistance. In particular, I want to thank Stephen Baker, the senior curate, and Stephen Bampfylde, the vice-chairman of the PCC, for taking over during that absence and for their spirit of understanding in doing so. Perhaps there are some Guildford folk who may recognise in these pages material they have heard in sermons and devotional addresses of late. Morag Reeve, of Darton, Longman and Todd, showed immediate interest in the project, and the libraries of Guildford Cathedral, Sion College, and Westminster Abbey have been unfailing in their help. The family have put up with me for long enough, and Sarah, my wife, read the script and asked astringent questions. On the production side, James, our son, was a patient and efficient tutor in word-processing technique – on a machine generously lent and tended by Philip Spencer, a friend and parishioner. For all this – and much more – I am deeply grateful.

KENNETH STEVENSON
Guildford, Holy Cross Day, 1993

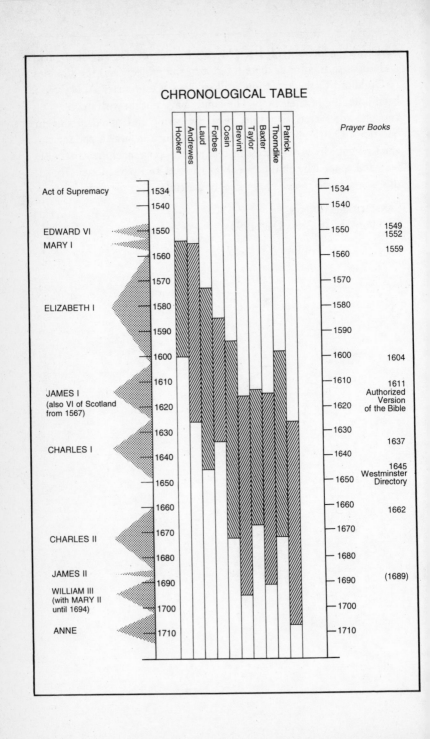

CHRONOLOGICAL TABLE

Hooker · Andrewes · Laud · Forbes · Cosin · Brevint · Taylor · Baxter · Thorndike · Patrick

Prayer Books

Act of Supremacy	1534
	1540
EDWARD VI	1550
MARY I	
	1560
	1570
ELIZABETH I	1580
	1590
	1600
	1610
JAMES I (also VI of Scotland from 1567)	1620
	1630
CHARLES I	1640
	1650
	1660
CHARLES II	1670
	1680
JAMES II	
WILLIAM III (with MARY II until 1694)	1690
	1700
ANNE	1710

Prayer Books:
1534
1540
1549
1552
1559
1604
1611 Authorized Version of the Bible
1637
1645 Westminster Directory
1662
(1689)

CHAPTER ONE

Setting the Scene

William Schellinks was a Dutch painter and poet who visited England in the company of two of his fellow-countrymen, Jacques and Jacobi Thierry, father and son, between the years 1661 and 1663. It was part of a grand tour of the continent of Europe. Fortunately for posterity, Schellinks has left behind a full chronicle of his stylish visit, in which he gives a neat and sometimes amusing account of what happened to them. On 11th September, 1662, on their journey from Winchester to the Isle of Wight, they stayed at Weston, where the following events took place:

> At six o'clock in the evening the Bishop of Winchester came into the town and was met and accompanied by the gentry; sitting in his carriage, he was welcomed in front of Holy Rood Church and the town hall by the aldermen and the mayor, and continued to his lodgings at the mayor's house, while all the church bells rang like possessed. There was not enough accommodation in the town for all his large suite. The Bishop came there to introduce the new order of service and to change and abolish the old customs.

Three days later, on the 14th, we find them on the island, having travelled there by ferry to East Cowes, and from there to Newport:

> When we got there we went to the church; the service was over and the Bishop proceeded with the confirmation of the people and blessing by laying on of hands: there was such an immense crowd

of people who, without any order, jostled each other as if they
were to get money.

Note: When I saw that every Tom, Dick, and Harry were
confirmed by the Bishop by the hundred, without any examination
or distinction, I joined the crowd and pushed into the choir and
received the blessing from Bishop Morley of Winchester. After
the blessing was done, he delivered a long oration to the listeners
in the church about the episcopal authorities' present form of
service, after that he went to the St George Inn and held there
a large banquet with the governor, the mayor, and many others.
Meanwhile all the militia remained at arms.[1]

What Schellinks so innocently describes here is a pair of local
implications of the event which dominates our study – the imposition
of The Book of Common Prayer on the Church of England in 1662.
Many of the ingredients are there: a new bishop, George Morley,
anxious to get about his diocese in the full style of his time in order
to associate his ministry with that new Book; the local populace in
both cases turning up to see him in action; and a mass-confirmation
without let or hindrance (which even includes our Dutch Calvinist
visitor), probably the first such for many years, and certainly quite
unknown in the years since the abolition of Prayer Book and bishops
by Parliament in 1645. In the intervening years, only Puritan forms of
worship were legal throughout the realm, and it was these practices
(dubbed 'old customs', now being abolished, by Schellinks) that were
to go. The Establishment had changed with the arrival on the throne
of Charles II, and with a new Establishment came inevitably the
kind of Church identified with the monarchy, which had bishops and
a strictly ordered book of worship.

Central to the Prayer Book was the service of holy communion. It
was full access to this act of worship that Morley ensured when he
confirmed so many persons at Newport. It was the communion practices
of the Church which had been debated so heatedly not only during
the reign of Charles I but right through the years going back to the
time of Edward VI in the preceding century. A case could be argued
for maintaining that the eucharist has always been disputed in some
way or other and that even the New Testament itself contains within
its pages signs of differences of emphasis and style over how the Lord's
Supper was to be celebrated and understood.[2] Of course, disputes over

forms of liturgy and type of doctrine had changed over the centuries. But while the details varied from century to century, in the west of Europe at least certain areas of dispute kept coming back.

These are many and varied, but some stand out as central at the Reformation. How is Christ present in the eucharist? In the bread and wine, or in the receiving of them? And how should either (or both) be described? Allied to those questions are other fundamental issues, like how one sees the eucharist as an offering. Is it a re-offering of Christ, or a sacrifice of thanksgiving, and/or a memorial-sacrifice? In that connection, should the bread and wine be somehow offered on the altar, or are they only to be placed there in a functional manner? How often should one receive holy communion? In one or two kinds (usually meaning bread only, or both bread and wine)? And then there is the issue that affects every celebration of the eucharist – how the order of service should be formulated and performed. That question is the one which continues to create controversy in the twentieth century, not least after an almost unprecedented era of liturgical change among all the Western Churches. Many a sixteenth-century Protestant would be not a little taken aback by the enthusiastic way in which the Roman Catholic Church took part in this cooperative area in our own time.

In a much-changed world, there is also the vital question of the relationship between the eucharist and the society in which it finds itself, for the Church is never meant to live in an enclosed ghetto, turning the gospel of the love of God manifest in Christ into an exercise in self-regard and gratuitous introspection. As we shall see, several of the writers highlighted in our study have bold expectations that the eucharist has the potential to make the world a better, more loving community, and, contrariwise, its wilful neglect runs the risk of creating a world allowed to walk on unchallenged by this feast of the sacrificial values of the Kingdom of God in bread and wine.

The Reformers

Schellinks was a Dutch Calvinist, and he came from a country which had been split apart earlier in the century by theological dispute – between strict followers of Calvin and a more liberal movement, whose followers were called Arminians. By the seventeenth century, it becomes hard to identify the different strands of the Continental European Reformation. But the legacy of the original Reformers has an indirect bearing on our study. It is therefore appropriate to summarise their views on the eucharist at this stage, since the emphases and piety which followed them, rather more than the precise theological views which they held, affected the debates and controversies in our period.[3]

Martin Luther (1483–1546) was in many respects the most conservative of the Reformers. A visitor to Scandinavia today, for example, is often surprised by the way in which many of the outward forms of traditional Catholic liturgical practice survived the Reformation; the stone altars, the use of wafer bread, the vestments used by the priest. For him, the eucharist was the sign of the promise of humanity's justification by God's forgiveness, and this is primarily about what God does for us, rather than what we do in return – we are the receivers. This underlined his whole theological and liturgical programme. The Latin mass was stripped of all references to sacrifice, because that was about what the Church 'did'. And the view of Christ's presence in the eucharist was based on the fact that he is present everywhere in his humanity, and on that basis, rather than on what the Church can do in the celebration, he is present in the bread and wine. This view was called 'consubstantiation', in reaction to the Roman Catholic 'transubstantiation'; the bread and the wine remain bread and wine, but Christ is present by faith alone.

For Luther Christ's command to repeat the actions at the Last Supper supplies the warrant for 'doing this'. As the other Reformers also stress, the Word of Christ forms the basis for saying why we should celebrate the eucharist. In Lutheran piety, this theology works out in a particularly solemn celebration, kneeling at an altar, contemplating the mystery of the presence of God, but the bread and wine that are left are not normally consumed in a special manner, as that would imply a 'higher' view of the presence of Christ. Luther's ideal, which was followed in many places long after his death and continues (without the need for any 'revival') in several parts of world-wide Lutheranism, was to celebrate the eucharist at least every Sunday.

Ulrich Zwingli (1484–1531) is the most radical of the Reformers. For Zwingli, the eucharist must be stripped of all outward symbolism and should be made to look as much like an ordinary meal as possible. While it is not easy to pin him down to a single consistent view, we know that he was in favour of a quarterly communion only. This may seem strange to many people today, but in the Middle Ages, while most people went to mass frequently, they very seldom took communion. The key to Zwingli's understanding of the presence of Christ lies in his emphasis on faith. Like Luther, he places everything on the sovereignty of God, and in his reaction against Roman Catholicism, he wanted as much freedom as possible, hence the bare form of liturgy that he and his followers in Zurich and elsewhere used. The eucharist was about 'the contemplation of faith', it was a 'sign of grace given'. But the presence of Christ cannot be powerfully sacramental, because that has already been given through faith.

John Calvin (1509–64) came last, and was therefore able to exercise a critical function not only on Roman Catholic faith and practice, but also on Luther and Zwingli. For him the key question is 'how does the body of Christ become ours?' Calvin's answer lay in the role of the Spirit. The presence of Christ is not made by 'doing sacraments' (Roman Catholic), or by physical presence (Luther), or by the contemplation of faith (Zwingli). It is the Spirit of Christ, uniting the Christian to him, and forming 'a kind of channel' between Christ and us. Calvin thus brings the Trinity into the eucharist in a special way. The eucharist is no 'vain and empty sign' (perhaps a reference to the Zwinglian view), but an action in which we feast in the banquet, celebrating Christ's sacrifice. Christ stands in heaven, as the high priest, interceding for his people, and his presence is given through the power of the Spirit. We shall come across some of Calvin's ideas later on as these are carefully adapted and supplemented by others in the course of time.

In liturgical practice, however, even though he wanted a weekly eucharist he had to make do with a monthly celebration. And although much Prayer Book worship at the local level could not get beyond a monthly eucharist, there is still a sense in which Calvinist piety is not entirely at home with the Prayer Book eucharist. None the less, for him the eucharist strengthens faith, and whereas he was negative about the language of sacrifice (though not as much as were Luther and Zwingli), he could see the Lord's Supper as a dynamic memorial, a renewal of the covenant. We shall encounter covenant language again. Calvin's liturgy, however, did not live up to the promise of his theology. It was much nearer that of Zwingli than Luther. It was bare and wordy, but unlike Zwingli's, it had scope for psalm-singing, just as Luther allowed ample scope for the singing of hymns, and opened up a whole doxological culture that enabled Lutheranism to develop a vigorous liturgical life which in its own way bears comparison with the Prayer Book tradition.

On the whole, the influence of these men and their followers was both mixed and regional. Luther's teaching affected a great deal of what became Protestant Germany, and also Scandinavia and the Baltic nations. Zwingli's following was less widespread, largely because Calvin's following absorbed and corrected it, spreading through Switzerland, Holland, and Scotland, as well as parts of Germany. In England, however, it is fair to say that the main influences were Zwingli and Calvin. It is impossible to place the English Prayer Books into either of these categories. But there are strong arguments for suggesting that the author of the first two Prayer Books, Thomas Cranmer (1489–1556), had leanings in both directions. His liturgical conservatism (or the influences that helped to keep the Prayer Book so conservative in comparison with Zwingli or Calvin) sowed the seeds for precisely the synthesis of tradition, reinterpretation and renewal which lies at the heart of our quest. It was Calvin's strongly Christ-centred emphasis that was to be the more influential of the three early Reformers on the theologians we shall be looking at. But even those influenced by him take care to distance themselves from him, as they accommodate themselves more and more to the views which they came to discern in the Fathers of the first few centuries, and are also affected by the regular use of the Prayer Book liturgy, so different from the forms of service which Calvin himself used.

The Ten Characters in Question
This study is intended to offer a kind of eucharistic counterpoint to the two situations into which William Schellinks stumbled in the Winchester diocese in the early autumn of 1662. Such a counterpoint is made up of the music played by ten selected characters who lived around Schellinks' time, and who made important contributions to the way the eucharist was celebrated and reflected upon. As is often the case, criteria for selection has not been easy to come by. It has to have an overture as well as a finale, otherwise the exercise would be unworkable.

Some are obvious choices, such as Richard Hooker and Lancelot Andrewes, because they are foundation figures, the former sitting in his rural vicarage writing a systematic theology of the Prayer Book while the latter becomes a prominent court preacher with a curious gift for the contemporary and the vivid, as well as a deep knowledge of the tradition. Then come a pair of different contrasts: William Laud, the ambitious prelate who was perhaps a more able theologian than a diplomat, and William Forbes, able Aberdonian and the most widely travelled of our collection of characters, and who in his eirenical writings is therefore perhaps one of the most interesting. In Cosin and Brevint we encounter two men of quite different backgrounds who were brought together by circumstances; Cosin was an up-and-coming churchman under Charles I, who had to go into exile in Paris, where he met Brevint, a Channel Islander of Huguenot stock, whom he took back with him to Durham at the Restoration. Cosin's main contribution is not confined to the revision of the Prayer Book, though that is significant in itself, whereas Brevint's part in our story consists in a short devotional treatise of penetrating quality, which came to be a fundamental influence on John and Charles Wesley when they wrote their eucharistic hymns. His Huguenot roots and the tradition he helped to inspire in the Wesley brothers thus mark him off as a figure of considerable ecumenical significance.

Then come Jeremy Taylor and Richard Baxter, two spiritual masters who are on opposite sides of the ecclesiastical fence. Taylor went underground during the Commonwealth but became a bishop in Ireland at the Restoration, whereas Baxter thrived during the Commonwealth, but was unable to remain in the Church of England under the terms of the new regime. Finally, Thorndike and Patrick, both survivors of the Commonwealth era who remained in England, provide us with more than ready writers who stood for firm principles but yet wanted to unite people around common purposes, Thorndike by looking afresh at antiquity, Patrick by a special blend of tradition and reason.

Others could have been included from the galaxy of writers in this era, like Henry Hammond, John Bramhall, or George Bull. Several of them merit a book in their own right, notably Thorndike and Patrick, who wrote on such a wide variety of issues. Some of them deserve further research on their background and thought, such as Forbes and Brevint, both of whom have the advantage of taking our study out of a potentially exclusive English milieu, a milieu that already embraces Ireland in Taylor's later exile and subsequent episcopate. Richard Baxter stands as the dominant (though not necessarily typical) figure in the developed Puritan movement because of the extent of his

writings, and his unique combination of a liturgy which he composed
to harmonise with the patterns set down for use during the Commonwealth and which has its own theological style.[4]

Their Context and Relationships

What, then, of the wider issues of context? Not only are our characters
different, so are their writings. In fact, the nature of the evidence used
in these pages reveals the not wholly surprising truth that there is
hardly a single exact correspondence between one writer and another.
Hooker's *Laws of Ecclesiastical Polity* are unique. On the other hand,
there are similarities in method and scope in Taylor's *Holy Living*, and
of approach (though hardly in style) in Thorndike's *Laws of the Church*.
And while all of them, with the exception of Forbes and Brevint, have
left us with printed copies of their sermons (which may not always
reflect the words actually used on the occasions in question but could
be special set-piece productions), it is notoriously difficult to lump
together sermons in an exact manner, since each preacher is contex-
tualised by his or her own style, and the particular occasion in question.
For example, Andrewes before King James on Easter Day 1622, is going
to be different from Richard Hooker preaching on the Epistle of St
Jude. Two classic treatments of the eucharist which appeared at the
Restoration in 1660, namely Taylor's *Worthy Communicant* and Patrick's
Mensa Mystica, have the same overall shape: a theological introduction
to set out the main understanding of the eucharist, followed by
extended devotional and pastoral explorations, with material for use
during the time of the eucharistic celebration. There are none the less
important areas of difference, for example in Taylor's propensity to link
the eucharistic action on earth alongside Christ's eternal intercession
in heaven, and Patrick's tendency to emphasise that transcendental,
heavenly action in history now. Yet nearly all our characters relate
their writing about the eucharist to the praying life of the Church,
hence all those references to the Prayer Book service, or the prayers
which they compose to be used in conjunction with their works.

In style, too, the evidence has many layers. Brevint was used to
writing against the Roman Catholic Church, in the shadow of which
he spent the formative years of exile in Paris. But he adopts a quite
different approach in *Christian Sacrament and Sacrifice*, in which the
life of prayer before the mystery of the holy communion is the starting-
point. Forbes, alas, has only come down to us in the posthumous form

of extended notes edited by Thomas Sydserff, his former episcopal colleague in Scotland. (Sydserff is a figure we shall encounter in the background on more than one occasion, not only in the work of Forbes, but in Laud's tactless Scottish encounters, as well as in Cosin's and Brevint's years in Paris during the Commonwealth, as a tame bishop for exiled Anglicans.) We shall have the chance to compare the devotional prayers written, for example, by Lancelot Andrewes, in his classic *Preces Privatae*, with John Cosin's *Collection of Private Devotions*, the former composed for the private use of the author himself, the latter compiled for a wider audience. And devotional prayers continue as an important liturgical genre throughout our study, for nearly all our characters wrote prayers of some kind to accompany their theological-devotional treatises, such as Brevint and Patrick.

Another feature that will emerge from our study has already been alluded to – namely the lack of any sense of English isolation among these writers. One only has to look at their citations to earlier writers (or else the notes offered by subsequent editors) to see the vast range of learning from the distant past. All of them show considerable familiarity with the Fathers, for example in Hooker's use of John Chrysostom or Basil of Caesarea. Many of them know a great deal of the theology of the later Middle Ages. But Andrewes, for example, is cautious about using material from such a late era, preferring the Undivided Church as a more reliable witness for theological norms. All are well versed in the Reformation Fathers, with Thorndike discussing the views of Luther, Zwingli, and Calvin. Some of them reveal openly their reading of Roman Catholic writers, as with Taylor's use in one small place of Francis de Sales' *Introduction to the Devout Life*. Forbes' array of sixteenth-century theologians extended to such little-known writers as Cassander and Witzel (usually latinised into Wicelius). Both of them were moderating figures who tried to answer Martin Luther's attack on the 'Babylonian Captivity' of the Church (1520) in a constructive way, and were therefore special heroes for him.

We are not, therefore, dealing with an introverted Anglo-Saxon world in this study of the evolution of Anglican tradition. In Andrewes, we have a Renaissance man who never actually left the shores of this country in body, but who was well acquainted with writers of any era, and knew many languages, European as well as Eastern. In Forbes, we have more than that – a scholar who spent five years near the start of the seventeenth century travelling and studying in Europe. This was a process that brought him into direct contact with some of the most brilliant scholars of his day, such as Joseph Scaliger, who ruled the emerging world of classical studies from Leiden University.

Another aspect of this wider perspective comes across in the fame these men received in their lifetime and after. We know that Andrewes' *Responsio* (1610) to Cardinal Bellarmine was read in Venice at the time. Forbes' *Considerationes Modestae* first appeared in London in 1658, and subsequently in Helmstedt in 1704 and Frankfurt in 1707. We owe a great deal to the editors and publishers of the nineteenth century for the thoroughness with which they brought these works (and many others) before the public. But although that process might have felt like a rediscovery at the time, it has to be pointed out that several of the works we shall be looking at were published and republished again and again in the years immediately after their original appearance. Taylor's *Holy Living* and Patrick's *Mensa Mystica* are two cases in point. They demonstrate the enduring character of seventeenth-century piety in succeeding generations.

Do Labels Fit?

Relationships with one's contemporaries play a vital role in the formation of a tradition, and in our ten characters we have a kind of chain of contacts. Hooker was known to Andrewes, who was a colleague of Laud, who knew Forbes in Scotland. Taylor as a young don knew Laud, and Baxter knew Sheldon as Bishop of London at the Restoration; and Sheldon had quarrelled with Taylor over his All Souls' College fellowship years before, which was perhaps one of the reasons for Taylor not being elevated to the English bench. Cosin, of course, knew Andrewes and Laud, and probably Forbes also. Brevint enters the scene as Cosin's protégé. Thorndike could not have failed to know Cosin in the latter's Cambridge years, and he met Baxter in 1661 at the 'Savoy' Conference for the revision of the Prayer Book before 1662, where Baxter was a representative of the Puritans. Patrick followed Thornlike as a canon of Westminster Abbey. Moreover, these relationships multiply. It is significant that Baxter should have met Thorndike at the 'Savoy' Conference in 1661 to discuss Prayer Book revision, because of the latter's enthusiasm for remodelling the office of bishop at the Restoration along primitive lines, a move which might have made Baxter less disinclined to accept the offer of the bishopric of Hereford in 1661. But neither Baxter's liturgy nor Thorndike's proposals to reform the Church saw the light of day. The Restoration, moreover, brings us face to face with coincidences. To take one example: George Morley was bishop first of Worcester and then of Winchester. At Worcester, he had to remove Baxter from his cure of souls in Kidderminster and later met Baxter, Thorndike and Cosin at the 'Savoy' Conference. Then as Bishop of Winchester he worked tirelessly to re-establish the life and learning of the Church – and he happened to visit the Isle of Wight one September day in 1662 and confirm a crowd among whom was a certain visitor from Holland called William Schellinks.

Relationships have a habit of producing a good climate for innovation, and with them, posterity (or contemporaries, if they get there first) begins to place them into schools and parties and groups. This is not always a happy development, because scorn and misunderstanding tend to produce a world of caricatures. ('Majorism' was admitted into the *Shorter Oxford English Dictionary* in 1993, named after the current Prime Minister, a term about which only one fact is certain – it was invented by journalists.) In the seventeenth century, many labels were used to describe people according to their theological hues. 'Laudian' came to be used to describe those who followed William Laud. But Laud was an able theologian, and in both his theology and his liturgical practice he owed more to Lancelot Andrewes than to any originality of his own. 'Laudian' has usually been interpreted to mean some kind of High Churchman. Laud was himself determined to raise the standards of public worship. He adorned buildings that had been denuded of decorations by Puritans. But in his doctrinal stance and liturgical practice he was first and foremost someone who adapted tradition. The charges of papism that clung to him at the time owe more to the atmosphere of invective that surrounded that sad era and to the manner in which Laud set about putting his ideas into practice than to the actual substance of what he was saying and doing. Similarly, Patrick has been dubbed a 'Latitudinarian', after the 'men of latitude' who emerged on the scene in the Restoration period, and who came to dominate the episcopal bench after the Revolution that brought down James II and placed William and Mary on the throne in 1689. Yet Patrick was his own man, whose use of 'reason' was more mystical and God-centred than the down-to-earth practical Christianity that became fashionable in the 'Latitudinarian' pulpits of the following century.

Perhaps it is the word 'Puritan' that is the biggest casualty in the use of labels. Originally coined to describe an attitude rather than a school of theology, its use became so widespread that it is indeed difficult to define. In fact, it has proved more useful to adopt a wider approach and take the view that there were some Puritans who wanted every local church to be independent and free to order its own life – the predecessors of Congregationalists. Then there were other Puritans, like Richard Baxter, who wanted congregations banded together in groups, under the leadership of ministers and elders – they became Presbyterians. Finally, there were Puritans who remained Anglicans. Edward Reynolds is one example of this group. He was made Bishop of Norwich at the Restoration, probably partly as a move to show that the new regime in the Church would try not to be exclusive in its sympathies. Reynolds attended the 'Savoy' Conference, and it is probably to him that we owe the much-loved 'General Thanksgiving' ('Almighty God, Father of all mercies . . .') and the general 'Prayer for all sorts and conditions of men' that were included in the revision of the Prayer Book for 1662.[5] Puritanism is a phenomenon that we shall encounter repeatedly in our study, because so many people were affected by it. Andrewes appears to have been under its influence as part of his background in his early days as a student. Usually our characters strove to look behind the issues which they saw being over-simplified by extreme Puritans, such as notions of church order. Thorndike's *Of the Government of the Churches* (1641), with its stress on the primitive character of the office of bishop, helped persuade the young Simon Patrick that he needed to be re-ordained.

Another kind of labelling that is fashionable in Anglicanism itself (though it is frequently used of other groups of Christians too) is to distinguish between 'High,' 'Middle' and 'Low' Churchmen. While these distinctions are often useful as a quick term of reference, on closer inspection they overstay their theological welcome. Thus, when looking at John Cosin,[6] shifts in his approach to the eucharist and his attitude to other Churches have been discerned in such a way as to label him a 'High Churchman' at the start of his career, when he was filling Durham Cathedral with candles to celebrate the Presentation in the Temple, and a 'Middle Churchman' when he returned to his native land at the Restoration after experiencing Calvinists in France who were more friendly to him than the Puritans in England (who had been the cause of his exile), to say nothing of the polemics of some of the French Roman Catholics towards converting him to their allegiance. There has also been a tendency for our nineteenth-century forebears in some way to claim the seventeenth-century divines as their own possession: Andrewes, man of tradition though he undoubtedly was, can hardly be viewed as an Anglo-Catholic before his time. They were all clear that they were not Roman Catholics, nor (except for Baxter) Puritans, and they sometimes had to fight for the Prayer Book spirit, discipline and ethos.

The main argument of this book is about the balance of continuity and discontinuity which evolved within what later came to be called Anglicanism. In every case that we shall look at, there is a strong sense of handling tradition creatively, of adapting the inheritance, and of avoiding extremes. It was Laud, who has been so often painted in lurid colours, who once wrote, 'Truth usually lies between two extremes.'[7] Forbes, towards the end of his *Considerationes Modestae* wrote, 'Extremes are to be avoided, and the truth which lies in the middle is to be embraced.'[8] And Patrick, near the start of his *Mensa Mystica* states that 'the truth commonly lies between two extremes, and being a peaceable thing, cannot join itself with either of the directly opposite parties. And therefore I shall seek for her in a middle path.'[9] The balance was not always identically placed, nor did our ten characters agree on everything. But in an age like ours in which the middle ground in many areas of life is despised, it is a sobering reflection for us to see how such very different people as Laud, Forbes, and Patrick should express their deepest convictions. They did so at a time when the religious atmosphere was often so heated that the Church as a whole needed to develop a theological cooling-system.

What Had Happened to the Eucharist?[10]

Under Henry VIII, the Church of England broke away from Rome and at first there was no thought of any substantial changes in the way churches were ordered, either theologically, liturgically, or architecturally. As far as the eucharist was concerned, it was not until the reign of young Edward VI that these alterations became the norm. In 1548, communion was to be received in both kinds, and communicants were to make their confession and receive absolution corporately just before receiving the consecrated bread and wine. Such changes as these appear to us as modest but their effects were far-reaching, for both of them had the force of reversing older customs, namely of making confession before communion privately, and of receiving only the bread. Those who instigated these changes knew full well that the custom in antiquity was universal – everyone in the early centuries who took communion received both the bread and the wine, unless the circumstances prevented it in some way, and the penitential practice of the early centuries was a corporate one.

Then, in 1549, the first Book of Common Prayer was issued, which contained all the main services of the Church in English – both of these innovations which from a practical point of view were probably welcome, for in the preceding era there were lots of different books for different kinds of services, such as the Missal for the eucharist, the Breviary for the daily office, the Manual for the pastoral offices (baptism, marriage, the sick, and funerals). The form of the eucharist made considerable changes apart from the language, though the main shape of the service was much along the lines of the old mass; indeed, the title of the service included the words 'commonly called the mass', as if this name would continue in use. (Lutherans in Scandinavia and elsewhere still talk of the main service as 'High Mass'.) The service was to be conducted from the altar as before, with the priest in the traditional vestments, though a cope was allowed as a substitute for the chasuble, probably because the cope was a ceremonial garment worn by many different types of minister in the Middle Ages, whereas the chasuble had sacrificial associations because of the prayer recited by the priest privately while he put it on in the vestry. The eucharistic prayer was stripped of much of its sacrificial language; the elements were solemnly placed on the altar beforehand without any special prayers of offering, the prayer of consecration stressed the memorial aspect of the celebration, though it prayed for the acceptance of 'our sacrifice of praise and thanksgiving', and made an offering of the people's souls and bodies – which had scriptural warrant (Romans 12:1).

Response to the book was mixed. The people of Cornwall, who doubtless could not understand the standard English of Archbishop Thomas Cranmer's prayers any better than the Latin, complained that the new service was a 'Christmas game' – probably a reference to the new custom of placing a coin in a box at the offertory, when they were expecting the priest to prepare the bread and wine with several sacrificial prayers at the altar. But as with all liturgical change, there were devotees of the new forms, led by townsfolk and the intelligentsia. Silversmiths were not slow to keep up with these developments, for as early as 1549 we have the first Reformation chalice and paten, made for St Mary Aldermary, London.[11] The chalice stands 7.5 inches high, half stem and half bowl, whereas the paten, with its generous upper part for the bread, has a small foot, for ease of handling. Thus was born the English Protestant chalice and paten, obviously a cup and a plate, but with clear affinities to the special ecclesiastical ware of the previous era.

However, the 1549 book did not last long, for in 1552, a second Book of Common Prayer was issued. It is likely that this was part of a two-phase scheme, unless those who criticised the 1549 book as insufficiently Protestant had more influence still. The order for Holy Communion in this new book was more radical. The table was to be placed side-ways in the church where people could most easily gather, which in practice meant a wooden table which stood in the old east end while not in use, and which was moved down into the chancel on those occasions when the eucharist was celebrated. The congregation thus gathered round the table in a way that they had not before. The priest was to wear only the surplice – a single white robe. Ordinary bread and wine are envisaged – though the transition from wafer bread to leavened bread took much longer than is generally supposed, for we find it a bone of contention in the following century. The eucharistic prayer was divided up; immediately after the words of Christ at the Last Supper, the bread and wine were distributed to the congregation, so that their act of 'remembrance', instead of being the prayer of the priest on their behalf in making the eucharistic memorial, was now their *act* of communion, an act consummated in the prayer of their self-offering ('we offer thee our souls and bodies') afterwards. Any bread and wine not consumed at communion was meant for the local cleric's 'own use' – which implied no particular doctrine of the presence of Christ in the sacramental elements, save for their actual *use*.

The 1552 Book had an even shorter life, as Edward VI died that year, bringing to the throne his Roman Catholic elder sister, Mary Tudor, who tried to turn the clock back. The old mass was re-imposed, the Protestant leaders either had to recant, risk being burnt at the stake (as happened to many of them, including Thomas Cranmer himself), or else go into exile. Among these was John Jewel, who was later to be of such importance in the next reign, and a lasting influence on Richard Hooker. The effect of exile in soundly Protestant places such as Frankfurt, Geneva, and Zurich (the most extreme of all) meant that when these theologically well-versed ecclesiastics returned after Mary's death (1558) to assist Elizabeth I in her Church arrangements, the Church of England hierarchy was strongly Protestant. The third Book of Common Prayer, of 1559, was much the same as 1552, though it is widely believed that Elizabeth, who liked candles, a crucifix, and vestments in her own chapel, would have preferred a return to the 1549 spirit. Some significant changes were made, for example in the words of distribution at communion, the 1549 and 1552 formulae were conjoined. This meant, in the instance of the bread, that the 1549 'The Body of our Lord Jesus Christ which was given for thee preserve thy body and soul unto everlasting life' was immediately followed by the 1552 'Take this in remembrance that Christ died for thee, and feed on him in thy heart by faith with thanksgiving.' By looking at these two versions in separation, one can see that 1549 implies a presence of Christ in what the bread is meant to be, whereas 1552 only speaks about what the communicant is supposed to do. By this conjunction, there is an attempt to steer a middle course between Roman Catholic and Protestant emphases of eucharistic piety. The Articles of 1563 and 1571 say this loud and clear when they affirm that 'the Body of Christ is given, taken, and eaten, in the Supper, only after an heavenly and spiritual manner. And the mean whereby the Body of Christ is received and eaten in the Supper is faith.'

What of the environment of worship? Not much Elizabethan church architecture remains.[12] However, Langley chapel, not far from Shrewsbury, Shropshire, stands in a field as a witness to this very era. It probably dates from 1564, and consists of a small single-room church, built of stone, with a timber roof. The two worship areas reflect the medieval ideas of nave and chancel-sanctuary. But there are subtle changes. At the very back stands a desk, perhaps from which singers read their music. Then come very basic bench pews which were intended for the servants of Langley Hall. Then come a few box pews, for the squirearchy, and a comfortable-looking reading desk, from which the minister would have presided at most of the liturgy, only walking over to the pulpit (a movable one) for the sermon. A single small step takes one to the communion area, where benches with kneeling-rails surround a simple wooden table on three sides, the open part on the westward face. Langley points to a balance of faith and doctrine. But the picture was obviously more varied, particularly at the start of Elizabeth's reign. There were places where some of the old medieval practices lingered,[13] just as there was an increasing number of places later on (e.g. Emmanuel College, Cambridge, founded in 1584), where the growing Puritan movement left its mark; the congregation would sit around a table and pass the elements from hand to hand. Not all Puritans favoured infrequent eucharists, for there were many whose sacramental practice put others to shame.[14] But liturgy is about doctrine as well as practice, and what we read in the hybrid 1559 communion formula, and sense behind the Elizabethan Articles, and see in the Langley chapel arrangements, amount to an eloquent testimony of a collective search for a constructive common mean between the warring factions at work in much of Christian Europe over what exactly it is when we 'do this in remembrance of me' – a celebration which is not primarily interior and mental, but exterior and embodied in the eucharistic action.

NOTES

1 *The Journal of William Schellinks' Travels in England 1661–1663* (translated from the Dutch, and edited by Maurice Exwood and H. L. Lehmann) (Camden Fifth Series Volume 1) (London: Royal Historical Society, 1993), pp. 138, 140.

2 See, for example, the classic study, J. Jeremias, *The Eucharistic Words of Jesus* (London: SCM, 1966).

3 The literature on this subject is prodigious; see the work of Christopher J. Cocksworth, *Evangelical Eucharistic Thought in the Church of England* (Cambridge: University Press, 1993), pp. 19–33, and, in general, the whole book.

4 See Bryan D. Spinks, *From the Lord and 'The Best Reformed Churches': A study of the eucharistic liturgy in the English Puritan and Separatist traditions 1550–1633* (Bibliotheca Ephemerides Liturgicae Subsidia 33) (Roma: Edizioni Liturgiche, 1984); and also by Spinks, *Freedom or Order? The Eucharistic Liturgy in English Congregationalism 1645–1980* (Pittsburgh Theological Monographs, New Series) (Allison Park: Pennsylvania, 1984).

5 See Geoffrey Cuming, 'Two Fragments of a Lost Liturgy?' in G. J. Cuming, *Studies in Church History* III (Leiden: Brill, 1966), pp. 247–53.

6 See, for example, the earlier classic, C. W. Dugmore, *Eucharistic Doctrine in England from Hooker to Waterland* (London: SPCK, 1942), pp. 102–10.

7 *The Works of William Laud* (Volume III) (Library of Anglo-Catholic Theology) (Oxford: Parker, 1849), pp. 138–9.

8 *Considerationes Modestae et Pacificae Controversiarum per Gulielum Forbesium* (Volume II) (Library of Anglo-Catholic Theology) (Oxford: 1846), p. 611.

9 See Alexander Taylor (ed.), *The Works of Simon Patrick* (Volume I) (Oxford: University Press, 1858), p. 94.

10 See Geoffrey Cuming, *A History of Anglican Liturgy* (London: Macmillan, 1982), pp. 45ff.

11 See Charles Oman, *English Church Plate* (London: Oxford University Press, 1959), plate 50.

12 See Nigel Yates, *Buildings, Faith and Worship: The Liturgical Arrangements of Anglican Churches 1600–1900* (Oxford: Clarendon Press, 1991). See also Mark Chatfield, *Churches the Victorians Forgot* (Ashbourne: Moorfield, 1989), pp. 110ff (with illustrations).

13 ibid., pp. 12ff.

14 See, for example, R. C. Richardson, *Puritanism in North-West England: A Regional Study of the Diocese of Chester to 1642* (Manchester: University Press, 1972), pp. 32ff, where the Puritan liturgical practice of such seated sharing of the eucharistic gifts by Joseph Midgley, vicar of Rochdale, is traced back to his time at Emmanuel College Cambridge (p. 32 n. 41).

CHAPTER TWO

Founding Fathers I
Richard Hooker (?1554–1600)

There are always dominant figures in any story and this is certainly true of Richard Hooker and Lancelot Andrewes. Different as they were in the kind of posts they held in the Church, they complement each other. This is true not just in the way that a country priest (on the one hand) and a highly-placed prelate (on the other) reflect different but necessary roles within the Church as a whole. It is more to do with the task they performed in bringing to birth the kind of tradition which our study is looking at. We have already seen the first stirrings of that in the Elizabethan Settlement, as it is called, and we shall shortly see how John Jewel acts as a kind of bridge between that Settlement and the flowering of theological writing that is expressed in the work of our ten characters. At face value, Hooker and Andrewes could not have been more different from each other in the kind of writing which they accomplished. Yet that is another symptom of the vicarage and the palace. In those days country clergy did have a lot of time for study, and Hooker made use of it. Andrewes, natural and obvious scholar that he was, still had countless other demands, with the result that he had to make time for his studies. Both are equally learned, Hooker perhaps showing more natural originality, Andrewes displaying more obvious energy in the way that his learning shines forth in his preaching.

Life
Much of what we know about the life of Hooker comes from the biography written many years after his death by Isaac Walton, who is

perhaps more famous for his *Compleat Angler*, which he published in 1653. The date of that publication suggests in itself that Walton did not actually know Hooker. Indeed he did not. And yet Hooker's fame and repute were so great that it was not hard for Walton, in the midst of the other biographies which he wrote (a list that includes the priest-poets John Donne and George Herbert), to gather enough in the way of information and anecdote to put together a life of Hooker. Walton's *Life* of Richard Hooker achieved such authority that it is normally printed with the editions of Hooker's Works. It is not nowadays regarded as wholly accurate, but it is still a classic in its own right.

Richard Hooker was born at Heavitree, near Exeter, about the year 1554 and died at Bishopsbourne, Kent, in 1600. Thus his life began half-way through the reign of Queen Mary and ended three years before the death of Queen Elizabeth. He was educated at Exeter Grammar School, where his uncle, John Hooker, was school-master. John was so impressed with his young nephew's potential that he was determined to do all in his power to further his career as a scholar. As it happens, John was a good friend of John Jewel, the Bishop of Salisbury. The two of them were summoned to Salisbury for an interview, whereupon Jewel decided that the poverty of the lad's parents should not stand in the way of his future. Richard Hooker was therefore granted an annual pension to pay for his education, and Jewel went so far as to obtain for him a place at Corpus Christi College, Oxford. The relationship between the two became a close one; Walton recounts that when they met for the last time before Jewel's death in 1571, Jewel forgot to give Hooker money, and sent a servant to bring him back to him. The story goes that Jewel then said to him: 'Richard, I sent for you back to lend you a horse which hath carried me many a mile, and, I thank God, with much ease.' Whatever the truth of the tale (and there seems little grounds for doubting it) it is clear that Jewel's influence on Hooker was considerable, more spiritual than equestrian.

At Oxford, Hooker distinguished himself, becoming a Fellow of his college in 1577. (The President of Corpus Christi was William Cole, like Jewel an old exile from the reign of Queen Mary, and a pronounced Protestant.) Hooker's brilliance was such that two years later he became deputy Hebrew professor, to stand in for Thomas Kingsmill, who was prevented by illness from fulfilling his duties. It is generally reckoned that Hooker was ordained about 1581, and continued as Fellow until his marriage to Joan Churchman. She was a woman who does not appear to have got on well with Hooker's friends when he left Oxford in 1584 for Drayton-Beauchamp, where he expected to serve his time as incumbent.

But Hooker was attracting attention from others. A sermon preached in the open air at St Paul's Cross (where many famous preachers made their mark at the time) had marked him out as a man who was critical of the growing influence of Calvinism on the part of the Puritans in the Church at large. Their emphasis on predestination, the effect of which was to underplay the importance of humanity's ability to decide and to act in the direction of good, was becoming increasingly strong. Hooker's prominent champions had their chance when the post of Master of the Temple Church, London, became vacant. There were many who thought that Walter Travers would succeed automatically to the Mastership, since he was the 'lecturer' (second presbyter with special duties to preach the afternoon sermons). But Edwin Sandys, Hooker's old Oxford friend, besought his father, who was Archbishop of York, to see if he could ensure that this attractive and influential post was offered to Hooker instead. Travers was a well-known Puritan, whereas the Archbishop of Canterbury, John Whitgift, was not. Accordingly, Hooker moved to the Temple.

Walton gives the impression that the two fought each other all the way through their time together at the Temple Church, 'insomuch that as St Paul withstood St Peter to his face, so did they withstand each other in their sermons; for as one hath pleasantly exprest it, "The forenoon sermon spake Canterbury, and the afternoon Geneva." '[1] (In fact, the two of them may not have been quite as far apart as has been generally thought.[2]) But there was obviously some considerable controversy in their different theological and liturgical approaches. Travers had been an exile during the reign of Queen Mary, but had refused to assent to the Thirty Nine Articles and so was not allowed even to preach, preferring instead to minister to the English congregation in Antwerp, where he received Presbyterian ordination. He had been allowed to be afternoon lecturer at the Temple, but he had refused to be ordained again by a bishop.

The theological clash between Hooker and Travers, however, was far from being a little local event. It was the playing out of a nation-wide tension within the Church between the aspiring Puritans and those keen on maintaining and even developing further the Elizabethan Settlement. In 1572, the *Admonition to Parliament* was published. Probably the work of the two prominent London Puritans, John Field and Thomas Wilcox, it was an uncompromising call to Parliament to change the constitution of the English Church, and to abolish such eucharistic practices as wafer bread (still in use in many places), receiving communion kneeling, and admitting Roman Catholics to the eucharist. However, early in the following year, Robert Johnson of Northampton was tried before the Queen's Commissioners for not consecrating additional wine for use at a service when the wine on the altar proved insufficient. For some extreme Puritans, even the prayers of the eucharist seemed superfluous, but the 'Johnson Case', as it is often called, highlighted the fact that there was a strong body of opinion in the Church at large that took a traditional view of eucharistic consecration as an objective fact, a setting apart of the elements. The stream of Puritan works, however, continued unabated, for in 1574 a work appeared entitled *Ecclesiasticae Disciplinae* ('Ecclesiastical Disciplines'), which took the view that the English Church should be presbyterianly governed. And it was written by Walter Travers.

It was, therefore, no surprise that a learned man such as Hooker should set his mind to writing about these controversies. It took the unusual form of a lengthy series of books on the nature and form of the Church. But its scope was to be far wider. We shall look later on at its general argument, for its structure is intricate. For now it is worth noting that Hooker's eye was very much on these disputes, from the theology of the eucharist itself to points of procedure in the liturgy, like kneeling, and giving communion to Roman Catholics, which were under attack. During the opening years at the Temple, he conceived the great work of his life, the *Laws of Ecclesiastical Polity*. Whereas his great patron, John Jewel, had had to answer criticisms of the Church of England from the Roman Catholic side, Hooker now had to face them from the Puritan. Jewel had written his *Apology of the Church of England* in 1562 (a work which was read all over Europe, including at the Council of Trent by the Roman Catholic theologians) against Thomas Harding. Now Hooker set out to refute the Puritan attack on the Church of England. The parallel between the two men is even stronger, for it was Jewel's sermon at St Paul's Cross in 1560 against the papists that drew attention to him – like Hooker's sermon in the same place just over twenty years later against extreme Calvinism.

Accordingly, Hooker set to work on this entirely new kind of book.

It is unique for its style and scope, and is clearly the result of wide reading and deep thought. Unlike so much other theological writing of the time which was openly aggressive in expression, Hooker takes on a more peaceful tone – his polemics are more subtle. But he shunned the public character of controversy and wanted to get away from the open gaze of the public. So he moved to country parishes to be the scholar-pastor that he probably felt was his true vocation. As Francis Paget wrote tellingly many years ago, of the move and the spirit in which Hooker set about his new tasks:

> It is rare to see a man still young (for Hooker was but thirty-eight when he resigned the Mastership) turning away from a sphere where he has borne a brilliant part, and betaking himself into comparative seclusion, with the simple and unselfish desire only to do before he dies as much as he can of that which he believes to be his proper task. But it is perhaps even more rare for the heart of controversy to kindle in a man the desire not to talk but to think. And in both ways the example of Hooker's life may claim as much attention as the strength of his theology and the grandeur of his style.[3]

By the time he moved to Boscombe, near Salisbury, to be rector and also Subdean and Prebendary of the cathedral, he had already begun the *Laws*. In 1594, Books I to IV appeared. In the following year he moved to Bishopsbourne, Kent, which he served as rector until his death in 1600. He had only been there two years when the famous *Fifth Book* of the *Laws* appeared. The remaining three were not properly completed; Books VI and VIII were not published until 1648, and Book VII in 1662, though there is some dispute over exactly how much Hooker there really is in Book VI.

The Laws of Ecclesiastical Polity

Hooker begins his great work not with some high-flown dedication but with an address to 'the reader'. Such a strategy bears out what one of his biographers, Vernon Staley, has said about the tenor and approach of the *Laws*: 'He showed that it was possible to write theology in English which should at once raise the level of thought in the learned, and be of interest to the public.'[4] Many have been the authors who have had that bold and ambitious design in mind as they began their literary careers! Hooker's opening words are worth quoting in full:

This unhappy controversy about the received ceremonies and discipline of the Church of England, which hath so long time withdrawn so many of her ministers from their principal work, and employed their studies in contentious oppositions; hath by the unnatural growth and dangerous fruits thereof, made known to the world, that it never received blessing from the Father of peace.[5]

Hooker's aim is explicitly stated: he wants to deal once and for all with the disputes in the Church about the Book of Common Prayer, its principles of church order and worship, and its attendant theological rationale, so that clergy can stop wasting their time on internal rows. Little seems to have changed in the intervening centuries in this regard but that is not to undermine the value of Hooker's intentions or his method. Because of the importance of this method, both here and in the remaining nine of our ten characters, we have set our face against plucking a few key quotations out of context and trying to create easy conclusions from them. What Paul Bradshaw has called the 'hit and run' approach to writing about the worship of the early Church is a pitfall as easy in other eras of history.[6] So what is Hooker up to in these first five Books, the ones which we can confidently ascribe to his authorship?

Hooker moves cunningly from the general to the specific. Book I sets out to define the nature of law in general and the eternal Laws of God in particular. These latter consist of 'directive rules unto goodness of operation',[7] in which the way the Church is ordered has its proper place. This latter is not to be set up by the whim of a passing age, nor it is, on the other hand, something that never changes. Having set out the nature of authority as intended and given by God to the Church, Hooker moves on in Book II to deal with the Puritan view that Scripture is the only rule, which directs all things, all aspects of human behaviour. To this claim Hooker replies by adopting a wider approach to the way God speaks to humanity, rebutting the superficial view that it is only done through Scripture: 'Wisdom hath diversely imparted her treasures unto the world. As her ways are of sundry kinds, so her manner of teaching is not merely one and the same.'[8] He goes on to make the important distinction between what is *necessary for salvation* and what he calls things which are *accessory* (what others called 'indifferent'), which vary from time and place according to

circumstance.[9] This becomes a vital criterion when he comes to answer
criticisms of the Prayer Book eucharist.

The scene is set for Book III, in which Hooker comes to another of
the main Puritan tenets, that Scripture must actually contain a form
of Church polity. Resisting the notion that one can define exactly who
is in the Church, Hooker wants the boundaries wide, so that they
open the Kingdom of God to the sinful and the wicked. He goes on
to defend the use of the word 'polity' as a better, less restrictive,
and more Christian term when speaking of church order than either
discipline or government. Human reason is a vital tool in the discernment of God's will and purposes. While he will not try to defend the
polity of the Church of England on biblical terms, he is clear that it
is better than the Puritan view – a series of local congregations, with
tightly defined boundaries between membership and non-membership,
and a presbyterian and less centralised form of government. Then in
Book IV he moves specifically to the Puritan attack on the Church of
England as having a corrupted polity, thanks to its traditional order
and liturgy, which should be purged of popish accretions. It is here
that he defends with some boldness the independence of the Church
of England to decide its own way of life; ceremonies are not to be
scoffed at, for in their right place they affirm the visible because they
are ways God communicates truths to his people. There is even a hint
of his love of the early Fathers when he writes: 'The ceremonies which
we have taken from such as were before us, are not things that belong
to this or that sect, but they are the ancient rites and customs of the
Church of Christ, whereof ourselves being a part, we have the selfsame
interest in them which our fathers before us had, from whom the same
are descended unto us.'[10]

Laws Book V – The Sacraments
We now come to Book V. Unlike the first four, it has a dedication, to
Archbishop Bancroft, his old friend, who had been Bishop of London
before, and was now once again Hooker's diocesan bishop. It is the
longest of all, being about a third as long again as Books I to IV put
together. Its purpose is to answer the criticism that much superstition
has been retained in the Prayer Book. He begins by asking what is
superstition (chs.1–4), goes on to give some axioms (5–10), and discusses the need for church buildings (11–16), and their use (18–22). He
then deals with the nature of prayer (23–49), the nature of sacraments

(50–57), baptism (58–65), confirmation (66), the eucharist (67–68), holy days and the pastoral offices (69–75), ordination and the discipline of the clergy (76–81).

It will be apparent that the eucharist is tucked away into the centre of this key volume in the series. But that is not to suggest any lack of importance. Hooker is a shrewd observer of the things of God, and on closer inspection it becomes clear that in his preliminary treatment of the sacraments, he discusses, for the first time, the central doctrines of the Trinity and the Incarnation. He opens with the assertion that 'sacraments are the powerful instruments of God to eternal life'[11] and then goes on to state how the Trinity and the Incarnation fit into this framework. His method is crucial here, for he is not trying to subordinate God to the Church, rather the reverse. 'The divine mystery is more true than plain.'[12] And of Christ he writes, 'these two natures are as causes and original grounds of all things which Christ hath done.'[13]

When he speaks of the way these two natures come together in Christ, he uses a traditional image from the early Fathers of how the unction of the deity glorifies the humanity, which lays further ground for his specific discussions of baptism and the eucharist. 'God from us can receive nothing, we by him have obtained much.' And then a keystone in the theology of the Anglican divines, the deification of humanity: 'God has deified our nature, though not by turning it to himself, yet by making it his own inseparable habitation.'[14] This is a way of expressing the union of the human and the divine in Christ, made available for all people, and is a significant approach to the whole area of Christian experience which avoids excessive and negative penitence, affirms the reality of the weakness of human nature, but places it always and everywhere in the hands of a loving and eternal God. It avoids mechanistic ways of approaching the sacraments, on the one hand, and also refuses to see them as exclusively human perceptions, on the other.

Sacraments, moreover, are part of God's presence. 'Presence everywhere is the sequel of an infinite and incomprehensible substance',[15] and a means whereby he is present in a powerful manner – 'a presence of force and efficacity throughout all generations of men.'[16] Hooker now moves into his favourite and fundamental theme for the sacraments – participation. 'Participation is that mutual inward hold which Christ hath of us and we of him.'[17] 'They which thus were in God eternally by their intended admission to life, have by vocation or adoption God actually now in them, as the artificer is in the work which his hand doth presently frame.'[18] This leads up to the key statement: 'We participate Christ partly by imputation, as when those things which he did and suffered for us are imputed unto us for righteousness; partly by habitual and real infusion, as when grace is inwardly bestowed while we are on earth.'[19]

What does this mean? Hooker is here dealing with an important item on the Reformation theological agenda, the distinction between *imputed righteousness*, which was the Reformers' emphasis on salvation outside humanity by Christ's work on the cross, and *imparted righteousness*, the Roman Catholic view that salvation worked through an indwelling power of God for good in Christ. It has, inevitably, become a somewhat technical aspect of ecumenical dialogue but it has important implications, for in this quotation, Hooker offers his own synthesis – as he will do with eucharistic theology. He places the work of Christ as central to the scheme of salvation (*imputed*), but at the same time gives to human beings the capacity to stand before God as redeemed, and therefore able to worship and serve him (his use of the term *infused*). It is all of a piece with what he goes on to say about baptism:

> Baptism is a sacrament which God hath instituted in his Church, to the end that they which received the same might thereby be incorporated into Christ, and so through his most precious merit obtain as well that grace of imputation which taketh away all former guiltiness, as also that infused divine virtue of the Holy Ghost, which giveth to the powers of the soul their first disposition towards future newness of life.[20]

Laws Book V – The Eucharist, Chapter 67

Hooker does not race us to the altar. He only takes us there after having set many other matters in order. 'It greatly offendeth, that some, when they labour to shew the use of the holy Sacraments, assign unto them no end but only *to teach* the mind, by other senses, that which the Word doth teach by hearing.'[21] Hooker's agenda is very much conditioned by extreme Puritans who want to make the Lord's Supper into a kind of visual aid. He offers two chapters only (67 and 68), the former on eucharistic theology, the latter answering certain specific criticisms of the Prayer Book rite. (He adopted the same

treatment with baptism in the preceding chapters.) In my own copy
of the *Laws*, which was printed in 1639, these chapters amount only
to sixteen pages. Yet they build on the foundations already laid.

Hooker begins by insisting on the relationship between baptism and
eucharist: 'The grace which we have by the holy Eucharist doth not
begin but continue life . . . Such as will live the life of God must eat
the flesh, and drink the blood of the Son of man, because this is a
part of that diet which if we want we cannot live.'[22] He then goes on
to address those who would regard the sacrament 'only as of a shadow,
destitute, empty and void of Christ.'[23] And he stresses the 'real participation' of Christ by means of the sacrament.[24] Participation is a word
that he uses no fewer than ten times in this chapter.[25] Addressing the
controversy about presence, he distances himself both from the
Lutheran view of consubstantiation, which he describes as trying to
incorporate Christ into the elements, and the Roman Catholic view
of transubstantiation, which he describes as changing the substance of
the elements into Christ himself. 'I wish that men would more give
themselves to meditate with silence what we have by the sacrament,
and less to dispute the manner how.'[26]

After a brief discussion of the appearance of the risen Christ in John
20, when the disciples recognised him without disputation, he observes
that at the Last Supper

> they saw their Lord and Master with hands and eyes uplifted first
> bless and consecrate for the endless good of all generations till
> the world's end the chosen elements of bread and wine, which
> elements made for ever the instruments of life by virtue of his
> divine benediction they being the first that were commanded to
> receive them . . . and . . . those mysteries should serve as conducts
> of life and conveyances of his body and blood.

Extending the aquatic imagery (one which, as we shall see, Andrewes
employs on more than one occasion), he remarks: 'They had at that
time a sea of comfort and joy to wade in, and we by that which they
did are taught that this heavenly food is given for the satisfying of our
empty souls, and not for the exercising of our curious and subtle wits.'[27]
He repeats the theme of presence and participation, and the eucharist
as 'the wellspring out of which this life floweth'.[28]

But it is not always easy to pin Hooker down. For he goes on to say,
from one corner of his mouth, that 'the real participation of Christ's

body and blood is not therefore to be sought for in the sacrament, but in the worthy receiver of the sacrament',[29] and yet later on he waxes even more lyrical than usual:

> Christ assisting this heavenly banquet with his personal and true presence doth by his own divine power add to the natural substance thereof supernatural efficacy, which addition to the nature of those consecrated elements changeth them and maketh them that unto us which otherwise they could not be; that to us they are thereby made such instruments as mystically yet truly, invisibly yet really work our communion or fellowship with the person of Jesus Christ as well in that he is man as God, our participation also in the fruit, grace and efficacy of his body and blood, whereupon there ensueth a kind of transubstantiation in us, a true change both of soul and body, an alteration from death to life.[30]

It is as if Hooker were (if the image is not inappropriate here) trying to have his eucharistic cake and eat it. In the former passage, he states implacably that Christ's presence is to be sought in the communicant. But in the latter he affirms that consecration does set the eucharistic gifts apart, and makes them into something else that they were not before. They become the means whereby our fellowship with one another and with Christ is built up in a manner that cannot be subjected to too great a human scrutiny. (One is reminded of a short statement in his discussion of sacraments in general: 'Sacraments serve as the instruments of God . . .moral instruments, the use whereof is in our hands, the effects in his.'[31])

Perhaps the key lies in what he states in the discussion between these potentially contradictory assertions. First of all, he outlines what he regards as a common ground between all Christians on the sacrament in terms of five truths; that it is a 'true and real participation of Christ'; that in the eucharist the Holy Spirit is given 'to sanctify them as it sanctifieth him which is their bread'; that 'what *merit, force or virtue soever there is in his sacrificed body and blood*, we freely, fully, and wholly have it by this sacrament'; the effect of the sacrament is '*a real transmutation of our souls and bodies* from sin to righteousness, from death and corruptibility to immortality and life'; and finally that although the bread and wine are meagre things in themselves, God's power is sufficient to bring about his promises.[32] (Italics in quotations are only used when in the original text, and are reproduced in order to convey the rhetorical emphasis of Hooker's style.)

In these five points, Hooker both reiterates what he has said before about participation, and brings the Holy Spirit into the eucharistic action. This lays the ground for later writers to make this more explicit in the eucharistic prayer, for in the 1549 Prayer Book there had been a petition for the 'Holy Spirit and Word' to come upon the eucharist, and this was to reappear in the following century both in proposed liturgies and in the writings of several divines. There is a link made between the eucharist and the sacrifice of Christ, though not in the form of actually describing the eucharist as an offering. He further uses a fresh word for the effect of the sacrament on the communicant – transmutation. And he refuses to let the bread and wine be demeaned. Hooker's theology is an astonishing and impressive tight-rope walk.

Criticising by implication those who seem to regard the sacrament as 'a bare sign or figure only',[33] he goes on to reapply his ideas to the controversies of the time. He tries to bring the best out of their approaches. 'All three do plead God's omnipotency: sacramentaries [i.e. the followers of Zwingli and perhaps also some Calvinists] to that alteration which the rest confess he accomplish; the patrons of transubstantiation over and besides that to the change of one substance to another; the followers of consubstantiation to the kneading up of both substances as it were into one lump.'[34] And he cites passages from three early Fathers to support his medial line on eucharistic presence. Then in a final section of this chapter, he indulges in an extended fancy, of presenting a rhetorical assertion in quotation marks. It is by far the longest of these in the entire *Laws*, which is a clear sign that it was of some importance to him. He uses for inspiration a work on the eucharist spuriously ascribed to the third-century North African bishop, Cyprian of Carthage, but actually written by Arnold of Chartres, who lived in the twelfth century and was abbot of Bonneval, and a friend of Bernard of Clairvaux. This leads him to provide an alternative view of the eucharist which might find agreement among Christians:

> ... *this hallowed food, through concurrence of divine power, is in verity and truth, unto faithful receivers, instrumentally a cause of that mystical participation, whereby as I make myself wholly theirs, so I give them in hand an actual possession of all such saving grace as my*

sacrificed body can yield, and as their souls do presently need, this is
to them and in them *my body*. [For some reason those five key
words are not printed in italics.]

This introduces into the lengthy concluding reflection, which perhaps ranks among the more wonderful and sublime passages in the
whole of Hooker. It ends thus:

... what these elements are in themselves it skilleth not, it is
enough that to me which take them they are the body and blood
of Christ, his promise in witness hereof sufficeth, his word he
knoweth which way to accomplish; why should any cogitation
possess the mind of a faithful communicant but this, O my God
thou art true, O my soul thou art happy![35]

Laws Book V – The Eucharist, Chapter 68

Before evaluating Hooker's theology, the whole picture must be given,
for in the following chapter, he deals with six key areas of criticism
from Puritans. They did not like words of distribution for each communicant. It will be remembered that these had originally been one
sentence long in the forms in which they appeared in the 1549 and
1552 Prayer Books, but for reasons of theological balance, they had
been brought together into a composite formula in 1559, where they
still are in the 1662 Prayer Book. 'The Body of our Lord Jesus Christ . . .
Take this in remembrance that Christ died for thee . . .' It may be that
this version merely added to the criticisms, but Hooker rebuts this on
the simple basis that in baptism the priest says 'I baptise thee', and so
a distribution formula for communion is right and proper.

Then there were complaints about kneeling for communion. In 1552
a carefully worded rubric was added at the end of the service pointing
out that kneeling implied no corporal presence of Christ in the sacrament. Posture at communion was to continue to be a thorny issue
until well into the ·following century and after, so it is well that we
should take note of the point at this stage in our study. Hooker's reply
was to say that kneeling was a 'gesture of piety'.

The next two criticisms concerned eucharistic discipline. Every communicant, Puritans maintained, should be examined. We have already
seen Hooker's impatience with over-indulgence in theological niceties,
and he was similarly ill-disposed to those who would impose 'superfluous scrupulosity lets and hindrances' before parents whose Christian

faith was not deemed sound.[36] Hooker did not think excluding the
apparently unworthy should be a policy, though he approves of discipline 'when need requireth it.' Another criticism concerned communicating those who were regarded as notorious offenders, including
papists. Hooker again deals with these points with characteristic clarity
and discretion, refusing to refuse Roman Catholics who present themselves for the eucharist. That in itself could not have endeared him to
his rigorist opponents.

The last two points concerned the practice of communion. First,
the Puritans complained about the comparatively small numbers of
communicants at Prayer Book services, which probably resulted from
the fact that these services were more frequent but those who did not
wish to communicate could withdraw after the first part of the service.
Secondly, they criticised the practice of giving communion to the sick
at home: Calvin defended it, but his followers opposed it, on the
dubious ground of diminishing the corporate nature of the sacrament.
Hooker stands firm by established custom. There is no need to deny
the service simply because few happen to turn up on that particular
day, nor is it right to deny it to those who may be dying.

Hooker on the Eucharist

It would be a rash person who dared to say anything original about
Hooker's theology in general, and his views on the eucharist in particular. In an important analysis of the whole of Hooker's theology, the
French scholar Olivier Loyer[37] sets Hooker's work in a wider perspective
than has often been the case. A previous generation of Anglicans
tended to place him on a pedestal, and perhaps even see him as a quasi-
Catholic figure. Loyer praises him for his simplicity, his ecumenical
aspiration, and his stress on the real-ness of the sacramental action
and experience. There is little doubt that for both Loyer and the
American scholar, John Booty,[38] Hooker's language seems deliberately
contrived to draw various strands together. When he speaks of 'merit,
force or virtue' he talks like a Calvinist, for whom the bread and wine
remain unchanged by consecration, yet for whom the virtue or power
of Christ's presence is conveyed in the eating and drinking. When he
speaks of 'the real presence . . . in the worthy receiver' he seems to
have a more 'receptionist' view, less dynamic on presence, yet locating
that presence in the communicant. But when he affirms that 'Christ
assisting this heavenly banquet . . . changeth them [previously referred

to as "those consecrated elements"] and maketh them that unto us which otherwise they could not be' he is moving in a more traditional direction.

In terms of his handling of sources, he could not know that the treatise on the Lord's Supper was not written by someone so ancient (and therefore reliable) as Cyprian of Carthage. He has an instinctive desire to walk with the early Fathers if he can: 'Touching the sentence of antiquity in this cause . . . they knew that the force of this sacrament doth not necessarily presuppose the verity of Christ's both body and blood.'[39] But he never lets his sources get on top of him. The Early Fathers whom he calls in for support in his yearnings for a dynamic but imprecise theology of eucharistic presence may not in fact deliver the goods,[40] yet one senses a desire to be faithful to the Reformation, where the main influence on him is probably Calvin. These he brings together and unites by adopting a kind of theological *mélange*, as well as his own special use of language. One must not forget, either, the sheer effect of the Prayer Book liturgy upon his piety, an interplay of faith and doctrine that we see particularly at the end of his discussion of eucharistic theology.

How successful is Hooker in this exercise? Clearly, he did not unite all Christians with his eucharistic synthesis. Perhaps he did not even think that he would manage it. And yet there is in his approach something both traditional and unusual. He sets the eucharist within a sacramental theology in which baptism has an essential place, and in the context of a Trinitarian theology in which Father, Son, and Spirit have a role that is vital. This explains his stress on the Spirit being given to the communicants, just as the Spirit consecrated Jesus himself – a clear reference to another image of the Trinity, at the baptism of Christ, a theme we shall encounter in the sermons of Lancelot Andrewes.

By using the notions of mystery and change, participation and indwelling, Hooker succeeds in providing an approach to eucharistic theology that he hoped would somehow break the deadlock of the Western Protestant–Roman Catholic divide. He uses it rather like a spotlight on a stage, which suddenly appears from a totally different direction in the middle of a great deal of confusion, so bringing to prominence a perspective that has not been seen so far. For Hooker, there are two essential foci in the eucharist, the individual's faith, and the Lord's gift of his presence, a gift of dynamic presence. These two ingredients are a matter of balance, but they are not determined by a desire on Hooker's part to sit on some kind of theological fence; rather they form part of the very nature of the eucharistic mystery itself. With his concepts of real and personal presence set within that wider perspective, with his novel ideas of transmutation of the soul and sanctification by the Spirit, he loosens up the eucharistic legacy he was addressing. This was, in the first instance, the extreme Puritans, who were to become a force to be reckoned with in the next two reigns. In the next instance, it was the Protestant and Roman Catholic theologians further afield, some of whom continue to admire this curious post-medieval man, this 'judicious Mr Hooker', who wrote theology with such conviction, prayerfulness, and detachment.

Over one area he is virtually silent – sacrifice. He is content to contemplate the sacrifice of Christ, and to see Christ's presence in the eucharist in terms that border on the sacrificial – all that language of death and new life. But when in a later chapter he discusses priesthood, he passes over in a somewhat embarrassed manner the fact that the Early Fathers themselves used sacrificial language of the eucharist.[41] It is also curious that he did not make anything of the Prayer Book's significant prayer after communion, in which the communicants offer themselves 'as a living sacrifice' (Romans 12:1). Perhaps this overarching view of participation, a scriptural image skilfully adapted from Calvin, was what he thought would cover everything. It certainly links in strongly with a dynamic notion of the nature of the Church, in which reason and tradition (whose importance had already been highlighted in his mentor, John Jewel's, *Apology*) have as large a part to play as Scripture itself.[42] It ties in, too, with Hooker's view of the mystical body of Christ, 'in number as the stars of heaven, divided successively by reason of their mortal condition into many generations.'[43] The communion of saints, underplayed in the 1552 and 1559 Prayer Book liturgies, keeps returning in our characters, and eventually makes a re-entry in the 1662 service.

Loyer's overall analysis of Hooker's eucharistic theology – remarkable in coming from a French Roman Catholic – is best summed up in the following:

> The mystical body is a body to share. It is not reducible to that solitary body, limited in time, localised in space, which was born of the Virgin and died under Pontius Pilate. It is the body of

which Christ is the head and we the members. The eucharistic presence is not a 'static' one, or even an 'immobile' one. From such a view as this are necessarily derived the notions of virtue, force, and efficacity, and in this respect Hooker takes up in his turn the better part of Calvin . . . The sacrament is an action, not a sign to be contemplated, and it is more, an action in no way taking place outside us, but with us and in us . . . The Roman error is to forget this Pauline line of thought, and, in consequence, to reduce the sacrament more or less to the consecration of the species on the one hand, and to make it a spectacle on the other, from which the faithful are excluded, because the action is done by the priest.[44]

Booty, on the other hand, captures the liturgical impact of Hooker's own spirituality on the doctrines he so reflectively enunciates:

Such an understanding . . . proceeds from the person who partakes of the body and blood of Christ in the public liturgy of the church, and it surely cannot be denied that the experience of participation in and through the liturgy works on the mind and heart of the faithful. Thus it is possible that the mightiest influence working on Hooker as he formulated his view of the eucharist was the *Book of Common Prayer* and its emphasis upon the sacrifice of Christ for us. In his homiletic-poetic conclusion to Chapter 67 Hooker seems to agree more with the early Fathers than he does in the section wherein he seeks to expound their views and this is possibly so because the liturgy as known and participated in has its own power and effect.[45]

One may therefore picture Hooker presiding at Prayer Book liturgies in his country churches, perhaps already filled with benches and pews, and with a reading desk from which, clad in a surplice, he read the prayers in his restrained manner. 'His voice was low, his stature little, gesture none at all'[46] was one account of how he performed in the pulpit. And then on Communion Sundays, perhaps once a month, he would stand at the north side of the communion table in the sanctuary and preside – for devoutly kneeling communicants – at this Supper which obviously held enough fascination in him to provoke from his pen that long devotional-theological soliloquy which ended, 'O my God thou art true, O my soul thou art happy.'

Hooker's writings left their mark firmly on virtually every Anglican theologian in the period after his death – and beyond. They are not to be gulped, but sipped. They are not for easy labelling, because the great little man's mind is too flexible and original for that. It is good to see the eucharist set like a nut within a large and complex shell. Not all commentators on the Lord's Supper have that insight – or humility. Let Hooker have the final words – this time taken from a sermon on the Epistle of Jude, in the course of which he reflects on the words 'edify yourselves in your most holy faith' (Jude 20):

> Receiving the Sacrament of the Supper of the Lord after this sort (you that are spiritual judge what I speak) is not all other wine like the water of Marah, being compared to the cup which we bless? Is not manna like to gall, and our bread like to manna? Is there not a taste, a taste of Christ Jesus in the heart of him that eateth? Doth not he which drinketh behold plainly in this cup, that his soul is bathed in the blood of the Lamb? O beloved in our Lord and saviour Jesus Christ, if ye will taste how sweet the Lord is, if ye will receive the King of Glory, 'build yourselves.'[47]

NOTES

1 See *The Works of that Learned and Judicious Divine, Mr Richard Hooker, with an account of his Life and Death by Isaac Walton* I (Oxford: University Press, 1845), p. 9.

2 See Richard Bauckham, 'Hooker, Travers and the Church of Rome in the 1580's', *Journal of Ecclesiastical History* 29 (1978), pp. 37–50.

3 Francis Paget, *An Introduction to the Fifth Book of Hooker's Treatise of the Laws of Ecclesiastical Polity* (Oxford: Clarendon Press, 1907), p. 9. See also Henry McAdoo, 'Richard Hooker', in Geoffrey Rowell (ed.), *The English Religious Tradition and the Genius of Anglicanism* (Wantage: Ikon, 1992), pp. 105–25.

4 Vernon Staley, *Richard Hooker* (London: Masters, 1907), pp. 106–7.

5 *Works* I, p. 85.

6 See Paul F. Bradshaw, 'Ancient Church Orders: A Continuing Enigma', in Gerard Austin (ed.), *Fountain of Life: In Memory of Niels K. Rasmussen*, OP (Washington: Pastoral Press, 1991), p. 19 (whole essay, pp. 3–22).

7 *Book* I, 8.4. (Citations to the *Laws* given by Book, Chapter, Section.)

8 *Book* II, 1.4.

9 Book II, 4.4.

10 Book IV, 9.1.

11 Book V, 50.3. See also William O. Green, 'Sacramental Theology in Hooker's *Laws*. A Structural Perspective', *Anglican Theological Review* 73 (1991), pp. 155–76.

12 Book V, 52.1.

13 Book V, 53.3.

14 Book V, 54.5. See also A. M. Allchin, *Participation in God: A Forgotten Strand in Anglican Tradition* (London: Darton, Longman & Todd, 1988), esp. pp. 7ff, on Hooker.

15 Book V, 55.4.

16 Book V, 55.9.

17 Book V, 56.1.

18 Book V, 56.7.

19 Book V, 56.11. On this issue, see Peter Toon, *Justification and Sanctification* (London: Marshall, Morgan and Scott, 1983), pp. 93ff. For a more detailed discussion of the ecumenical aspects, see Edward Yarnold, 'Duplex iustitia: The Sixteenth Century and the Twentieth', in G.R. Evans, *Christian Authority: Essays in Honour of Henry Chadwick* (Oxford: Clarendon Press, 1988), pp. 204–23.

20 Book V, 60.2. Cf. Wilhelm Niesel, *The Theology of Calvin* (Lutterworth Library Vol. XLVIII) (London: Lutterworth, 1956), pp. 120–39 for a discussion of the issue of grace and righteousness. I am indebted to Christopher Cocksworth for drawing my attention to this work.

21 Book V, 57.1.

22 Book V, 67.1.

23 Book V, 67.2.

24 Book V, 67.2 and 5.

25 See Book V, 67. 2, 5, 6 (twice), 7, 9, 10, 11 (twice), and 12. Cf. 'Participation is that mutual inward hold which Christ hath of us and we of him', Book V, 66.1.

26 Book V, 67.3.

27 Book V, 67.4.

28 Book V, 67.5.

29 Book V, 67.6.

30 Book V, 67.11.

31 Book V, 57.5.

32 Book V, 67.7.

33 Book V, 67.8.

34 Book V, 67.10.

35 Book V, 67.12.

36 Book V, 60.7.

37 See Olivier Loyer, 'Hooker et la doctrine eucharistique de l'église anglicane', *Revue des sciences philosophiques et théologiques* 58 (1974), pp. 213–41.

See also his _magnum opus_, _L'anglicanisme de Richard Hooker_ (2 vols) (thèse présentée devant l'universitée de Paris III – le 1 juin, 1977) (Paris: Librairie Champion, 1979). The article cited is contained in the dissertation, pp. 509–42; see also his excellent discussion of 'participation', pp. 485ff. It is a great loss to the English-speaking world that this interesting and original thesis was not translated into Hooker's native language before the author's death.

38 See John E. Booty, 'Hooker's Understanding of the Presence of Christ in the Eucharist', in John E. Booty (ed.), _The Divine Drama in History and Liturgy: Essays in Honor of Horton Davies on his Retirement from Princeton University_ (Pittsburgh Theological Monographs, New Series) (Allison Park: Pickwick Publications, 1984), pp. 123–48, for a seminal discussion of the issues involved.

39 _Book V_, 67.11.

40 See Booty, art. cit., pp. 138f.

41 _Book V_, 78.2.

42 See Paul Avis, _Anglicanism and the Christian Church_ (Edinburgh: T and T Clark, 1989), pp. 47ff.

43 _Laws V_, 56.11.

44 Loyer, op. cit., p. 534 (my translation).

45 Booty, op. cit., p. 144.

46 Quoted from John Gauden's _History of Britain_ (1662) from Staley, op. cit., p. 264.

47 See _The Works of Richard Hooker_, II, p. 779.

CHAPTER THREE

Founding Fathers II

Lancelot Andrewes (1555–1626)

In 1919 a special ceremony took place near the high altar of Southwark Cathedral. Just to the south of the altar, a canopy was placed over the tomb of Lancelot Andrewes, designed by the church architect, Reginald Theodore Blomfield.[1] A symbolic action such as this conveyed a signal to the outside world that Andrewes was being given the special recognition that he deserved, and also that this was to be his lasting resting place. For when he died on 25th September 1626, he had been buried in what was then simply St Saviour's Church, Southwark, the main parish church in that northernmost tip of the Winchester diocese next to his London residence, appropriately called Winchester House. But the site of his burial was in a chapel that once stood beyond the present retro-choir.

Then in 1832 a new London Bridge was built, and in order to get the levels right, the municipal authorities had this chapel pulled down – an action which a more conservation-minded generation would not have countenanced. Andrewes' tomb was accordingly moved a few yards west, to stand in the present retro-choir. This was not to last long, for by 1919 new fashions were stirring in the Church, which caused the retro-choir to be restored into an area containing four chapels. Andrewes' tomb was therefore moved once more, to its present resting-place. The canopy serves as a kind of apology for this restlessness. But it also marks the site where one of the greatest men of his age was buried.

Andrewes would probably like being so near a high altar because he was above all a man of the eucharist. As we shall see in this study, he made a not inconsiderable contribution to virtually every area which affects the eucharist. He wrote theological treatises. He preached sermons for the eucharist that were the main source of his fame. He composed some finely-wrought devotional prayers for his own use at communion, which are contained in the famous *Preces Privatae*, his private prayers. And he had carefully-worked out views on how the eucharist should be celebrated in his chapel, which are reflected in his notes on the Prayer Book.

Life

The life of Lancelot Andrewes is aptly summed up by a modern biographer in the following words:

> He was born in 1555, the year when the Marian persecution produced many Protestant martyrs, he was a school-boy when Elizabeth was excommunicated, he went up to Cambridge a year after Cartwright had been deprived of the Professorship [for Puritan views]. At the University he found himself in the midst of the Puritan ferment and was later drawn into the controversy on predestination. After his ordination he was engaged in disputation with both recusants and Separatists. When James became king, Andrewes himself was on the road to becoming a national figure. He was present at the Hampton Court Conference [about Prayer Book revision], he was one of the translators of the Authorised Version, he became the leading apologist against Rome, and he thus contributed to the new school of theology which was providing the Church of England with a sound historical and theological basis. He emphasised the need for order in public worship, and he had a high conception of episcopacy. At the same time, however, he was one of the foremost preachers of the divine right of kings and he was active in the Court of High Commission. He thus played his part in preparing for the rupture to come. One year after James died and Charles had begun his tragic career, Andrewes himself passed from the stage.[2]

It is clear from this rapid tour of Andrewes' life that we are dealing with another giant, though one of different style and proportions to Hooker. Born at Barking, the son of a merchant seaman, Andrewes was educated at Merchant Taylors' School, and was by all accounts a very serious and studious young boy. So hard did he work that his

parents had to try to force him to play. Latin and Greek were part of
him and he had a natural flair for languages, taking advantage of his
father's profession by widening his linguistic horizons. Here one sees
the seeds of the future prelate who spent several hours each morning
in prayer and study, refusing any appointments to see people. He is
reputed to have had a daily discipline of working late and rising early
– at 4.00 a.m.

At Pembroke Hall, Cambridge, he lived and worked among enthusiastic Puritans. But his love of the classics led him into another direction
of theology which was to leave its imprint on almost everything he
wrote. He took to the early Fathers like a duck to water. This is not
to say that the Puritans, or indeed the early Reformers, had no liking
for the Fathers – indeed they did. But with Andrewes one senses that
reading them was a little like coming home. He did not idolise them,
for he held a high view of that critical judgement, the 'reason' which
was so prominent a first principle in Hooker. Graduating in 1578, he
became a Fellow of his college and was ordained four years later,
immediately taking on the post of Catechist, which meant preaching
teaching sermons on Saturday and Sunday afternoons. Through his
contacts he tried to convince both Roman Catholics and Separatists
that the Church of England could be their home, and there is evidence that he attended some 'prophesying' meetings with Puritans.
But it was probably the extreme Puritans, actively encouraged in the
new foundation, Emmanuel College, that gave him the real inklings
that this approach to Christianity was not for him. In Holland, the
softer and controversial form of Calvinism being pioneered by Jakob
Hermans – latinised into Jakobus Arminius – was a sign, if not also
an influence, of a reaction against predestination and its attendant
attitudes in the Church. 'Arminian' soon became a term of abuse
towards the unsound, and Andrewes and others so minded were accused
of these leanings.

His preaching was bringing him into prominence. In 1589, only
about eight years after Hooker's famous St Paul's Cross sermon,
Andrewes was invited to preach the celebrated 'Spittal Sermon' on
Easter Wednesday at St Mary's Hospital, London. The custom was for
the Monday sermon to be preached by a bishop, the Tuesday sermon
by a dean, and the Wednesday sermon by a doctor. Andrewes was, we
may surmise, by this time a doctor of divinity, in standing if not also
in rank. In 1589 he took over the living of St Giles, Cripplegate, and

also a prebendal stall at St Paul's Cathedral which by tradition had
the ministry to penitents attached to it. Andrewes, who was also made
Master of his old college in that year, threw himself into these many
tasks with that mixture of energy and reflectiveness that was to be the
hallmark of his career. He kept a foot in both the theological and
the ecclesiastical areas of interest, and when the *Lambeth Articles*
appeared in 1595, with their Puritan leanings towards predestination,
Andrewes declared his hand in a firm but tactful manner in his *Judgement of the Lambeth Articles*. He had held back thus far from the
controversy but now had to come out against predestination, not so
much because it might or might not be true, but because of the way
it was being interpreted and applied by avid Puritans who were intent
on turning the Church into an exclusive group, in which the mind of
God seemed clearly made up.

In 1601, Andrewes was made Dean of Westminster and in that
capacity took part both in the funeral of Queen Elizabeth I and the
coronation of King James VI of Scotland as James I of England. He
and the new monarch struck up a strong relationship. Andrewes was
invited to attend the Hampton Court Conference, which was convened
by the King to listen to the complaints of the Puritans about the
Prayer Book of 1559. They hoped for a more austere form of worship
and a presbyterian kind of church government – more like the Church
of Scotland that James had known than the Church of England as
he was increasingly to appreciate. Andrewes was on the side of the
Elizabethan Settlement. He went on, however, to take part in the main
fruit of the Hampton Court Conference – the new translation of the
Bible, the so-called Authorised Version, which appeared in 1611. The
more reactive result of the conference was the publication of the 1604
Canons, which attempted to settle in an anti-Puritan manner many
of the disputes concerning worship. Among these were the enforce-
ment of the surplice and the direction that the communion table had
to be placed at the east end of the church, where it was to be covered
with a 'carpet of silk', and a 'fair linen cloth' during the service itself.
Enthusiasts for the less formal style of Lord's Supper which was common
at the time would not have found these Canons to their liking, but
we may be sure that Andrewes did.

Andrewes kept his old friends, among them Richard Hooker, whom
he would almost certainly have known personally during the latter's
time at the Temple Church, and with whom he worked as one of the

select band of examiners at the Merchant Taylors' School. When Hooker died, in 1600, Andrewes was most anxious that his papers should be secured. Hooker's house had, in fact, been burgled before his death, which does not appear to have perturbed the owner, as no books were stolen. Andrewes was right to be solicitous in this regard, for at that stage only five of the Books of the *Laws of Ecclesiastical Polity* had been published, and it was known that more was on the way. Whatever the precise details of how the remaining notes of the other Books in the series reached the printing press, Andrewes' concern shows that he was – to say the least – an admirer of the theological parish priest in Kent. We shall return to this point later, since it is of some importance in assessing the relationship between these two quite different men.

Andrewes was clearly destined for the episcopate. The old Queen had tried to promote him in that direction but he had refused to surrender part of the episcopal revenues which had been one of Elizabeth's means of building up her own finances. King James did not try those tricks, and Andrewes was accordingly made Bishop of Chichester in 1605, moving on to Ely in 1609, and finally becoming Bishop of Winchester in 1619. When Bancroft died in 1610, many people expected him to become the next Archbishop of Canterbury, but instead the job went to George Abbot, of London. However, Andrewes was already well established at court, and also had a number of friendships that brought him into contact with developments overseas, notably with two interesting scholar-diplomats, Hugo Grotius, from Holland, and Isaac Casaubon, from France.

As Bishop of Ely, Andrewes retained his interest in his old University, and as Bishop of Winchester he was ex officio Visitor of several Oxford colleges. Andrewes was thus able to keep directly in touch with university life virtually all the way through his ministry. His relationship with James was important for both parties. Although their views were by no means identical, James relied on Andrewes' support for his notion of the unity of the monarchy and the episcopate (James's famous dictum, 'nae bishop, nae king'). And Andrewes was given the unprecedented opportunity as preacher to deliver sermons before the King and the court from 1605 until his death, on virtually every major festival as well as on the other special commemorations, including the anniversaries of the Gunpowder Plot. Although he became James's confessor and spiritual adviser, he was too frail to attend upon him on his deathbed, nor was he present at the King's funeral. Charles I, whose arrogant attitude Andrewes is supposed to have commented upon when he was a young prince, did consult him, but Andrewes' days were (perhaps fortunately) over by the time the new reign got into its stride.

Theological Works

Among Andrewes' works, two stand out as of particular importance for the purposes of the present study.

The first is his *Responsio ad Apologiam Cardinalis Bellarmine* which appeared in 1610. It was written as part of King James's defence of the monarchy and the Church in England as then constituted. Andrewes had already written, at James's insistence, his *Tortura Torturi* in 1609 as a more political statement. The *Responsio*, however, was directed at one of the Pope's theologians, Robert Bellarmine, a Jesuit, and a keen controversialist, who had been told by the Pope to write a riposte to the King's own statement of his position, the *Triplici Nodo, Triplex Cuneus, or an Apology for the Oath of Allegiance* (1608). That James himself wrote it may be partly in reaction to the famous Gunpowder Plot of history and mythology three years before.

The *Responsio* does not bear the marks of the kind of systematic monumentality that we saw in Hooker's *Laws*, because Andrewes decided to answer Bellarmine point by point. Theological controversy is, in any case, often most effective in the short term when it is specific, and the readers know exactly who is saying what and against whom. There are two sections which are central to our concern, eucharistic sacrifice and presence, where Andrewes shows his subtle powers of historical perspective and synthesis. (Andrewes wrote the work in Latin, and we are using the translation by Darwell Stone.)[3]

> Our men believe that the Eucharist was instituted by the Lord for a memorial of Himself, even of His Sacrifice, and, if it be lawful so to speak, to be a commemorative sacrifice, not only to be a Sacrament and for spiritual nourishment. Though they allow this, yet they deny that either of these uses (thus instituted by the Lord together), can be derived from the other by man either because of the negligence of the people or because of the avarice of the priests. The sacrifice which is there is Eucharistic, of which sacrifice the law is that he who offers it is to partake of it, and

that he partake by receiving and eating, as the Saviour ordered. For to partake by sharing in the prayer, that indeed is a fresh and novel way of partaking, much more even than the private Mass itself.

Then he goes on to one of his more trenchant and suggestive comments:

Do you take away from the Mass your transubstantiation; and there will not long be any strife with us about the sacrifice. Willingly we allow that a memory of the sacrifice is made there. That your Christ made of bread is sacrificed there we will never allow.

Andrewes is more adventurous than Hooker in allowing the eucharist a sacrificial character – a memorial of the sacrifice of Christ, but not a re-offering of Christ – which was one of the main areas of piety which the Reformers found unpalatable. By a careful argument, Andrewes concedes the sacrificial nature, in a softened manner. He insists that everyone should partake – a clear reference to the frequent practice of non-communicating attendance at mass. But he will not have transubstantiation at any price, and he considers that if that were removed, and communicating attendance restored, there would be fewer points on which to disagree.

On the presence of Christ Andrewes is firm:

We place it among the theories of the school, but not among the articles of the faith.

We believe no less than you that the presence is real. Concerning the method of the presence, we define nothing rashly, and, I add, we do not anxiously enquire, any more than how the blood of Christ washes in our Baptism, any more than how the human and divine natures are united in one Person in the Incarnation of Christ.

Again, one can see the influence of Hooker, but Andrewes goes further. There is the historical perspective, but also the conviction that it is not possible to define exactly how Christ is present.

The other work is the *Two Answers to Cardinal Perron* (Cardinal Jacques du Perron, the French Roman Catholic controversialist) which was not published until after his death, in 1629.[4] In it Andrewes covers similar ground to the *Responsio*, and also deals with such matters as the acceptability of incense (which, as we shall see, he used in his private chapel), the term altar (which he employed when describing his own chapel), the practice of reserving the sacrament for the sick, and the intercession at the eucharist for the whole Church, living and departed. All these he admitted on primitive grounds. But he was careful in each case to tone down that acceptability in terms of what he saw as the custom of the Church of many centuries before – antiquity itself. Incense had no theological grounds, other than as symbol of prayer; the altar was for the memorial of the sacrifice of Christ, not its repetition; reservation of the consecrated bread and wine was for the communion of the sick, not for the purposes of adoration; and prayer in the communion of saints implies no doctrine of purgatory. In each case, Andrewes is generous in spirit but uncompromising over essentials.

The Preacher

Andrewes' fame as a pulpit-orator lived on until well after his death. For example, in an entry for 4th April, 1679, John Evelyn notes: 'The Bishop of Gloucester [John Pritchett] preach'd, in a manner very like Bishop Andrews, full of divisions, and scholastical, and that with much quicknesse.'

And four years later, on 15th July, he writes:

> A stranger, an old man, preach'd on 6 Jerem.8. the not hearkening to instruction, portentous of desolation to a people; much after Bp. Andrews's method, full of logical divisions, in short and broken periods, and Latine sentences, now quite out of fashion in the pulpit, which is grown into a far more profitable way, of plaine and practical discourses . . .

A more nuanced, specifically appreciative, and oft-quoted verdict appeared in 1842, the year of the republication of the *Sermons*, from James Mozley, the Oxford theologian:

> He is so quick and varied, so dexterous and rich in his combinations; he brings facts, types, prophecies, and doctrines together with such rapidity; groups, arranges, systematises, sets and resets them with such readiness and multiplicity of movement, that he

seems to have a kind of ubiquity, and to be everywhere and in every part of the system at the same time.[5]

On the other hand, the Puritan Richard Baxter once remarked that 'when I read such a book as Bishop Andrewes *Sermons*, or heard such kind of preaching, I felt no life in it: methought they did but play with holy things.'

But T. S. Eliot, who as a layman could not read Andrewes as a model for sermon-composition, did more than anyone else to bring Andrewes' preaching back into popular religious awareness earlier this century: 'Andrewes' emotion is purely contemplative; it is not personal, it is wholly evoked by the subject of contemplation to which it is adequate; his emotion is wholly contained in and explained by its object.'[6]

From these disparate evaluations of Andrewes, it will have become clear that not only is preaching often a matter of fashion and taste, but that Andrewes himself was an unusual man in the pulpit, and that it was probably just as well that few tried deliberately to imitate his style. There are so many features that are drawn together, not just the words, the images, the ideas, but those intangible qualities which relate to the actual day of delivery and not the previous or subsequent preparation of the manuscript. Evelyn's reference to 'much quicknesse' probably needs to be born in mind, not so much because of the speed of delivery as the style itself. And I would add my own strong impression from reading and rereading these works of art that Andrewes' warmth must surely demonstrate a man with a strong sense of humour, not unaffected by another seminal result, a sense of the irony of things.

It says something for the stature of Hooker and Andrewes that they have each been the subject of careful and loving scrutiny in recent years not from their own country, but from French scholars. We have already observed Olivier Loyer's views on the theology of Hooker. Another Frenchman, Nicholas Lossky, has recently made a study of Andrewes' *Sermons* which is now an indispensable tool for those who would look deeply into Andrewes' person. His own analysis is neatly summed up:

With James I's accession to the throne of England, Lancelot Andrewes was given the occasion of expressing the whole of his theological vision in extended preaching, with still more freedom

than in the preceding reign (Andrewes had preached before Elizabeth on a number of occasions), and of bringing to maturity the
best intuitions already present in the work of his friend, Richard
Hooker.[7]

What, then, of these much-commented-upon sermons? By no means
all have come down to us, but there are two main collections. The
famous 96 *Sermons* were published after his death at the request of
Charles I in 1629, together with the funeral sermon delivered by John
Buckeridge, Bishop of Rochester. They were edited by William Laud,
at the time Bishop of London, and Buckeridge himself, who had
become Bishop of Ely. The other collection is the *Apospasmatia Sacra*,
which are some of the sermons and lectures given during Andrewes'
time at St Giles' Cripplegate and St Paul's Cathedral, which were
published in 1657. Although there is more than enough material from
which to build a picture of Andrewes, it is still a shame that not more
of his ordinary sermons have survived. There is inevitably something of
the 'set-piece' about the published versions. Nonetheless, we are
fortunate to have what we have, and in a quest for his understanding
of the eucharist there is ample material.

One of his endearing habits in the festival sermons is to lead into a
reference to the eucharist near the end, which in turn would introduce
another favourite ending-motif, the hope of heaven. Thus, of the
Christmas Day sermons preached between 1605 and 1624, all except
those for 1622 and 1624 make explicit reference to the eucharist, and
of these, nearly all lead into a direct reference to the banquet in
heaven. Of the Easter Day sermons preached between 1606 and 1623,
every single one refers either directly or indirectly to the eucharist, as
does the sermon prepared for Easter Day 1624 but not delivered in the
event because of Andrewes' failing health. And nearly all these end
in heaven. As far as the Pentecost sermons go, of the fourteen delivered
between 1606 and 1621, all except the last makes direct reference to
the eucharist; the one prepared for 1622 does not include one; but all
of them end on the heavenly note. The device will no doubt have
strengthened the intricate connection between Word and Sacrament,
and perhaps even have encouraged any waverers among the potential
communicants in the congregation to come up to the altar for the
sacrament. But this device will have had another effect, too, namely
to set the eucharistic banquet within the context of eternity.

By one of those feats of versatility, Andrewes always manages to link these eucharistic teachings to his texts; which vary a great deal and only occasionally use one of the set readings for the eucharist on the day in question. A typical example is the sermon for Christmas Day, 1618, whose text is Luke 2:12–14 – finding Christ. With consummate directness he brings that message to the eucharist, drawing together the need to draw near, the poverty of the elements, and the reality of the presence of Christ feeding body and soul, all themes dear to Hooker's heart:

> You say well, for that we have heard we may, but not for any sign we. Yes, for that too. The Sacrament we shall have besides, and of the Sacrament we may well say, *Hoc erit signum* [this shall be the sign]. For a sign it is, and by it is *invenietis Puerum*, 'ye shall find this Child.' For finding His flesh and blood, ye cannot miss but find Him too. And a sign, not much from this here. For Christ in the Sacrament is not altogether unlike Christ in the cratch [crib]. To the cratch we may well liken the husk or outward symbols of it. Outwardly it seems little worth but it is rich of contents, as was the crib this day with Christ in it. For what are they, but *infra et egena elementa*, 'weak and poor elements' of themselves? yet in them we find Christ. Even as they did this day *in praesepi jumentorum panem Angelorum*, 'in the beasts' crib the food of Angels;' which very food our signs both represent, and present to us.[8]

The reader becomes accustomed to the style, with the mixture of jerky movements of thought and subtle blendings of image, of which the little Latin tags (doubtless familiar to his élite congregation at court) are a feature. We may note, too, the use of 'represent' and 'present' to describe Christ in the eucharist.

The Easter sermons, as one might expect, reflect on the relationship between the offering of Christ and the eucharistic memorial. Preaching on Easter Day 1611, on the text, Psalm 118:22 ('the stone which the builders rejected has become the corner-stone'), he produces this observation:

> Many ways was Christ, our blessed Saviour, a 'Corner-stone.' . . .
> One chief corner-point of His was, 'when He joined the Lamb of the Passover and the Bread of the Eucharist, ending the one and

beginning the other, recapitulating both Lamb and Bread into Himself;' making that Sacrament, by the very institution of it, to be as it were the very corner-stone of both the Testaments. No act then more fit for this feast, the feast of the passover, than that act which is itself the passage over from the Old Testament to the New. No way better to express our thanks for this Corner-stone, than by the holy Eucharist, which itself is the corner-stone of the Law and the Gospel.[9]

Not only does he build together notions of Easter and Eucharist. He uses the traditional association of the Old and New Testaments, of the passover and the Lord's Supper, in order to portray Christ – and by implication the eucharist – as the centre-point of the gospel. In his Christmas Day sermon in 1623, he uses a similar vivid picture of Christ being 'summed up' in the eucharist.[10]

The Pentecost sermons are marked by a particularly strong focus on the Trinity. In both the 1612 and 1615 preachings, he weaves baptism into his discourses in a way that is based on the baptism of Christ, in Eastern iconography always an image of the Trinity: 'The Father in the voice, the Son in the flood, the Holy Ghost in the shape of a dove' (1612), and 'The son in the water, the Holy Ghost in the dove, the Father in the voice' (1615). This provides him with the opportunity of drawing baptism into the scheme of things, not for the only time, either. The prominence of baptism in the life of the Christian is a central feature of Andrewes' teaching. Moreover, it is quite within his powers of ingenuity to bring the two dominical sacraments together, as a passage from the concluding portion of the 1616 sermon, on John 20:22 ('receive the Holy Ghost'), for Pentecost shows:

Fond, ignorant men! for hath not the Church long since defined it positively, that the baptism Peter gave was no better than that which Judas; and exemplified it, that a seal of iron will give as perfect a stamp, as one of gold? That as the carpenters that built the ark wherein Noah was saved, were themselves drowned in the flood; that as the water of baptism that sends the child to heaven, is itself cast down the kennel [drain]; semblably is it with these: and they that by the word, the Sacraments, the keys, are unto other the conduits of grace, to make them fructify in all good works, may well so be, though themselves remain unfruitful, as do the pipes of wood or lead, that by transmitting the water make the garden to bear both herbs and flowers, though themselves never bear any. And let that content us, that what is here received, for us it is received; that what is given them, is given them for us, and is given us by them. Sever the office from the men; leave the men to God to whom they stand or fall; let the ordinance of God stand fast. This breath, though not into them for themselves, yet goeth into and through every act of their office or ministry, and them conveyeth His saving grace into us all.[11]

In a tightly-packed paragraph, Andrewes deals with just about everything; the sacramental elements of water, bread and wine, the triumph of God in the weakness of humanity by the power of the Spirit; the redeemability of that humanity (shades of Hooker, with his 'imputed' and 'infused' righteousnesses); and all served up with another dose of Old Testament typology – the reference to Noah and the ark, an ancient image of baptism. Moreover, he does this through an extended use of the image of the conveying of grace, through 'conduit-pipes'. We have already noted Hooker's use of water-language focused on his 'conducts of life and conveyances of his body and blood'.[12] Exactly the same word, 'conduit-pipes', has already been used by Andrewes of the graces of the eucharist in the Christmas Day sermons for 1610 and 1611; and he will employ the same word to describe the gifts of the Spirit and the sacraments in the Pentecost sermon for 1621.[13]

Andrewes' use of language can be as unconventional as Hooker's, yet both are obviously standing within an evolving tradition, which is being consciously adapted for new needs. I know that sermons are, in one sense, out of date the moment they have been preached, which makes me wonder how I would have felt actually listening to them, for they must have been demanding on the concentration. But Andrewes is not trying to hector his hearers; and I suspect that most of his congregations went away with a profound sense that the Christian faith is interesting, challenging, and profound. He surely could not have wanted them to leave church having remembered everything he said. Like Hooker, he was suspicious of those who would turn the pulpit into the lecturing desk. His mind is always ready to absorb new images. Unlike Hooker, who no doubt thought that his notion of 'participation' would suffice (why not? he surely evolves it richly), Andrewes even employs the image of the eucharist as covenant – a theme of which we shall hear much more in Thorndike and Patrick – as at Pentecost in 1610:

> To a covenant there is nothing more requisite, than to put the seal. And we know the Sacrament is the seal of the new covenant, as it was of the old. Thus, by undertaking the duty He requireth, we are entitled to the comfort which here He promiseth. And 'do this' He would have us, as is plain by His *hoc facite* [do this].[14]

Andrewes was by no means the first to use this image, which goes right back to the Bible itself. But he will have been aware of Puritans like William Perkins[15] who were applying it in an exclusive manner to the God who predestines those who are in the covenant and those who are not. By the very nature of his language, Andrewes makes it clear that this is a covenant with two partners, with obligations on both sides: the one the divine initiator, the other the received who may have responsibilities in discipleship but who is always able to return to the Lord in order to renew that covenant as a forgiven and new creation.

Finally, Andrewes is acutely aware of the need to place the eucharistic memorial in its biblical framework. We have seen how he insisted on the 'commemorative sacrifice' in his dealings with Cardinal Bellarmine in 1610. Two years later, on Easter Day, he returns to this very matter:

> And that sacrifice [i.e., Christ's] but once actually performed at His death, but ever before represented in figure, from the beginning; and ever since repeated in memory, to the world's end. That only absolute, all else relative to it, representative of it, operative by it.[16]

We shall be returning to this treatment of the eucharistic memorial – 'representation' is a favourite term in the writings of Taylor. But it shows up Andrewes in a strangely prophetic light, when one thinks of the way in which this very notion of relating the historical eucharist to the eternal sacrifice of Christ has been described in the ecumenical convergence of this century.

In 1617, Andrewes preached his Pentecost sermon before the King – at Holyrood, in Edinburgh, during James's return visit there since moving south after Elizabeth's death in 1603. The principal purpose of the visit was to celebrate the fiftieth anniversary of his coronation as

King of Scotland. James had probably been somewhat provocative in his directions for the way in which the worship of the Chapel Royal should be carried out – a mite too Anglican for the more Calvinistic Scots. (Andrewes may not have had all that good a name among some of the presbyterian-minded in Scotland, for when some of their elected bishops came south for consecration in 1610, Andrewes, who was to take part in the service, had wanted them to be re-ordained as priests, on the grounds that their presbyterian orders were not valid; he had been over-ruled.) In a sermon of typical vivacity, Andrewes preached on the grace and unction of the Holy Spirit, and towards the end applied this to the grace conveyed at ordination. But just before that, he expounded his view of authority, taking the Bible first, but giving the Fathers a special prominence:

> This Booke chiefly; but in a good part also, by the books of the ancient Fathers, in whom the scent of this ointment was fresh, and the temper true; on whose writings it lyeth thick, and we thence strike it off, and gather it safely.[17]

It may well be that it was such a compendium of views on tradition that provoked the comment from a Scottish laird: 'No doubt your Majesty's bishop is a learned man, but he cannot preach. He rather plays with his text than preaches on it.'[18]

Sermons, as we have admitted, are often a matter of taste. And perhaps Andrewes' manner was too vivid and unconventional for the sober-minded, who preferred something more straightforward, less allusive. But Andrewes was not straightforward. Nicholas Lossky captures the potential of his approach so craftily worked out when he writes:

> For Andrewes, an authentic witness to the apostolic faith is not simply someone who is content to think more or less correctly. It is someone who, like him, has made deeply his own the experience of the Church. It is someone for whom theology is not a system of thought, an intellectual construction, but a progression in the experience of the mystery, the way of union with God in the communion of the Church.[19]

The Preces Privatae

During his lifetime, Andrewes compiled a book of private devotions for his own personal use, culled from many sources, biblical, liturgical, Latin and Greek. It was so precious to him that it was virtually the only book in his hands during his last days. He gave a copy to William Laud, and there were other manuscripts of it in circulation. Perhaps because of its essentially private nature, it was not published until 1675, since which time it has been edited and translated by several scholars. The most notable of these are, first, the work of John Henry Newman, who prepared a version of the Greek prayers which appeared as the 88th in the series of the *Tracts for the Times*, after which it was reprinted as a separate book. Secondly, F. E. Brightman made a more scientific study of all the manuscripts, and translated them into traditional Prayer Book English. He also included copious notes, which guide the reader through Andrewes' principal sources in the course of the text, and, in an extended section at the back, provide a host of quotations from Andrewes' sermons to demonstrate correspondences of thought and idea between the two. This significant work of scholarship has shown beyond all doubt that Andrewes prayed how he preached, and preached how he prayed.

Nearly half-way through the devotions is a short section containing Andrewes' own prayers at the eucharist. There are four sections: preparation beforehand, the offertory, after the consecration, and after the blessing. The private origin of these prayers is apt to be overlooked by those who might be tempted to place them on an equal footing with, for example, the prayers provided by Jeremy Taylor or Simon Patrick in their devotional books. Moreover, for obvious reasons of context, those who have used them in English have used the older style of the language. Our own age has seen some considerable changes in the language of the Church in public worship. It therefore seems logical and appropriate that if Andrewes can be translated into Cranmerian-style English in the nineteenth and early twentieth centuries, there is no reason why he should not be translated afresh into contemporary English. David Scott has recently brought out a selection of prayers from the daily sections in the *Preces Privatae*,[20] and he graciously agreed to make a translation of the eucharistic devotions in the same style for this study. They follow now in full, the layout corresponding to that of Andrewes' original Greek.

THE HOLY MYSTERIES

(Preparation)

LORD

I am not worthy, nor sufficient
because of the decrepit state of the roof
of the house of my soul
    to receive you
and there is nowhere in me worthy
    to lay your head.

But as you took it on yourself
    to be born
in a cave, in the manger of a cattle shed
    as you did not refuse
the invitation to the house of Simon the leper
    as you did not reject
the sinner, who like me
    turned to you and touched you
    as you did not turn away from
    that corrupt and sinful kiss
    nor from the thief on the cross
        who confessed you
        so I broken
    worn out, miserable
    the greatest of sinners
ask to be brought to the touch and taste
of the perfect, awesome, life-giving,
    and saving mysteries
    of your all holy body
    and your costly blood.

(At the Offertory)

Look upon us, Lord, our God
    from your holy dwelling
and from the glorious throne of your kingdom
    reach out to make us holy.
You live both with the Father above

and with us invisibly below
come to make holy these gifts set out before you
and make perfect both the cause and the people
for whom and by whom
they are presented here.
And give us fellowship to bring about
bold faith
pure love
a keeping of the commandments
alertness to spiritual gifts
a turning from all hostility
the healing of soul and body
a symbol of unity
a memory of the upper room
a foretaste of death
communion of body and blood
a sense of the spiritual
forgiveness of sins
a turning from the old ways
a ceasing from mental turmoil
the clearing of debts
the cleansing of consciences
healing of the sickness of the soul
renewal of the covenant
supplies of the life-giving Spirit

an increase of { being clothed with grace
                 consolation for the soul in facing death

an arousal { of repentance
            of thought

a preparation for humility
a sign of our faith
a fulness of wisdom
the binding of love
a concern for the poor
armour for endurance
a readiness to give thanks
a freedom to pray
a dwelling in one another
a promise of the resurrection

a real defense in judgement
a portion in the covenant
a type of perfection
So that we with all the saints
who from the beginning have pleased you
   may be partakers
   of your pure and everlasting blessings
which you have prepared for those who love you
   in whom you are glorified for ever.
      LAMB OF GOD
   you take away the sin of the world
     take away my grievous sin.

(After the Consecration)
   Even we then Great Lord, remember
   (in the presence of your holy Mysteries)
     the saving passion of your CHRIST
     the life-giving cross
     the precious death
     the three days buried
     the resurrection from the dead
     the ascension into heaven
     the sitting on the right hand of your Father
     the glorious and fearful coming again
  We pray to you, Lord
  with the witness of our conscience clean
  we may receive our share of your holiness
  and we may be united with the holy body and blood
    of your CHRIST
  and receive them not unworthily
   and that we may have CHRIST dwelling in our hearts
  and let us become temples
   of your holy Spirit
   say YES, our God.
  And make none of us unworthy
    of these terrifying
   and heavenly mysteries
   nor weaken our bodies and souls
    by receiving them

                unworthily.
                But give us
            to the last and final drawing of our breath
                worthiness to receive the hope
                    of your holy things
                            unto
        holiness, vision, strength
        and a lightening of the cargo of my many
                        sins
            protection from all the works of evil
            and a turning away from a trampling on the wickedness
                    of my conscience
                the dying to passions
                a keeping of commandments
                an increase of your divine grace
        and a making of Your Kingdom my home.

(After the Blessing)
                Finished and completed
            as much as lies in our power
                CHRIST, our God,
            is the mystery of your purpose and being.

        We have held the memory of your death
        we have seen the image of your resurrection
        we have been fed with your unending life
        we have been filled with all the delights you possess
            so that in the world to come
                all of us may receive
                    your blessing

                May the good Lord God
                    grant pardon
                to every heart
                who makes a practice of seeking guidance
                    of the Lord, the God
                        of his forebears
                    even if he has not observed
                    all the rules of the holy place.

There are many Andrewes' themes in these prayers, such as indwelling, union with Christ, the fruits of communion (which even include the 'renewal of the covenant' and 'a portion in the covenant' in the preparation), and a sense of the reality of the eucharist as something which is happening in the midst of human beings. Andrewes' penchant for vivid language, which we noted over his 'conduit-pipes' in the sermons, asserts itself in the use of words like 'the cargo of my many sins' at the end. He places the eucharist within the orbit of the communion of saints ('we with all the saints' ... after the consecration). Above all, there is a recurring emphasis on the holy: 'your all holy body' in the preparation; 'make us holy' and 'make holy these gifts' at the offertory; 'your holy Mysteries', 'your holiness', 'the holy body and blood', 'your holy Spirit', 'your holy things' and 'holiness' after the consecration; and 'the holy place' after the blessing. One can sense in the background the phrase from the Greek liturgies just before communion – 'holy things for holy persons'.

There is, too, a progression of ideas. The preparation is clearly penitential in style – we shall come across Simon the leper in Jeremy Taylor's liturgy. It is only in the course of the liturgy that the holiness language appears, at the offertory asking for the hallowing of self and eucharistic gifts, and after the consecration for the receiving the hallowed things, for holy resolutions. The concluding prayer looks back to what has taken place in 'the holy place' – doubtless a deliberate rhetorical device.

Andrewes' main liturgical source is the Greek Liturgy of St Basil, including the opening part of the concluding prayer ('finished and completed'), which we shall also encounter in Jeremy Taylor's devotional writings. But it is interesting to note how, in the prayer following the consecration, Andrewes weaves together two complementary thoughts. The first is the memorial of Christ's death, resurrection and ascension – all straight from the Liturgy of St Basil. The second is the notion of union with Christ, with participation in God, which may well have been inspired by Hooker's ideas, though recast for present purposes. Yet again, Andrewes adapts tradition. Participation is the purpose of the eucharistic memorial; the gifts have been set before the Lord on the altar, and the action of the Church is to celebrate the work of Christ and to pray for fruitful communion.

These prayers provide us with a unique flavour of Andrewes' inner life and it is good that they have the chance of continuing to nourish others in our own day. That they reproduce many of the motifs of the *Sermons* is perhaps no surprise. It is now appropriate to look at how he actually celebrated the liturgy in his chapel.

Andrewes' Liturgical Practice[21]

For Andrewes, church architecture was of great importance, for he provided the first order for consecrating a church. His private chapel in London as Bishop of Winchester – a thirteenth-century building – was commodiously furnished. The altar was placed at the east end, in line with the practice of his school of thought. There were kneelers at the north and south end, and seats for assisting clergy and visiting prelates in the sanctuary, as well as a credence table. The altar had two candlesticks and a large dish for the offerings on it, together with a handsomely-bound copy of the service-book. On the credence table there was a canister for the wafers (Andrewes used wafer-bread), like a wicker-basket, with a cambric laced liner.

There was a small barrel for the communion wine, and a dish for the water, with three pipes, as well as a chalice and paten, the former with the Good Shepherd engraved on it, the latter with the 'wisemen's star' on the cover. These designs were significant for Andrewes because he composed a form for consecrating communion plate. The decorations are equally significant: in the case of the chalice, the Good Shepherd is mentioned as a chalice-motif by Tertullian as early as the third century, the eucharistic symbolism of which Andrewes explained in his Easter Day sermon in 1624. As far as the paten-lid star is concerned, Andrewes refers to its association with the 'asterisk' placed over the paten in the Greek liturgy when he preached on Christmas Day in 1620.[22] The design of the chalice was different from the more normal secular-inspired beakers in general use, as it was deliberately modelled on the medieval cup, with a traditional stem and bowl. Andrewes was to set in motion a fashion here, in both the design and the Good Shepherd image.[23] An additional table held the ewer and bowl for the washing of hands before the consecration. Outside the sanctuary, which had altar-rails, there were seats set collegiate-style to north and south, facing inwards. In the centre stood a lectern, and before it, on the altar side, a table on which stood a standing censer, which had its own incense boat.

How did it all work? Andrewes left some notes about the Prayer Book rite, from which we can reconstruct his own liturgical practice.

Nothing was to be chanted, he notes at the start. (Cosin was keen on this custom in Durham, as we shall see in a future chapter.) The celebrant led the opening prayer at the north side kneeler, but, after a low bow, recited the ten commandments from the centre of the altar-rail. The collect of the day was recited at the altar again, the Epistle and Gospel from the altar-rail centre. After the creed, the basin was filled with the alms of the people, and the wafer bread and the wine in the barrel were offered on the altar (this was to be done by the bishop himself if he were present). He also provides his own additional offertory sentences, one of which includes the concluding portion of the offertory prayer at the dedication of the Temple in Jerusalem, 'All things come of Thee, O Lord, and of thine own we give unto thee' – 1 Chronicles 29:14, its first appearance in Anglican liturgy at this point. In all this, Andrewes makes a clear distinction between the offering of alms, by the people, coming up to the altar, and the presentation of the bread and wine, by the chief pastor present. After the prayer for the Church, Andrewes, who was a great believer in private confession, draws attention to the Prayer Book exhortation which urges those with troubled consciences to seek out some godly minister for spiritual counsel and forgiveness.

The service proceeds through the confession and the comfortable words, right up to the end of the prayer of humble access ('We do not presume'), and only then does the priest go to the side-table, pour water *over the napkin* and cleanse his hands, reciting Psalm 26:6 ('I will wash my hands in innocence'). This method of cleansing is entirely novel, while the use of the psalter verse is taken straight from traditional Roman Catholic practice. Then the priest returns to the altar and takes from the canister sufficient bread for communion, and from the flagon sufficient wine, being careful to mix the chalice with some water – a custom not laid down in any of the Prayer Books, and again reflecting traditional custom from the Middle Ages. The service proceeds, the bread being broken at the appropriate words in the consecration prayer. Every communicant is to say Amen at each of the words of distribution. This was not laid down in the Prayer Book, but was an old custom (revived in our own century). We shall encounter this recommendation again.

What are we to make of this? It is clear that Andrewes likes what he likes. In Fuller's *Church History of Britain* (1655), comes this opinion of Lancelot Andrewes' personal style: 'This I dare affirm that wheresoever he was a parson, a dean, or bishop, he never troubleth parish, college, or diocese with pressing other ceremonies upon them than such which he found used before his coming thither.'

Andrewes' Visitation Articles as a diocesan bishop could be quite detailed, but one suspects that he simply got away with his personal innovations, which were surely not confined to his private chapel. In any case, the influence of private chapels during the period in question must not be underestimated. They attracted a great deal of notice – not least when the owner was royal, aristocratic, or a Church prelate. In the case of Andrewes, the hand of a skilful adapter of tradition is at work. Taking bread from a silver wicker-basket and wine from a barrel (made to his own designs) is a way of stating one's independence and originality. The standing-thurible, which Cosin was to use later on at Peterhouse, Cambridge, and thereby scandalise the Puritans, is another sign of Andrewes' ingenuity; the preacher who loves the Old Testament's relationship with the New, not least in the sacraments, has incense rising from a table on the altar-side of the lectern. Inspired both by Jewish temple-usage and Catholic tradition, he branches off on his own, and although the more exotic of these practices do not seem to have been imitated much elsewhere, others (e.g., wafer-bread, and turning east) were, and became the subject of debate at the 'Savoy' Conference in 1661, as the Puritans wanted them abolished once and for all.

Moreover, while many of his fellow-churchmen were using ordinary cups and plates at communion, Andrewes appears to be taking the more delicate line, of making special the ordinary rather than simply using the ordinary in a special context. He loves tradition, but is ready to add to it through organic development rather than radical change. In any case, we can see in these arrangements the same mind that answered Bellarmine point by point, that preached those sermons, and that put together those remarkable prayers. In all these respects, we can discern the strands of tradition and innovation imaginatively meeting together to form a coherent whole.

But there is another side to these directions, especially if we compare them with the *Preces Privatae*, and that concerns the growing debates about changes to the Prayer Book. Andrewes wants to make a sharp distinction between the people's alms and the presentation of the bread and the wine, which becomes a favourite theme later on. We shall come across, too, the practice of reciting the prayer of oblation (in which 'we offer thee our souls and bodies') immediately after the prayer of consecration and before communion, instead of after it. The effect of this is to make the consecration feel more like the old eucharistic prayer from the 1549 Prayer Book. Although this was not Andrewes' practice, he anticipated it and in some ways went beyond it in the *Preces Privatae*, when he prays (by himself) immediately after the consecration a slightly different sort of prayer, remembering the work of Christ and asking for the benefits of communion. The two are not all that far apart, especially when one considers such a passage in the prayer of oblation that asks 'that we and all thy whole Church may obtain remission of our sins, and all other benefits of his passion'.

Conclusion

Andrewes is a man with many interests, and it is right that we should look at all four areas where he clearly had an effect on eucharistic thought and practice both during his lifetime and after. We have seen the influence of Hooker on his emerging theology, and also those instincts that took him a little beyond Hooker's scheme, though the two stand in direct relation. As Henry McAdoo has written in his seminal study of the seventeenth-century Anglican theologians: 'Neither Hooker nor Andrewes refused to meet the situations in which their times placed them, for both produced able expositions of the basis of their position in Scripture, reason, and antiquity, and both saw the need to establish and vindicate it.'[24]

We may equate, too, their determination of what are called 'the two righteousnesses', namely that we are made holy through a loving God, and that holiness was won on the cross, but is active now. Hence the fact that Christians in no way add to Calvary when they celebrate the eucharist (replying to Rome at her most polemical), but they can do more than just call to mind Jesus at his Supper (replying to Calvinism in its extreme form). The 'doing' of the eucharist, distinct from 'offering Christ' (on the one hand) and basking in his cross (on the other), provided for Andrewes the road towards seeing the Lord's Supper in terms of that 'commemorative sacrifice'. It was a variant of tradition, a reaching back to the early Fathers, and a development fed on Hooker's equally dynamic focus on 'participation'. But if there is a significant difference from Hooker in the substance of his teaching, it lies in Andrewes' much more open attachment to the Fathers, who were quoted so freely in his sermons and used so extensively in his devotions.

For Andrewes, this led him to delve into the past, but with a judicious eye on the present. It enabled him, too, to see this holiness as both beyond and yet in our midst – hence those references to the holy in his eucharistic devotions, and his enthusiasm for vivid language of an aquatic style to point beyond towards a loving God, always 'conveying' his grace abundantly through the visible and living signs of the sacraments. And all of this is set within the framework of eternity, and the work of God the Holy Trinity, manifested at the baptism of Christ ('the Father in the voice, the Son in the flood, the Holy Ghost in the shape of a dove' in the Pentecost sermon of 1612), and mediated in the eucharist ('Even we then, Great Lord, remember . . . the saving passion of your Christ . . . let us become temples of your holy Spirit' in the devotions).

But, as Donald Allchin has pointed out, and as we have seen in the extraordinarily broad scope of the fruits of communion in the eucharistic devotions, Andrewes always places the eucharist within the wider spectrum of Christian *living*.[25] It starts in faith, and ends in love, love as the key of all virtues, love as made flesh in Christ. Near the end of his Christmas Day sermon in 1616, preaching on the heavenly virtues from a Psalm long associated with the incarnation (Psalm 85:10,11 – mercy and truth, righteousness and peace), he has this to say:

> What is then the proper work of this day, but still to renew this meeting on it? For Christ's birth we cannot entertain, but all these we must too, necessary attendants upon it every one. They be the virtues of His Nativity, these. At His birth Christ bethought Himself of all the virtues which He would have to attend on Him then; and these he made choice of then, and for ever, to be the virtues of this feast.[26]

NOTES

1 Information supplied by Guy Rowston, and Canons Dudley Hodges and Peter Penwarden.
2 Paul Welsby, *Lancelot Andrewes 1555–1626* (London: SPCK, 1958), p. 7.

3 Translation in Darwell Stone, *A History of the Doctrine of the Holy Eucharist* II (London: Longmans, 1909), pp. 264ff.

4 *The Works of Lancelot Andrewes: Minor Works* (Library of Anglo-Catholic Theology) (Oxford, Parker, 1854).

5 Quoted from Nicholas Lossky, *Lancelot Andrewes The Preacher (1555–1626)* (Oxford: Clarendon Press, 1991), p. 34.

6 T. S. Eliot, *For Lancelot Andrewes: Essays on Style and Order* (London: Faber, 1928), p. 18.

7 See Lossky, op. cit. p. 17. It is noteworthy that Lossky has had his work translated from French into English. See also Nicholas Lossky, 'Y-a-t-il une mystagogie Anglicane?' in A. M. Triacca and A. Pistoia (eds.), *Mystagogie: pensée liturgique d'aujourdhui et liturgie ancienne* (Bibliotheca Ephemerides Liturgiae Subsidia 70) (Roma: Edizioni Liturgiche, 1993) pp. 189–99, where Lossky elaborates further this thesis of comparing Andrewes to the 'mysta-gogical' writers of Eastern tradition.

8 *Ninety-Six Sermons by Lancelot Andrewes* (Volume I) (Library of Anglo-Catholic Theology) (Oxford: Parker, 1841) p. 213. (This work will here-after be referred to as *Sermons* with the Volume number.) See also Marianne Dorman, *The Liturgical Sermons of Lancelot Andrewes: Volume One: Nativity, Lenten, and Passion* (Edinburgh: Pentland Press, 1992) for an edited series of lengthy extracts of these sermons; a further volume is in preparation.

9 *Sermons* II, p. 288.

10 *Sermons* I, pp. 281f.

11 *Sermons* III, pp. 199, 242.

12 Hooker, *Laws* V, 67.4 and 5.

13 *Sermons* I, pp. 83, 99, and III, p. 362. The term is found in a sermon on absolution preached on the Sunday after Easter 1600, where it expresses abundant sacramental grace, and is inspired by Ps. 87:7, see *Sermons* III, p. 98.

14 *Sermons* III, p. 161.

15 See Peter Toon, *The Emergence of Hyper-Calvinism in English Nonconformity 1689–1765* (London: Olive Tree, 1967), pp. 18–29. See Hooker, *Laws* V, 64.3 and 4, where Hooker uses covenant-theology language but in relation to baptism, and in his defence of the use of godparents against his Puritan critics. It needs to be noted that he does not use the term in chapter 63, which is the specifically theological of the two chapters devoted to baptism.

16 *Sermons* II, p. 300.

17 *Sermons* III, p. 287.

18 Quoted from Horton Davies, *Worship and Theology in England from Andrewes to Baxter and Fox, 1603–1690* (Princeton: University Press, 1975), p. 147.

19 Lossky, op. cit., p. 345.

20 See *The Preces Privatae by Lancelot Andrewes: the introductions to each day's prayers in Greek edited with an English translation by David Scott* (Blewbury: Rocket Press, 1993). For the older translations of the eucharistic devotions,

see *The Devotions of Bishop Andrewes* Part I (Oxford: Parker, 1856), pp. 141–6 (Newman) and *The Preces Privatae of Lancelot Andrewes Bishop of Winchester* (London: Methuen, 1906), pp. 121–4 (text) and pp. 228–42 (notes) (Brightman).

21 See Vernon Staley, *Hierurgia Anglicana: Documents and Extracts illustrative of the Ceremonial of the Anglican Church after the Reformation* (Part I) (London: De La More Press, 1902), pp. 92ff. For the liturgical directions, see 'Notes on The Book of Common Prayer', *The Works of Lancelot Andrewes: Minor Works* (Library of Anglo-Catholic Theology) (Oxford: Parker, 1854) pp. 151–8; the order for consecrating communion plate used by Andrewes in Worcester Cathedral on a special occasion follows on pp. 159ff.

22 *Sermons* III, pp. 89–90 and I, p. 247. See Tertullian, *de pudicitia*, x.

23 See Charles Oman, *English Church Plate*, pp. 226f. Oman points out Andrewes' love for these images, which were not used on communion silver in the Middle Ages. See also pp. 178f for a discussion of Andrewes' communion plate in general. They were all of gilt, which was common at the time.

24 H. R. McAdoo, *The Spirit of Anglicanism: A Study of Anglican Theological Method in the Seventeenth Century* (London: A. and C. Black, 1965), p. 332.

25 See A. M. Allchin, 'Lancelot Andrewes', in Geoffrey Rowell (ed.), *The English Religious Tradition and the Genius of Anglicanism*, p. 158 (whole essay, pp. 145–64).

26 *Sermons* I, p. 194.

CHAPTER FOUR

Caroline Prelates

William Laud (1573–1645) and

William Forbes (1585–1634)

About a quarter of the way down the Royal Mile from Edinburgh Castle to Holyrood Palace stands St Giles', the High Kirk of Edinburgh. A church is supposed to have stood on the site since the ninth century, though a larger structure was built half-way through the twelfth. Scotland and England have long acted like two nations bordering on each other, and when one of the many raids on England was being planned, the instigators are supposed to have met in St Giles' itself. King Richard II retaliated by leading a counter-raid and one of his acts of vengeance was to have St Giles' burnt to the ground. Rebuilding commenced almost immediately and the present dignified aisled church was completed by the mid-fifteenth century, and it received the honour of being made a 'collegiate' church, served by a college of clergy, in 1467.

St Giles' felt the early stirrings of the Scottish Reformation. In 1561 the first communion service according to the new 'Book of Common Order' was celebrated there; all the trappings of Roman Catholic worship had disappeared, for the 'Book' was a Calvinist liturgy, based on Calvin's Genevan service-book, and brought to Scotland under the influence of John Knox, the prominent Scottish Reformer. At this service, long tables were laid down the nave with bleached linen cloths; the communicants came forward to sit around those tables, passing the loaf of bread and the common cup from hand to hand.[1]

But the character of the Scottish Church was not to be finally settled until near the end of the following century. There was still a limited attachment to the office of bishop, encouraged by the young King James VI, and when he came to England in 1603, he did all in his power to get the Kirk to agree to episcopacy. Accordingly, new Scottish bishops were consecrated in London in 1610, by the Bishop of London, George Abbot, instead of the Archbishop, in order to avoid implying any canonical subjugation of Scotland to Canterbury. James set to work on trying to introduce practices reminiscent to many Scots of the old order which were part of the English Prayer Book tradition: in the 'Articles of Perth' agreed at the General Assembly there in 1618, kneeling at communion, confirmation by the bishop, saints' days, and communion for the sick were agreed. (All these were matters Hooker had defended against Puritan attack in his *Laws*.) A new liturgy was issued in 1619 – two years after James's first visit to Scotland since his move to England – a kind of half-way house between Presbyterian and Anglican styles. But it was becoming apparent to the more perceptive observers of the two countries that many Scots might have been content with their earlier, more moderate form of reformed episcopacy, but now saw James's version of it as closely tied to his style of rule. To put it bluntly, bishops came to be identified with an English desire to dominate Scotland.

James wisely backed off further encroachments on the independence of the Church of his native country. But his son, Charles I, was not so wise. Coming north in 1633 to be crowned at Holyrood (he had succeeded his father seven years before) he surrounded himself with English prelates. Two events ensued. He met one William Forbes and was so impressed by his preaching that when he decided to found a new diocese of Edinburgh, carving it out of the older one of St Andrews, Forbes was made its first bishop. The other event came in 1637 when a new Prayer Book was forced upon the Kirk, the reaction to which was so violent that it helped begin the national revolt against Charles. William Laud, rightly or wrongly, was associated with that book, and by 1641 he was in the Tower of London on a charge of impeachment. St Giles' short life as a cathedral is accordingly where our two such different Caroline prelates meet.

WILLIAM LAUD

Life
It is hard for people of an age in which religion is a matter of freedom and option to understand the violent background to the seventeenth

century, and harder still to understand why an Archbishop of Canterbury should be beheaded. Moreover, because of Laud's tragic end, and the fact that he became a scapegoat for a Parliament intent on self-assertion against an untrustworthy and haughty monarch, his strengths are usually lost in the face of his weaknesses. He was arrogant, ambitious, and not adept at working with people for whom he had little affection or understanding. He had a morbid streak to his character, and he was frequently haunted by dreams. He was a tough disciplinarian prepared to go to any lengths to enforce a new regulation on a diocese or a college. But although he was probably promoted beyond his real ability, he was an incisive theologian, a devout man of prayer, and he had a strong sense of obedience to his King.

William Laud was born in Reading in 1573, the son of a cloth merchant. When he went up to St John's College, Oxford in 1589, so began a career that brought out both the best and the worst in such an able young man. After graduating, he took a fellowship and was ordained, and in 1601 he was made the senior fellow and given the college lectureship in divinity. Theologically he had Arminian leanings, which were associated with Lancelot Andrewes, whom he knew through the latter's close friendship with John Buckeridge, President of St John's, who as Bishop of Rochester preached at Andrewes' funeral. Laud succeeded Buckeridge as President of St John's, where he enforced discipline; and here we have the essential difference between Andrewes and Laud. Whereas Andrewes had definite ideas but a greater self-confidence in others' ability to adopt or reject them, Laud always had to enforce his views. His assertive character and royalist convictions came to the King's attention when he preached at court, and he was made Dean of Gloucester in 1616. James took him north on his Scottish trip in the following year. Laud's tactless nature did not go down well. According to Charles Carlton's recent biography, he insisted on wearing a surplice at the funeral of one of the King's guards, which was technically correct. But he behaved so obnoxiously to the craftsman who installed an organ in the Chapel Royal – a sensitive move to make in a country where organs were regard as popish and indecorous by devout presbyterians – that the craftsman complained that he would have been better treated by a Turk.[2]

In 1621, Laud was appointed Bishop of St David's, which had the effect of moving him from an Oxford Common Room to the House of Lords. It was from this vantage-point that he began to encounter the House of Commons, so that when they voiced anti-monarchist sentiment, his reaction was as the college president to ill-behaved students. In the following year, he was asked to take part in public disputation with John Fisher, a Jesuit who had influence among Roman Catholics at court, on the claims of the Roman Catholic Church over the Church of England. We shall be looking at that document later; it was the most substantial piece of theological work undertaken by Laud, and it showed methods similar to those which we have observed with Andrewes. Laud's career flourished in the next reign. He preached the sermon at the openings of successive Parliaments, voicing the claims of the King by divine right. He became Bishop of Bath and Wells in 1626, and was translated to London in 1628. In 1630 he was made Chancellor of the University of Oxford.

When, in 1633, George Abbot finally died at the end of an archiepiscopate saddened by the stigma of a shooting accident on a hunt in the course of which a stray arrow from Abbot's bow killed a gamekeeper, everyone knew that Laud would succeed him. As Archbishop, Laud did all in his power to strengthen the position of the Church, for example by ensuring that all eleven of the bishops appointed during his time were his theological allies, and by energetically visiting dioceses to uphold discipline. There was a good side to such interference; Abbot had not been as able an administrator as his predecessor, John Bancroft, and there were many instances of poverty among the clergy and neglect of church buildings, always a difficult issue to settle in an age when responsibility is not as clear as it might be, and when the layout and even use of a church is a matter of uncertainty. Laud, however, was certain about what churches were for: worship and sacraments. One of his great crusades was for St Paul's Cathedral, which was badly in need of structural repair. As usual, the principle may be generally accepted, but where the money comes from not. Laud persuaded the King to agree that fines imposed by the Court of High Commission should go towards this needed work. And he got Inigo Jones, who also designed the new St Paul's, Covent Garden (where Simon Patrick was to serve as rector in years to come), to design a new west front, modelled on that of Il Gesu in Rome. Neither move was exactly calculated to endear him to his critics.

The steps that led to Laud's impeachment were as much political as ecclesiastical. Parliament had enough of the King, and Laud was very much the King's man. Laud had handled religious dissent in often brutal ways, tacitly agreeing, for example, to three Puritans having their ears cut off as the sentence of the Court of Star Chamber for writing virulent attacks on monarchy and Church that were clearly aimed at King and Archbishop. At his trial, Laud was allowed no counsel at all. He conducted his defence himself, and behaved with dignity, perhaps even arousing some sympathy for the way in which one of his principal Puritan opponents, William Prynne, had his diary (which was full of personal secrets from a very private man) removed from his room in the Tower and published. When his book of *Devotions* was returned to him after also being removed, he knew that the end was inevitable, and he wrote a prayer commending his soul to God. He was beheaded on 10th January, 1645.

Works

Because Laud is best known for his views on the *practice of liturgy*, it is perhaps appropriate to begin with them, although – as may become clear – this is by no means the most important area of his work. At his trial, he was blamed for at least two things for which he had no responsibility. These were the use of water-bread and incense, neither of which were practised by him – but both were the custom of Lancelot Andrewes and John Cosin. Wafer-bread had never died out in some places, and there are Elizabethan patens that are clearly designed for wafer-cakes rather than lumps of bread. But the kind of bread used at the eucharist never became a matter of discipline. For example, in Archbishop Bancroft's Visitation Articles in 1605, enquiry is simply made into whether 'a sufficient quantity of fine Whit Bread' is available for communion. Westminster Abbey, however, appears to have known no other custom than wafer-bread until the Commonwealth. But it was a matter of Puritan complaint, for the House of Commons resolved on 14th April not to take communion in Westminster Abbey but at St Margaret's, 'for feare of copes and wafer cakes.'[3] On the question of incense, we have already noted Andrewes' practice, and it appears to be a relatively isolated instance. A third complaint against Laud was having the Good Shepherd engraved on chalices, to which Laud retorted with the quotation from Tertullian used by Andrewes in one of his sermons, 'that shepherd will play the patron whom you depict on your chalice.'[4]

So what were Laud's views? They were indeed toughly applied. As

President of St John's College, Oxford, he caused a new chalice and paten to be made in 1615, and this is one of the 'Gothic' kind, with a longer stem than many of the later Elizabethan ones, and with star-like legs springing from the base. It has the Good Shepherd on the bowl and it is clearly designed to harmonise with later medieval designs, rather than the many other communion-cups that were being made along secular lines. These 'Gothic' chalices never became universal by any means, nor were they necessarily a badge of the 'Laudian' school. But Andrewes and Laud helped to popularise them. Then, as soon as he was made Dean of Gloucester, Laud had the altar moved back against the east wall and railed off, an action that caused controversy among the Chapter. He also had some handsome candlesticks made for the high altar.

Similar enthusiasms are known elsewhere, and were reflected in his private chapel. But it is in the public arena of church order that he came to the fore, and this explains the virulence of the Puritan reaction against him when he was at last no longer a dominant lord but a prisoner on trial. As a junior bishop, he helped to frame James's *Directions* in 1622 regarding the ordering of church discipline and the interior of churches. The 1604 *Canons* which laid down the procedure Laud adopted in Gloucester were widely disregarded. 'The altar is the greatest place of God's residence on earth, greater than the pulpit' are words Laud used in defence of this arrangement.[5] As if to symbolise further that 'residence', a 'carpet of silk' thrown over it became the 'Laudian' practice, although as we have seen, this custom goes back to the 1604 *Canons* and was doubtless not new then. It was the permanence and the symbolic character of the east end table which excited devout Puritans, who preferred to have a table set up only when communion was celebrated. In a later chapter, we shall be looking at Richard Baxter's practice in this regard. Meanwhile, it is worth noting the ideological polarisation between the Arminian pro-monarchist bench of bishops, led by Laud, with his enthusiasm for the altar fixed at the far end of the church, and the influential, strongly Calvinist, anti-monarchist Puritans, with their temporary communion tables only brought out when needed. It is easy to exaggerate the constituencies of both 'sides'; a recent estimate gives just under 17 per cent as a generous figure for the number of clergy who could be described as Puritan during Laud's archiepiscopate. But it is disingenuous to regard

Laud as the originator of these ideas. He was simply the applier of ideas not new.

The second area lies in Laud's *eucharistic devotions*. Like Andrewes and many others of his time, Laud had his own private prayer book, which he called his 'summarie of devotions',[6] and which was first published in 1666 with the imprimatur of Archbishop Gilbert Sheldon, a veritable symbol of the triumph of 'Laudian' ideals at the Restoration. Like Andrewes' *Preces Privatae*, it provides prayers for every day of the week, and for many other circumstances and occasions. But the style could not be more different. Andrewes loves to pray in blank verse form, using sources from many different strands, and in Greek, Latin, and Hebrew. Laud, on the other hand, writes in ordinary prose, often with straight collects as his base. He uses far fewer sources than Andrewes, and he confines himself to English and Latin. Two thirds of the way through the collection are some prayers entitled '*eucharistia*'. From the margin-directions (which are minimal) it seems that, as with Andrewes, these divide into two sections, preparation, and prayers for use during the service.

The preparatory prayers begin with a short confession, taken from one of Andrewes' devotions. There follow two prayers of self-examination. And the last in this preparatory section is a prayer the like of which we have not seen before, though its sentiments certainly reflect the troubled spirit of the time over eucharistic controversy:

> O Lord God, hear my prayers, I come to Thee in a steadfast faith: yet for the clearness of my faith, Lord, enlighten it; for the strength of my faith, Lord, increase it. And, behold, I quarrel not the words of Thy Son my Saviour's blessed institution. I know His words are no gross unnatural conceit, but they are spirit and life, and supernatural. While the world disputes, I believe. He hath promised me, if I come worthily, that I shall receive His most precious Body and Blood, with all the benefits of His passion. If I can receive it and retain it, (Lord, make me able, make me worthy,) I know I can no more die eternally, than that Body and Blood can die, and be shed again. My Saviour is willing in this tender of them both unto me: Lord, so wash and cleanse my soul, that I may now, and at all times else, come prepared by hearty prayers and devotion, and be made worthy by Thy grace of this infinite blessing, the pledge and earnest of eternal life, in the

merits of the same Jesus Christ, who gave His body and blood for
me. Amen.

There are three features to this prayer that deserve attention. First,
Laud makes explicit reference to disputes about the nature of the
eucharistic presence. The fact is nothing new – we have seen enough
evidence of it so far. It is the context that is startling. There is, frankly,
a flavour of the Pharisaical about some of the innuendos here. Second,
Laud uses Prayer Book allusions ('His most precious Body and Blood',
from the consecration, and 'the benefits of His passion', from the prayer
of oblation after communion). Third, in describing the nature of the
presence of Christ, Laud uses language that affirms the reality but
underlines the mystery, and he does this latter in such a way that
perhaps places him in a more Protestant light than Andrewes, who
would probably speak more definitely.

In the prayers for use during the service itself, we begin with the
collect for purity, and continue with prayers of adoration and intercession to the Trinity, which lead into some strongly penitential devotions, reminiscent of Andrewes in content, though not in style.
(Andrewes is an acknowledged source by the editor.) Laud's pusilla-
nimity comes to the fore when he includes the prayer for 'Turks,
Infidels, and Heretics' from the Good Friday collects in the Prayer
Book. But his piety speaks with a simple eloquence with which
Andrewes would hardly have been content in the prayer immediately
after receiving Communion (the margin notes *'utriusque specie'* – 'in
each kind', no doubt a mild anti-Catholic polemic):

> Lord, I have received this Sacrament of the Body and Blood of
> my dear Saviour. His mercy hath given it, and my faith received
> it into my soul. I humbly beseech Thee speak mercy and peace
> unto my conscience, and enrich me with all those graces which
> come from that precious Body and Blood, even till I be possessed
> of eternal life in Christ. Amen.

Laud knew Andrewes' sermons well, having performed the role of
editing them. It is therefore difficult not to see in the background
of his mind the Christmas preaching for 1617 on the virtues in Psalm
85:10. In the sermon, it was a case of celebrating the great meeting of
all things in Christ, here it is the feeding of a penitent sinner.

Just as easily forgotten in the maelstrom of Laud's trial and death is his main contribution to the debate about the rationale for the Church of England. Written up by him and published in 1639, the end of which year saw his arrest, it is an account of two public conferences held mainly between himself and John Fisher. Such public debates were by no means rare, especially on religious matters. James I loved a good discussion, and Henry IV of France himself convoked a disputation at Fontainbleau between Cardinal du Perron, to whom Andrewes had addressed his 'Answers', and the leading French Protestant, Philippe du Plessis-Mornay, founder of the Protestant Church at Saumur, where the young Daniel Brevint (of whom we shall hear more) came as a student towards the end of his life.

The original context for the confrontation with Fisher was the threatened defection to Rome of the mother of the Duke of Buckingham, Mary Villiers. Laud published them as *A Relation of the Conference between William Laud and Mr Fisher the Jesuit by the command of King James*.[7] Laud had first disputed privately with Fisher before Mary Villiers in 1622 and then subsequently did so in public, so that the two men knew each other's minds. The key to Laud's theological method lies in his assertion that 'the Church of England is nearest of any Church now in being to the Primitive Church.' In other words, antiquity is to be the judge of whether a Church is authentic. This was a bold claim, but it was one which others made for their Churches at the time. However, it became a peculiarly Anglican ground for belief in the years and centuries to come, not without a touch of romanticism. This proved the grounds on which he argued against transubstantiation:

> For all sides agree in the faith of the Church of England, That in the most Blessed Sacrament, the worthy receiver is, by his faith, made spiritually partaker of the 'true and real Body and Blood of Christ, truly and really,' and of all the benefits of His passion. Your Roman Catholics add a manner of this His presence, 'Transubstantiation,' which many deny; and the Lutherans, a manner of this presence, 'Consubstantiation,' which more deny. If this argument be good, then, even for this consent, it is safer communicating with the Church of England than with the Roman or Lutheran; because all agree in this truth, not in any other opinion.

While it is a moot point whether all the 'sides' to which he refers did in fact 'agree', the words 'truly and really' he later points out are

taken from Calvin, and one sees again the reference to 'the benefits of His passion' from the prayer of oblation after communion.
But what is most striking is the way in which, following in the
method of Hooker, he aims to establish a consensus, working for common ground where all may agree on basics, instead of using what he
regards as later terminologies. He builds on that common ground when
he affirms:

> Protestants of all sorts maintain a true and real presence of Christ
> in the Eucharist; and then, where is any known or damnable
> heresy here? As for the learned of those zealous men that died in
> this cause in Queen Mary's days, they denied not the real presence
> simply taken, but as their opposites forced transubstantiation upon
> them, as if that and the real presence had been all one.

When it comes to sacrifice, Laud is similarly motivated towards an
eirenic but firm approach:

> ... as Christ offered up Himself once for all, a full and all-
> sufficient sacrifice for the sin of the whole world, so did He
> institute and command a memory of this sacrifice in a sacrament,
> even till His coming again. For at and in the Eucharist, we offer
> up to God three sacrifices: One by the priest only; that is the
> commemorative sacrifice of Christ's death, represented in bread
> broken and wine poured out. Another by the priest and the people
> jointly; and that is, the sacrifice of praise and thanksgiving for all
> the benefits and graces we receive by the precious death of Christ.
> The third, by every particular man for himself only; and that is,
> the sacrifice of every man's body and soul, to serve Him in both
> all the rest of his life, for this blessing thus bestowed on him.
> Now, thus far these dissenting Churches agree, that in the Euchar-
> ist there is a sacrifice of duty, and a sacrifice of praise, and a
> sacrifice of commemoration of Christ.

We may find the careful distinction of roles (priest, priest and people,
every person on their own) schematic and contrived. As we shall see
later, Thorndike places the whole eucharistic action firmly in the
congregation's hands, presided over by the priest. But Laud here argues
on the basis of overlapping concepts (the different kinds of sacrifice)
and the Prayer Book rite itself, supplementing his statements with the

Reformation emphasis on the sacrifice once for all, and the symbols of broken bread and poured out wine.

What are we to make of Laud? He is inevitably overshadowed by Andrewes, and in all three areas outstripped by him, as Andrewes was a more tactful practitioner of the liturgy, a more original composer of devotions, and a more widely-read theologian. But all that this says of Laud is that he had great powers of synthesis. And yet his theological writing showed a tactical side: if for one moment he had taken the view that the Church of England should be defended, and made out to be different from the other Churches of the Reformation, his case would have been far weaker. Loyal to the Reformation sensitivities about the centrality of the cross, the graciousness of God, and the inner feeding of the soul, Laud is also confident about the role of the liturgy as the context in which that cross, graciousness and feeding meet in the eucharist. History may remember him as one of the few occupants of the see of Canterbury to end his life in a violent death. His personal aggressive style, too, left its mark in the pages of his prayers. His relationship with Andrewes is, perhaps, best summed up in the loving way in which he and Buckeridge edited the *Sermons*: he was obviously proud of this achievement, for when Elizabeth of Bohemia, King Charles' sister, asked for assistance in the plight of her husband, she received a presentation copy instead. But his enduring legacy as a theologian has not received the appreciation it deserves, perhaps because people approach him above all with labels in mind that only serve to distance him from the much more moderate stance that history ought to give him.

WILLIAM FORBES

Life

From the notorious Laud we move to a figure virtually unknown outside the confines of the specialist's enclave; which is a great pity. Unlike Cosin and Brevint, who were exiles, and the remainder of our characters, who stayed at home, Forbes is the only one who wilfully left his native land in order to travel and learn. It is the breadth of his knowledge and the personal contact with theology on the mainland of Europe that mark him off in a special way from all the others.

In 1658, there appeared in London a book entitled the *Considerationes Modestae et Pacificae Controversiarum de Justificatione, Purgatorio, Invocatione Sanctorum, Christo Mediatore et Eucharistia* (Modest and Pacific Considerations on Justification, Purgatory, Invocation of the Saints, Christ as Mediator, and the Eucharist). It was published by Thomas Rycroft and there is a copy in Sion College Library. In an age when printing was relatively easy, and even allowing for the theological stance of the author at the time of the Commonwealth, it is still a tightly compact book, with small print, packing as much of the material as possible into pages that cannot be said to be generous in size. It begins with a preface, and continues with a life of the author (both in Latin), which is signed 'T. G.' – Thomas Galloway, i.e. Thomas Sydserff (1581–1663), who was one of the Charles I Scottish bishops, and therefore a colleague of Forbes during his short time as Bishop of Edinburgh. The following narrative is based on Sydserff's account, supplemented from other sources.[8]

Forbes was born in Aberdeen in 1585, and after the traditional school education in the classics, he went on to Marischal College, Aberdeen, where he studied philosophy. Sydserff indicates that he was a hard worker (*'minus foeliciter quam obstinate'* – not so much happily as diligently). Graduating in 1601, he moved straight to teaching philosophy at the university, but in 1606 he resigned and began to travel, in order to study theology. This took him to Prussia, Poland, Germany, and Holland. In these places he not only studied – and, apparently, taught – the Fathers, the late medieval scholastic writers, as well as Hebrew, but he also got to know some of the leading lights of his day; men like Joseph Scaliger, Huig de Groot (Grotius), and Gerhard Jan Voss (Vossius), all of them teaching at one stage or another at Leiden. This kind of interchange clearly had a considerable effect on him; it gave him a width of perspective that can rival (if not supersede) even Andrewes. In the *Considerationes* he mentions at one stage discussing in person the beliefs of the Greek Orthodox Church with the Greek Bishop of Dyrrachium (Durres, in Albania). Nor was his desire to move around any kind of reaction against a supposed narrow upbringing. Aberdeen had long had rich and varied contacts with the rest of Europe.

Forbes was perhaps over-ambitious to travel. He wanted to take in

France and Italy but his health was not up to it, and he decided to return home. On the way back, he stayed in Oxford, where he was offered the Hebrew professorship, but it was evident that he needed to get back to the fresh air of Aberdeen. Ordained in 1611, he served two countryside parishes nearby, and in 1617 met King James on his visit to Scotland, when (along with certain others) he was awarded a DD by St Andrews University. At the Perth General Assembly in 1618 he defended the controversial 'Articles' which were being pressed on the gathering by the King: kneeling at communion, episcopal confirmation, saints' days, and communion for the sick. He also championed prayers for the dead, which involved him in controversy with the Principal of Marischal College, a factor which prompted the Principal's resignation. In 1620, however, Forbes was elected to succeed him, and was also made Rector of the University and Dean of the Divinity Faculty. Forbes was now recognisably one of the foremost theologians of his Church and nation, a veritable pride in what Allchin has described as the 'Aberdeen Doctors'. However, in 1621 Forbes was prevailed upon to forsake Aberdeen in favour of parish work in Edinburgh, but his enthusiasm for the King's mild but definite 'anglicanising' policy of the Kirk was not as acceptable there as it appears to have been in his native town, and so he returned to his former post in Aberdeen in 1626.

He was back in Edinburgh in 1633 for the coronation of Charles I at Holyrood and preached before him, doubtless meeting Laud at the same time. (It is not certain if the two had met on the 1617 visit, since Laud was apparently allowed to return to England early.) The King was so struck by the man and his preaching that he virtually chose him as the first Bishop of Edinburgh. He was consecrated in February 1634. He at once took up the liturgical cause and directed that there should be an Easter Eucharist in St Giles', that the communicants should kneel, and have the consecrated bread and wine given to each one of them individually. But his health did not survive long, and he died on the Saturday after Easter.

We may judge in retrospect that it was perhaps just as well that he did not survive to see the Scottish Prayer Book of 1637 provoke the anti-monarch and anti-anglican furore in the capital city. (For Sydserff and for the other Scottish bishops it was the end.) However, we may be sure that Forbes knew about the plans for this book, which had been in the air for some time. On one level, therefore, Forbes' tale is a sad one.

The Considerationes Modestae[9]

The *Considerationes* form one of the most unusual works of theology in the seventeenth century. While we have already encountered significant posthumous works, like Andrewes' *Devotions*, the *Considerationes* were left completed, which means that they lack the full impact that they might otherwise have. Further, they clearly circulated in different manuscripts, and John Cosin made a copy of three sections, on the eucharist, purgatory, and the invocation of the saints, in Paris in 1646. It no doubt assisted him with his work on transubstantiation, which we shall hear about in the next chapter. That copy is now in the Cosin Library at Durham. When did Forbes write the *Considerationes*? My suspicions are that they were written up in Aberdeen when he returned from his foreign travels, which is suggested by the fact that he refers to Andrewes as Bishop of Ely – where he was from 1609 until 1619. Being the work of a lively mind, intent on building up a huge collection of texts and quotations, he probably could never finish it. But it is as well that Sydserff somehow gained possession of it, an appropriate home for the work of a colleague on the bench. Perhaps it was Sydserff who drew it to Cosin's attention. As we shall see, Cosin and Sydserff knew each other.

While our concern here is with the eucharist, and therefore we stop short even of Cosin's selection from them, it is important to note that the eucharist comes last, and that by far the longest part of the work is the first item – justification. We have met this theme several times already, and it is interesting to note how the 'two righteousnesses' of Hooker and Andrewes (and others) come to play a part in Forbes' discussion of this topic, though he works it out in a much more closely-argued manner. This demonstrates Forbes' general manner, which is to deal with issues according to where the problems lie and annotate them with numerous references to scholars, Roman Catholic and Protestant. His overall approach, however, is to go for consensus: there is some fine biblical exegesis, and we read repeatedly of 'the more rigid Protestants' and of Catholics who give more leeway to controversial topics than the Council of Trent. Here is the result of Forbes' early classical education, a university training in philosophy, followed by a theological experience that was essentially 'ecumenical'.

That part of the *Considerationes* dealing with the eucharist is divided into three chapters.[10] These concern, first, the real presence and participation of Christ in the eucharist, secondly, communion in one or both kinds, and other matters such as reservation, and, thirdly, eucharistic sacrifice. His opening words comment sadly on the divisions of Christianity: 'May the merciful God grant in Christ with the Holy Ghost, that, all contention being done away, all Christians may again, on this matter as in all others, return to unity with concord in their hearts, without the loss of any verity necessary to be believed.'[11]

He rejects Zwingli's view of the eucharist as too weak, and too dismissive of tradition, but has more time for Calvin, although he is led by instinct to the early Fathers, who are freer with their 'realist' language but avoid the precision (over-precisions to him?) of the later medieval period. He quotes Andrewes with warmth when he wrote on one occasion, 'We as little follow Calvin as we do the Pope, where either the one or the other departs from the footprints of the Fathers.'[12] But it is the extreme Protestants who are rejected on three grounds. First, he does not like an overemphasis on faith ('faith, as is well known, is more properly said to receive and apprehend, than to promise or bestow'[13]). Second, one must not maintain that Christ is just as present in preaching as in the sacrament ('in baptism there is a layer, but here an aliment. Baptism is the entrance into the Church; the Supper is our nourishment and preservation in the Church'[14]). Third, Christ can be present in such weak things as bread and wine ('this presence is not natural, corporeal, carnal, in itself local &c., but without any departure from heaven and supernatural'[15]). We have been somewhere near these insights before with Hooker. When it comes to discussing transubstantiation, he covers the same issues that we have already met, though in much greater detail, and he calls to his aid some of the more moderate Roman Catholic theologians. This leads him to move towards the Eastern emphasis on the role of the Holy Spirit in the eucharistic prayer – the *epiclesis*. With his historical perspective, Forbes can see how the doctrine of transubstantiation developed, but (with Martin Chemnitz, the Lutheran) he rejects it, largely because it has been made an article of faith, rather than one explanation among several.

In the second book, he insists on communion in both kinds and defends reservation for the sick, using Patristic evidence to support his case. Although the main issues are clearer in this part of the discussion,

Forbes carefully chronicles the less extreme writers on the Roman Catholic and Protestant divides. One of his favourites is Georg Witzel, who admitted that communion ought to be in both kinds. Another is George Cassander, who thought that eucharistic adoration should be defined in the terms of the ancient Church. Witzel and Cassander were theologians in the first part of the sixteenth century who tried to defend in a constructive manner the attacks of early Protestantism, and whose works were subsequently regarded with suspicion by their own Church.

When it comes to eucharistic sacrifice in the third book, he quotes Andrewes' *Responsio* when he said that if transubstantiation were removed, there would not be many quarrels about sacrifice for long. But although the Bible does not in any clear way teach that the bread and the wine are offered to God, Forbes can still maintain, with antiquity, that the eucharist has a sacrificial aspect:

> The holy Fathers say very often that in the Eucharist Christ's Body itself is offered and sacrificed, as appears from almost numberless places, but so, that not all the properties of a sacrifice are properly and really preserved; but by way of commemoration and representation of that which was performed once for all in that one only Sacrifice of the Cross, whereby Christ our High Priest consummated all other sacrifices, and by pious prayer; by which the ministers of the Church most humbly beseech God the Father on account of the perpetual Victim of that one only Sacrifice, Which is seated in heaven on the right hand of the Father, and in an ineffable manner present on the holy table, that He would grant that the virtue and grace of this perpetual Victim may be efficacious and salutary to His Church for all the necessities of body and soul.[16]

Such a wide-sweeping picture unites heaven and earth, centring all on the work of Christ, but at the same time giving the Church a positive action in the celebration of the eucharist. Unlike Andrewes or Laud, he does not use the Prayer Book as a framework to his deliberations. He is working on a broader canvas still, searching for balance and integrity, blending the essential insights of Calvin on the ascended Christ and the virtue of the presence with the Patristic conviction that the eucharist is a visible action of the Church, 'efficacious and salutary'. And this leads him to affirm the union of the living with the departed in the eucharist, in a way similar to what we have seen in Andrewes: 'The sacrifice which is performed in the Supper is not merely Eucharistic, but also in a sound sense propitiatory, and is profitable not only to very many of the living, but of the departed also.'[17]

Forbes is not suggesting that the eucharist 'propitiates' God, only that it is such a close encounter between the human beings of history and the gracious God of eternity that in it and through it we are brought together, living and departed, in an act of praise and inter-cession. The 'profitability' of the eucharist is precisely that union of purpose, cause and effect, in the communion of saints.

Forbes is reputed once to have remarked to Sydserff that had there been more people like Cassander and Witzel, there would have been no need for Luther or Calvin. I would hazard a guess that Forbes, though not necessarily correct in such an assertion, has far more ecumenical potential in his writings than has been so far appreciated. Together with the other 'Aberdeen Doctors', his namesake Patrick Forbes, who was Bishop of Aberdeen from 1618–35, Patrick's son, John, and the equally distinguished James Sibbald, a significant group is formed of native Scottish Anglicanism. It is not for nothing that William Forbes ended the first of the three books on the eucharist that are contained in his *Considerationes* with the prayer: 'May God grant that avoiding every extreme we may all seek in love for pious truth, which very often lies in the *via media*.'[18]

NOTES

1 See the strongly devotional and theological sermons preached on the eucharist by Robert Bruce, minister of St Giles', in February and March, 1589, *The Mystery of the Lord's Supper, Sermons on the Sacrament preached in the Kirk of Edinburgh by Robert Bruce in A.D. 1589* (translated and edited by Thomas F. Torrance) (London: Clarke, 1958). My own personal copy is a gift from one of Bruce's twentieth-century successors, Dr Harry Whitley, whose sermons and communion services in St Giles' I remember well as a young episcopalian guest.

2 Charles Carlton, *Archbishop William Laud* (London and New York: Rout-ledge and Kegan Paul: 1987), p. 24.

3 See R. M. Woolley, *The Bread of the Eucharist* (Alcuin Club Tracts X) (London: Mowbrays, 1923), pp. 30–43, esp. p. 40.

4 See Chapter 3 n. 22. See also Charles Oman, *English Church Plate*, p. 226 and n. The St John's College Chalice is illustrated on plate 80.

5 See *The Works of William Laud* (Library of Anglo-Catholic Theology) (Volume VI), p. 478. See also Richard Buxton, *Eucharist and Institution Narrative: A Study in the Roman and Anglican Tradition of the Consecration of the Eucharist from the Eighth to the Twentieth Centuries* (Alcuin Collections 58) (Great Wakering: Mayhew-McCrimmon, 1976), pp. 124ff.

6 *Works* (Volume III) pp. 72–5 (the whole of the 'summarie of devotions' is to be found on pp. 1–107). See McAdoo, *The Spirit of Anglicanism*, p. 338 for a similar verdict.

7 *Works* (Volume II), quotations on pp. 320f, 328ff, and 339ff.

8 See below n. 9. See also A. M. Allchin, *The Dynamic of Tradition* (London: Darton, Longman, and Todd, 1981), pp. 63ff.

9 The edition actually used in this study is *Considerationes Modestae et Pacificae* (same title as given in the text) (Library of Anglo-Catholic Theology) (Oxford: Parker, 1846). The original Latin preface and life by Sydserff remain in Latin, but the main body of the text has been translated by the editor, G. H. Forbes. The life is on pp. 11–21.

10 ibid., pp. 368–613. (Latin and English on alternate pages – the references are therefore to Latin and English together.)

11 ibid., pp. 380–1.

12 ibid., pp. 388–9.

13 ibid., pp. 416–17.

14 ibid., pp. 420–21.

15 ibid., pp. 422–3.

16 ibid., pp. 576–9.

17 ibid., pp. 612–13.

18 ibid., pp. 506–7.

CHAPTER FIVE

Exiles Returned

John Cosin (1594–1672) and

Daniel Brevint (1616–1695)

Being Trinity Sunday the Dean of Peterborough preach'd; after which there was an ordination of two Divines, Durell and Brevent (the one was afterwards Deane of Windsor, the other of Durham, both very learned persons). The Bishop of Galloway officiated with greate gravity, after a pious and learned exhortation declaring the weight and dignitie of their function, especially now in a time of the poor Church of England's affliction; he magnified the sublimity of the calling, from the object, viz. the salvation of men's soules, and the glory of God; producing many humane instances of the transitorinesse and vanitie of all other dignities; that of all the triumphs the Roman Conquerors made, none was comparable to that of our Blessed Saviour's when he lead captivitie captive, and gave gifts to men, namely that of the Holy Spirit, by which his faithful and painefull Ministers triumphed over Satan as oft as they reduc'd a sinner from the error of his ways.

He then proceeded to the ordination. They were presented in their surplices before the altar, the Bishop sitting in a chaire at one side; and so were made both Deacons and Priests at the same time, in reguard to the necessitie of the times, there being so few Bishops left in England, and consequently danger of a failure of both functions. Lastly they proceeded to the Communion. This was all perform'd in Sir Rich. Browne's Chapell in Paris.

Such is the account given by the diarist, John Evelyn, of one of the more dramatic events in the life of the English congregation in exile in Paris. The date is 25th June, 1651, and in keeping with the traditions of the Church Trinity Sunday is chosen as the occasion for this ordination. But it is no ordinary ordination. The setting is the private chapel in Sir Richard Browne's residence in Paris. Browne was the 'English Resident' (ambassador) in Paris during the exile. It was a home Evelyn knew well, for he had married Mary Browne, Sir Richard's daughter, a few years before. This was the place where Anglicans worshipped, in a setting which is reputed to have been an impressive one.

Charles I has been dead two years. 1651 was one of the lowest points for the exile community, partly because of financial strains, a situation not helped by the attitude of Queen Henrietta Maria, who was a Roman Catholic. The preacher is John Cosin, still referred to as Dean of Peterborough, for all that he has been (illegally) deprived of that office by Parliament, an event which led to his exile seven years before. Cosin is a leading light of the exiled Anglicans, and he has with him two protégés, Durel and Brevint, both Jersey Huguenots by upbringing, who are now living proof of the enduring quality of Anglicans in such circumstances. Both will return to prominent positions at the Restoration (though Evelyn is in error over Brevint's preferment: he was made a Prebendary of Durham, but was subsequently Dean of *Lincoln*). The presiding bishop is one of the Scottish bishops, he who edited Forbes' *Considerationes Modestae*, Thomas Sydserff. Unlike Forbes, Sydserff lived to see the appearance of the ill-fated Scottish Prayer Book of 1637, and was deposed as a result of the national storm that ensued. One can sense the atmosphere of the service from Evelyn's description, brought out by the way he alludes to the address by Sydserff himself about the significance of the service. Exile has a strange effect on people. For our purposes, it brought together two very unlikely people – John Cosin and Daniel Brevint.

JOHN COSIN

Life

John Cosin[1] was born in Norwich in 1595, and after early education at the grammar school, went to Gonville and Caius College, Cambridge, graduating in 1614. As a learned young man, he was invited by two bishops (John Overall of Lichfield, and Lancelot Andrewes, then of

Ely) to come to London and serve as librarian. It was a strange double invitation, and it is evidence that Cosin had been noticed by two members of the bench who were of the 'Arminian' persuasion. In the end Cosin chose to work for Overall. It was a fateful decision indeed for two reasons. First, Overall had considerable liturgical interests, and secondly, when he was translated to Norwich in 1618, Cosin was taken over by another prelate, Richard Neile, who had become Bishop of Durham the previous year. Thus began Cosin's long association with that see. It is striking that Neile should have picked on Cosin, for he had the reputation of being one of the most ambitious prelates of his age, moving from one diocese to another with apparent ease: Rochester in 1608, Lichfield in 1610, Lincoln in 1613, Durham in 1617, and then, finally, York in 1631.

As domestic chaplain at Durham, Cosin established himself in the area. In 1624, he was made Master of Greatham Hospital, Rector of Elwick, a small parish near Hartlepool, and also a Prebendary of Durham Cathedral. Elwick was soon exchanged for a larger parish, that of Brancepeth. Rapid promotion followed, for in 1625 he was made Archdeacon of the East Riding. But the real mark of favour came at Charles I's coronation in 1626. Laud was one of the officiants and needed a master of ceremonies who was up to his own – and the new King's – standards. That Cosin should be selected for such a prominent role was a mark of the kind of confidence placed in him. The King was also impressed with the solemn liturgical arrangements made by Cosin on a visit to Durham Cathedral on his way to Scotland for his coronation at Holyrood in 1633.

Royal and prelatical concern for dignified ceremonial was not, however, to the liking of everyone. An attack on him which was to become of national importance was voiced by one of his fellow-prebends. Peter Smart was a strong Puritan and he had been chaplain to a previous Bishop of Durham. He had no liking for the liturgical enrichments that were being introduced in the cathedral, and on 27th July, 1628, he preached a sermon there in which he made a virulent attack on what had happened there on February 2nd (Candlemas) the previous year, including the number of candles that were lit. Smart went further and brought the matter before Parliament, but instead of having Cosin deprived, he was himself ejected. He was to have his revenge in due course.

In 1636, Cosin was made Master of Peterhouse, succeeding Matthew

Wren (uncle of Sir Christopher, the celebrated architect), who had been made Bishop of Hereford in that year. Wren was of the same school as Cosin, for the services in Peterhouse chapel were of such a reputation that it was rumoured that students were chosen for their musical ability in order to enrich the liturgy there. Peterhouse was nicknamed 'the Wren's nest' in certain quarters. Cosin carried on the tradition, beautifying the chapel further. In 1639, he was appointed Vice-Chancellor of the university, and the following year, Dean of Peterborough. However, political events were taking another turn, and in 1640 Smart brought the case of Cosin before the Long Parliament, which was also preparing for the trial of William Laud. Cosin's close association with the monarchy was well known. It persisted, for in 1642, he sent the Peterhouse plate to the King, in order to bolster up his position as the Civil War began.

The tide turned completely for Cosin when he was ejected from the Mastership of Peterhouse by Parliamentary visitation, the same process that was to deprive Herbert Thorndike of his fellowship, and Taylor of his living. So began the long, difficult period of exile in Paris, where Cosin's abilities were stretched in a way that he probably had not known before, as he helped to organise the little band of Anglicans there, and kept in touch with other distressed religious exiles.[2] It is no wonder that Evelyn took such pains to describe the ordination, at which Cosin both preached, and, as Cosin himself tells us, presented the candidates to be ordained. (This latter was a task normally performed by the archdeacon, which shows Cosin's seniority, an exiled dean standing in for an unavailable archdeacon.)

Someone so close to the royalist cause was bound to benefit from the Restoration. Returning to London shortly after Charles II, he was duly appointed to one of the most senior sees in the Church of England – his beloved Durham. Accordingly, on 2nd December, 1600, he was consecrated bishop along with six others, as the ranks of vacant bishoprics were filled up. As Bishop of Durham, he was energetic and tough, a trait in his character that had always been present, but which was perhaps exacerbated by the sixteen years of exile. His experience of French Huguenots may have softened his approach to nonconformists back at home, but he still tried to drive them to their parish churches. He made personal levies for small favours, from which he financed the repair of buildings. The diocese of Durham then included Northumberland, and was therefore adjacent to the country which had provided him with an ordaining bishop in exile. Reputedly a somewhat irascible man, Cosin could never forgive his son, also called John, for becoming a Roman Catholic. He had twelve years as bishop to make up for lost time, and died in 1672.

Works

When a change is made in what people do in worship, it is likely to cause more comment than alterations in the text.[3] As in the case of Laud, *liturgical practice* is appropriately at the head of our list.[4] In Durham Cathedral, copes were used in abundance, though it is a little hard to tell if Cosin is to be held directly responsible for this. Also introduced at Durham during his time was the full choral service of the Prayer Book, something Smart would have found against his convictions. The choir frequently sang anthems, and on special occasions, the *sanctus* and some other parts of the eucharist were also chorally rendered. As Archdeacon of the East Riding, his Visitation Articles of 1627 enquire whether each parish church had a 'comely and a large surplice, with wide and long sleeves' – a stipulation he was also to make as Bishop in 1662. He also enquired in 1627 into whether the priest says the words of distribution to each communicant when he 'delivers the Body and Blood of the Lord' to them, a clear sign of his understanding of eucharistic presence. He liked lecterns, but was not averse to reading desks, and at Brancepeth church he had two low pulpit-like fittings installed to north and south of the entrance to the chancel, for the reading of the service and for the preaching. Although only one remains, they must have appeared like the two 'ambos' of earlier tradition; Cosin wanted the word and the prayers to appear equal in importance to the congregation. This was not, in fact, an innovation; for example, George Herbert had a similar arrangement in Leighton Bromswold. It was a way of stating in architectural terms that the sermon was not the most important part of the service, as the Puritans believed.

The Smart sermon, however, drew attention to his liturgical actions in a dramatic fashion. Smart's account is as follows:

> On Candlemas Day last Mr Cosens, in renewing that Popish ceremony of burning candles to the honour of Our Lady, busied himself from two of the clock in the afternoon till four in climbing long ladders to stick up wax candles in the said Cathedral Church.

> The number of all the candles burnt that evening was 220, besides
> 16 torches, 60 of those burning tapers and torches standing upon
> or near the High Altar.

We may be correct in guessing that there is a certain element of
exaggeration in this account. Candles were obviously *de rigeur* for
Cosin, but in this instance as in so many others he is not simply taking
over tradition but he is adapting it. The use of candles on February
2nd according to Catholic tradition was not concerned with evensong
(as here) but as a prelude to the eucharist. Furthermore, as is apparent
from the alterations made to the Prayer Book in 1662, February 2nd
was not just the Feast of the Purification of the Virgin Mary, it was
also the Presentation of the Lord in the Temple – a change for which
Cosin was no doubt responsible. Indeed, the Gospel passage on
which this festival is based is a rich and subtle scene involving not
only Mary and Joseph, but Simeon and Anna (Luke 2:22–40).

When it came to his impeachment, Cosin answered his attackers by
denying responsibility for having the communion table in the cathedral
set up against the east wall of the sanctuary – such had been the
custom long before. The same was the case with the use of copes. The
candles were a practice deputed to him by the Dean and Chapter.
Choral singing need not exclude the congregation, though some of it
is in fact directed by the Prayer Book as an 'anthem'. We have a hint
here of the kind of attacks made on Laud at his trial. Cosin had
become a scapegoat as well. He adorned the chapel at Peterhouse with
cherubim and angels, a popular innovation in his school of thought,
and one which gave eloquent expression to the view that heaven and
earth are united in worship. This was particularly seen in the eucharist,
which is celebrated in a building that is more than a meeting house,
nearer a place where worshippers experience a sense of the transcendental. Cosin was able to indulge himself even further. He used
Andrewes' standing-censer, and had two candlesticks and a flagon
made. His interests in plate continued into the exile, for he brought
back from Paris a chalice which is now in Auckland Castle. The
climax to his work, however, came on 29th June, 1665, when the new
chapel was consecrated at Auckland Castle. The dedication to St
Peter could not have been a coincidence, for he had been Master of
Peterhouse, and Dean of Peterborough, and the parish church in Auckland answered with an old dedication to St Andrew. Inviting local

dignitaries and clergy to the occasion only served to draw to their attention the example of the old Great Hall now refurbished, with a screen, stalls in the chancel, and a finely appointed altar in the sanctuary. The example was there to be followed. The plate was sumptuous, too: a pair of candlesticks and flagons (one with an engraved depiction of the resurrection, the other with the ascension). Also included in the set was an alms-dish with an elaborate scene of the Last Supper on it, and two beautifully bound copies of the Prayer Book. There are signs that Cosin used his friendship with the famous silversmith, Sir Robert Vyner, whom he knew from Paris days, to obtain fine communion plate quickly.[5]

The next area of Cosin's work is his *Collection of Private Devotions*.

Cosin's *Devotions* are the real example in his works of gunpowder wrapped up in cotton wool. Published in 1627, the *Devotions* were written for the use of the ladies at court who were not Roman Catholics. The book was intended to serve as a kind of Anglican version of the 'books of hours' which those Roman Catholic members of court were in the habit of using. There was a need to fill a gap and to show that the Church of England could be an equal to the Church of Rome. It is a remarkable book, and although it can be compared in some respects with Andrewes' and Laud's books of private prayers, Cosin's *Devotions* may reflect his own personal use. But they were originally intended for the public domain. In spite of the opposition which it drew from Puritan detractors, the book was reprinted several times and it has influenced liturgical revision in several parts of the Anglican world in the period since. One of its most famous ingredients is Cosin's own translation of the medieval hymn, *'Veni Creator Spiritus'* – 'Come, Holy Ghost, our souls inspire', which Cosin had made at least in the previous year, as he had it included in a special copy of the Coronation service for the personal use of the new King.

In the latter part of the *Devotions*, there is a group of four sets of prayers for use in connection with the eucharist.[6] These are, first, 'prayers before receiving of the Blessed Sacrament'; secondly, 'heavenly aspirations immediately before the receiving of the Blessed Sacrament'; thirdly, 'thanksgiving after we have received the Blessed Sacrament'; and finally, 'meditations whilest others are communicated'.

The first section takes us from entering church to the consecration. It begins with verses 8 and 6 from Psalm 26 – 'the habitation of thine House' and 'I will wash mine hands in innocency' – the verse used by the priest when washing his hands in the medieval mass. Cosin may have had a special attachment to this particular verse, because there is an anthem consisting of these words which was composed and sung at Durham at the time, in which all the voices come together for the first time on a resounding finale with the word *altar*. Prayers of adoration follow, and part of Psalm 51 as an act of penitence. At the consecration, Cosin supplies his own metrical version of part of Thomas Aquinas' famous eucharistic hymn, '*Lauda Sion*'. It is interesting to note the way in which the theology of the presence of Christ is softened somewhat from the original in the third verse:

> A Speciall Theme of Praise is read,
> True living and life giving Bread
> Is now to be exhibited:
> Within the Supper of the Lord
> To Twelve Disciples at his bord,
> As doubtlesse 'twas delivered.
>
> What at Supper Christ performed
> To be done he straightly charged
> For his eternall memorie.
> Guided by his sacred orders
> Heavenly food upon our Altars
> For our soules we sanctifie.
>
> Christians are by Faith assured
> That by Faith Christ is received
> Flesh and bloud most precious.
> What no duller sense conceiveth
> Firme and grounded Faith beleeveth;
> In strange effects not curious.

Not an entirely successful piece of poetry, it none the less demonstrates how Catholic tradition is being handled. Like Andrewes and Laud, Cosin is convinced that when the priest recites the prayer containing the narrative of the Supper, what is going on is a 'consecration' – though that title is not to appear in the Prayer Book until 1662. Cosin seems more at home in formulating prayers, for in the three which follow, he uses ideas from the Prayer Book eucharist as inspiration for his work. The first concentrates on the cross, the second on the benefits of communion, and the third on the union of the earthly and the heavenly. This latter is worth quoting in full:

> Be pleased, O God, to accept of this our bounden duty and service, and command that the Prayers and supplications, together with the remembrance of Christ's Passion, which we now offer up unto thee, may by the ministry of thy Holy Angels be brought up into thy Heavenly Tabernacle: and that thou not weighing our owne merits, but looking upon the blessed Sacrifice of our Saviour, which was once fully and perfectly made for us all, mayst pardon our offences, and replenish us with thy grace and heavenly benediction, through the same Jesus Christ our Lord.

Some of the ideas come from the 1549 Prayer Book, of which he was an enthusiast, as we shall shortly see. What Cosin is expressing here is a theme we saw in Calvin, the way in which the Church participates in the high priestly work of Christ; the sacrifice is once and for all, but the Church 'offers up' 'the remembrance of Christ's passion'. We are near the memorial sacrifice so eloquently described by Andrewes, Laud and Forbes.

The remaining prayers are short – what are sometimes called 'ejaculations'. Immediately before receiving communion, there are verses inspired by the Psalms, and the *agnus dei*; when receiving the sacrament, the communicants must say the first part of the distribution formula ('The Body of our Lord Jesus Christ which was given for thee . . .') when the priest has finished. The thanksgiving after communion begins with an adapted version of Hooker's final words to his discussion of the theology of the eucharist: 'Oh my God, thou art true and holy; Oh my soule thou art blessed and happie' – whereas Hooker has 'O my God, thou art true, O my soule thou art happie.'

One could have no greater proof than this that Hooker was read for his devotional as well as his doctrinal worth.

The meditations after communion form a deliberate sequence of ideas: the coming of Christ (Luke 12:37); we are the temple of God (1 Corinthians 3:16,17a); being made whole (John 5:14); worship in spirit and in truth (John 4:23); and being followers of God (Ephesians 5:1f). Of these, perhaps the most significant are the temple of God and wholeness, both of which appear in Andrewes.

The third area of concern is Cosin's thinking about *changes in the*

Prayer Book. Cosin was an adept note-taker and at various stages in his life he made three series, as well as a set which we now call the 'Particulars', which were compiled in 1660 just before the revision process began at the Restoration. Then there is the famous 'Durham Book' (now in the Cosin Library, Durham) which was a copy of the English Prayer Book from the previous reign with copious annotations and suggestions which are largely the work of Cosin himself, some of which were adopted in the alterations made for the 1662 Book of Common Prayer. As far as the eucharist is concerned, these are too numerous even to begin to summarise. Through them, and through other sources, we gain the impression that he had some influence on the Scottish Prayer Book of 1637.[7] The extent of Cosin's influence is uncertain, but two things need to be said at this stage about that Book.

On the one hand, it was intended to be a liturgy specially composed for Scotland, on which basis it might commend itself to its people. On the other hand, by its actual contents, it embodies the kind of eucharistic practice which many of the seventeenth-century divines espoused. This constituency included some Scots, notably the small group of bishops, Sydserff included, who were keen on its production. The trouble was, however, that they were not representative of the Church at large, nor even did they command total support from the other Scottish bishops. The most significant feature of the 1637 Prayer Book, and the 'Durham Book', concerns the structure of the prayers at the consecration.

It will be remembered that one of the most dramatic changes made in 1552 from the 1549 rite is that instead of the priest reciting a lengthy 'eucharistic prayer', with thanksgiving, the *sanctus*, the words of Christ at the Supper, and a prayer 'remembering' the works of Christ, this sequence was split up into separate units, so that the communion followed immediately after the words of the bread and cup. Thanks to their interest in the ancient liturgies, people like Cosin wanted to draw those separate features together again, in order to reunite the 'eucharistic prayer'. (From Overall, Cosin learnt to recite the prayer of oblation immediately after the consecration, instead of after the communion, as a kind of half-way house, a practice which others adopted, and which shows how dissatisfied many people were with the 1552–9 liturgy, particularly in the way it moved directly from the words of Christ at the Supper to the distribution of the elements, instead of praying about what the eucharist was intended to mean, as in all the traditional liturgies.) In the event, this move proved too controversial, not just in Scotland (where the way in which the changes had been conceived and were to be implemented were bound to produce a counter-reaction) but in England as well. Abortive though this move proved to be then, it came to be of some importance when Scottish and American rites were being formulated in the following century – to say nothing of the work of revision all over the Anglican Communion in our own century.

Cosin's importance to the production of the 1662 Prayer Book was considerable. He took part in the conference that met at the Savoy in the Strand in the spring of 1661 at the command of Charles II in order to discuss the question of liturgical revision. No fewer than forty-four persons were involved, equally divided between episcopalian and presbyterian. Among the latter were Richard Baxter, whose work at this conference we shall see in the next chapter. Baxter produced a liturgy that he thought would find acceptance. At the other end of the scale, here was Cosin, championing ideas contained in the 1637 Scottish book – a book whose intrinsic merits were unappreciated by many for the reason that it was so identified with the late King's downfall. Cosin's wishes probably contained the whiff of popery. He was ahead of his time.

Apart from this major change, what else did Cosin want? Among the changes that were carried through into 1662 were the following: standing for the reading of the Gospel, with a response; having a proper thanksgiving for the departed (in 1552, the intercession ended with the sick, since the departed were untouchable – at least by Protestants); and a number of alterations to the rubrics. Most important among the latter was the description of the prayer over the bread and cup as the 'consecration'. There could now be no ambiguity about the fact that when that prayer was recited, the mind of the Church stated that something happened, that the bread and wine were set apart. The 1645 *Westminster Directory* had a similar view. But it was a significant change, building on the theological exploration and reinterpretation that we have looked at thus far.

Cosin was interested, too, in the liturgical year, and it is probably to him that we owe the readings for Candlemas, which we have already heard was a favourite festival of his. In the Middle Ages, the Gospel reading told us of Mary, Joseph and Jesus going into the temple and meeting Simeon, but the narrative stopped short of Anna, the prophetess. In the Eastern liturgies she is always included, and included she was in 1662. (Cosin's further interest in this feast is demonstrated by the fact that until 1662, there was no proper first reading at the eucharist.)

The final area is Cosin's work on *eucharistic theology*. Life in Paris had its demands, one of which was to make some kind of defence of the Church of England as it had been ordered. It was no easy task, given the fact that a new regime was in charge during the Commonwealth, and that Cosin and his followers were in a Roman Catholic land, whose Protestant minority was very small indeed; there were constant attempts to convert the little band of Anglicans. Cosin made two important attempts in this direction. The first was his *Regni Angliae Religio Catholica* ('The Catholic Religion of the English Kingdom'),[8] which was an attempt to justify the order and teaching of the Church. In it, he describes the way in which the eucharist is celebrated, usually once a month, and explains the meaning of the main parts of the service.

But it is the second which was the longer and more focused. Written in 1656, it is entitled *Historia Transubstantiationis Papalis* ('The History of Papal Transubstantiation').[9] Like the previous work, it was written in Latin. It was published posthumously in 1675, edited by Jean Durel, by then Dean of Windsor and who had been ordained by Sydserff in Paris alongside Daniel Brevint, – no doubt an act of *pietas*; it was incomplete without an English translation, which appeared in the next year. Following Laud's pacific line in working for a Protestant consensus rather than scoring needless points against other offspring of the Reformation, Cosin affirms near the start: 'The bread and the cup are in no way changed in substance, or removed, or destroyed; but they are solemnly consecrated by the words of Christ for this purpose, that they may most surely serve for the communication of His body and blood.'

He continues in a mode that is somewhat reminiscent of Calvin, but which also reflects the devotional prayers and the hymn we have just looked at: 'The result is that the body and blood of Christ are sacramentally united to the bread and wine in such a way that Christ is really presented to believers, yet not to be considered by any sense or by reason of this world, but by faith resting on the words of the gospel.'

In his series of 'Notes on the Prayer Book' we come across a similarly balanced view of sacrifice:

The Eucharist may by allusion, analogy, and extrinsical denomination, be fitly called a sacrifice, and the Lord's Table an altar, the one relating to the other, though neither of them can be strictly and properly so termed. It is the custom of Scripture to describe the service of God under the New Testament, be it internal or external, by the terms that otherwise most properly belonged to the Old, as immolation, offering, sacrifice, and altar.[10]

And he goes on to describe the eucharist as 'the unbloody offering up of this same sacrifice'. This is a term which was mainly but not exclusively used in the East, where it appears in a number of liturgies, but it was discussed by a number of Reformation theologians as a way of distinguishing between the 'bloody' sacrifice of Christ on the cross and the 'unbloody' offering of the Church in the eucharist.[11] Hooker, Andrewes, Laud and Forbes were all aware of its existence. We shall encounter it again.

In his second series of Notes, Cosin gives the following interpretation of the petition in the prayer of oblation 'that we and all thy whole Church may obtain remission of our sins, and all other benefits of his passion':

the virtue of this sacrifice (which is in this prayer of oblation commemorated and represented) doth not only extend itself to the living, and those that are present, but likewise to them that are absent, and them that be already departed, or shall in time to come live and die in the faith of Christ.[12]

Words such as these place the eucharist firmly in the context of the eternal, not only in what it gives thanks for, but also in what it beseeches God to grant through earnest prayer in union with Christ. We shall see that heavenly intercession of Christ developing in fresh ways in the writings of Brevint and Taylor.

In sum, Cosin's contribution covers many areas: how the liturgy is celebrated, how the devotional life relates to it, how the existing service-book could be changed, as well as how the doctrine of the eucharist should be understood. In all those areas, he shows himself an adapter of the inheritance, not as original perhaps as Andrewes, but thorough and well thought out. The eucharist should be celebrated with proper dignity; it should be backed up by prayers that feed the inner life of the Christian; it should be improved and it expresses a

doctrine. It is conceivable that there was a subtle shift in his understanding of the eucharist between the young Cosin and the older one,
as Dugmore suggests,[13] but my own inclinations are to view the man's
thought as an integrated whole. People do change, especially after a
time of great trial, such as befell him in Paris. But the carefully nuanced
adaptation of Reformation and Roman Catholic heritage that we saw
in the *Devotions* is much the same as what is to be read in the *Historia*.
It would seem that the man who (no doubt for diplomatic reasons)
did not take up the use of incense as Bishop of Durham that he had
done as Master of Peterhouse in Cambridge is the same man who
championed Candlemas in 1627 and ensured its more proper provision
in the Prayer Book of 1662.

DANIEL BREVINT

Life

Daniel Brevint was born on the island of Jersey in 1616 of a Huguenot
family. His father was the parish minister of St John's, and he was
baptised there on 11th May, 1616. When the Reformation swept
through the structures and worship of the English Church, it was the
French Reformed version that took hold on the Channel Islands.
Queen Elizabeth accordingly transferred these Islands from the (still
Roman Catholic) diocese of Coutances to the (now Protestant) diocese
of Winchester. The French Reformed influence remained strong and
it was not until the Restoration that the Prayer Book order and worship
were fully established there. Brevint went to study at the Protestant
University at Saumur, on the Loire, which had been founded by the
influential statesman Philippe du Plessis-Mornay in 1593. Saumur was
a stronghold for the French Protestants, and here Brevint will have
had the opportunity to meet the theological leaders of his Church,
including the scholar Jean Daillé, whose work on the early Fathers
had some influence in England, including on Jeremy Taylor. He graduated in 1624, having distinguished himself in the study of philosophy.

   Then in 1636, at the suggestion of Laud, Charles I founded three
fellowships at Oxford for Channel Islanders. Brevint was duly selected
by the inhabitants of Jersey, and he arrived in Oxford the following
year. It is one thing to start something new, it is another to deal with
its implications. Brevint naturally expected his degree from Saumur to

be fully recognised, but when Laud heard of this in his capacity as Chancellor, he tried to make the university insist that Brevint take an Oxford degree first. The Vice-Chancellor and his colleagues were not to be led into such a provincial attitude and Brevint was 'incorporated' with an Oxford MA in 1638. He carried on his work as a fellow until the Parliamentary Commissioners deprived him of his post, just as they deprived John Cosin at Cambridge. He returned to Jersey, but as the Civil War swept through the Channel Islands, he fled to France in 1651.

Brevint arrived in Paris with Durel, and others, convinced of the need to impress the Huguenots with the Anglican solution to the Reformation, and in due course he came across the English community, among whom was numbered another ex-don, John Cosin. The end result of these encounters was his ordination in Paris by Sydserff in the circumstances related above. He is supposed to have struck up a good relationship with Charles II, and this ensured his position at the Restoration, for when Cosin was made Bishop of Durham, Brevint succeeded to Cosin's two old Durham jobs, rector of Brancepeth and prebendary of the Cathedral. When Michael Honywood, the Dean of Lincoln and another Commonwealth exile, died in 1681, the King had Brevint succeed. This new post he held until his death in 1695.

Work

Brevint wrote various books, but his main work for the purposes of this study is his *The Christian Sacrament and Sacrifice*, which first appeared in English in 1673. But before we discuss its contents, it is important to take note of the more controversial side to Brevint, namely his polemical works against the Roman Catholic Church. In 1674, he published his *Missale Romanum: or the Depth and Mystery of the Roman Mass laid open and explained, for the use both of Reformed and Unreformed Christians*. There are parts of it that are strong in language, and their strength comes across all the more so in the somewhat different atmosphere of the twentieth century. The other reason for taking note of it is that much of the work is directed against the Roman Catholic understanding of the sacrifice of the mass. Since his purpose in *Christian Sacrament and Sacrifice* is to restore (what he sees as) a more primitive and biblical notion of sacrifice, a key paragraph in his argument in *Missale Romanum* is relevant to our discussion:

Because it was the general custom of primitive Christians, never to receive the Holy Sacrament, but after they had made their offerings, out of which the two elements of bread and wine, being set apart, and consecrated, and then by an ordinary manner of speech, called the Body and Blood of Christ; the word, as well as the act of offering, got so large and common a use in two distinct offices, as to signify the whole service, which St Augustine more distinctly calls offering and receiving; that is, offering the bread and wine before, and receiving part of it after it was consecrated. And really the whole service was little more than a continued oblation. For Christians before the Sacrament offered their gifts, and after it, offered their prayers, their praises, and themselves. And this was the constant and solemn oblation of the Church, until dark and stupid ages which by degrees have hatched transubstantiation in the bosom of the Roman church, have at last improved it to this horrid direful service, which mainly aims at this, to offer upon an altar, not the bread and the wine as before, but the very Body and Blood of Christ.[14]

Brevint's agenda is thus plain and clear. He wants to get back to a 'purer' and more ancient understanding of the eucharist, and it is interesting to note the citations to Augustine which he uses in this quest. The Reformation is about that process of purification. How did he set about it?

The answer lies in a book which he had written in Paris for the wife of Henri Turenne, the French military commander who led the French forces in the Thirty Years War. Turenne had been brought up a Protestant and his wife was a strongly religious person. Turenne made Brevint his chaplain after he came to Paris in 1651, and it was his contact with the countess and another prominent lady, the Duchess of Bouillon, that elicited *Christian Sacrament and Sacrifice*. The book obviously achieved a reputation. It was duly published in English many years later, in 1672, this edition being dedicated to Lady Elizabeth Carteret. Brevint knew the Cartearets: Sir George was a royalist who came from an old Jersey family. He had been Governor of his native island when the Parliamentary forces invaded, and became Treasurer to the Navy at the Restoration.

These aristocratic connections, however, in no way contextualise the real greatness of Brevint's work. Just as we had to take Laud's less appealing private prayers into account when they implied censure of those who did not share his views on the eucharist, so we have to accept Brevint's fiery writings against the Roman Church. They form the basis for his motivations in writing this short but profound work on the eucharist.

The work comes in four main parts, spread out over eight sections. In tone it could not be further from the clamour of controversy. It is the first work on the eucharist we have seen that has something of the style and approach of Hooker. Although not without repetition, it is exclusively about the eucharist, and it is interspersed with prayers at the end of each chapter (and one additional prayer not far from the end of chapter 7). The four parts concern the eucharist as, first, a memorial, second, a feeding of the Church, and third a pledge of the future; and the final part looks at the self-offering of the Christian. Ironically, one sees in that threefold scheme of memorial, food, pledge, the teaching of Thomas Aquinas.[15]

Brevint begins on a peaceful note, which expresses his intended approach to the issues concerned:

> The Sacrament instituted by Christ at the eve of his passion, which *St Paul* calls the *Lord's Supper* is, without controversy, one of the greatest mysteries of godliness, and the most solemn festival of the Christian religion. The holy table, or altar, which presents this sacred banquet, may, as well as the old tabernacle, take to itself the title of *meeting*, since there the people must appear to worship God, and there certainly God is present to meet and to bless his people.[16]

It is clear from the outset that the Old Testament background is important to him. His main line of argument is that Christ's sacrifice stands central and is eternal ('this eternal sacrifice'). This means that the Old Testament sacrifices prefigure the supper. Thus the eucharist is the sign used by God to portray that sacrifice in the bread broken and wine outpoured (the death of Christ), in the solemnity of the bread and wine so consecrated (God dwelling in the sanctuary), and in the bread and wine evoking by their context the sacrifice of Christ. The purpose of the eucharist is 'to enrich this *memorial* with such an effectual and real presence of continuing atonement and strength, as may both "evidently set forth Christ Himself crucified before our eyes" (Galatians 3:1) and invite us to his sacrifice, not as done and gone many years since, but, as to expiating grace and mercy, still lasting, still new, still the same that it was when it was first offered to us.'[17]

Brevint stresses throughout the present reality of the sacrifice. Just as Andrewes liked to use the water-image (his 'conduit-pipes'), so Brevint uses several times the word 'efflux' (channels of outflow), such as 'the true efflux of that Sacrifice'.[18] Nor is the comparison with Andrewes without profit. Both want to place the grace of God as supreme. But whereas Andrewes uses 'conduit-pipes' to illustrate the reality of that grace in the sacraments of the Church, Brevint employs the more specific image of that grace pouring out, in the blood of Christ. Central, too, to Brevint's thoughts is the link that he keeps making between that eternal sacrifice of Christ and the Church's memorial. He achieves this in two approaches. He compares it with the Old Testament temple-practice, such as the daily sacrifices, where a cereal-offering was poured over the lamb (Exodus 29:38ff). But more specifically, he stresses the work of Christ interceding in heaven and the way in which worshippers on earth share in that offering:

> This victim having been offered up both in the fulness of time and in the midst of the habitable world, which properly is Christ's great temple, and thence being carried up to heaven, which is his proper sanctuary, thence he spreads all about us salvation, as the burnt-offering did its smoke, as the golden altar did its perfumes, and as the burning candlestick its lights. And thus Christ's body and blood have every where, but especially at the holy Communion, a most true and *real presence*. When He offered himself upon earth, the vapour of his atonement went up and darkened the very sun; and by rending the great veil, it clearly shewed He had made a way into heaven.
>
> Now since He is gone up to heaven, thence He sends down on earth the graces that spring continually both from his everlasting Sacrifice, and from the continual intercession which attend it. So that it is vain to say, *who will go up into heaven?* since, without either ascending or descending, this sacred body of Jesus fills with atonement and blessing the remotest parts of this temple.[19]

This is the most elaborately worked out expression we have had so far of the union of the earthly and the heavenly, which we shall see developed in a similar way in Jeremy Taylor, with whom Brevint has much in common in his use of such key terms as 'mystery' of the sacrament, 'cloud' of God's revelation, and expressions like 'worthy communicant' and the image of the tree of life. Underneath his complex edifice, Brevint relies strongly on a sacrificial view of the work of Christ, and he feels no need to defend his case; no religion, he maintains, exists without some form of sacrifice. Several times, Brevint uses strongly virtualist language of the eucharistic presence, but in the next section, he goes one step further: 'The body and blood of Jesus Christ is, in *full value*, and heaven with all its fulness is, in *sure title*, instated as true Christians by those small portions which they receive at the blessed Communion.'[20]

One notes the language of 'value' (which is new) and the way he unites the faith of the communicant with the gift of Christ's presence, in a manner similar to Hooker. His comments in *Missale Romanum*, however, spring to mind on reading the following comparison between the ancient Church and what Christians of his own day should be doing:

> One may see both the great use and advantage of more frequent Communion, and how much it concerns us, whensoever we go to receive it, to lay out all our wants, and pour out all our grief, our prayers, and our praises before the Lord, in so happy a conjuncture. The primitive Christians did it so, who did as seldom meet to preach or pray without a Communion, as did the old Israelites to worship without a Sacrifice. On solemn days especially, or upon great exigencies, they ever used this help of sacramental oblation, as the most powerful means the Church had to strengthen their supplications, to open the gates of heaven, and to force, in a manner, God and his Christ to have compassion on them.[21]

When he comes to discuss the self-offering of the Christian, his ground is already prepared:

> But the Sacrifice of Christ, though it was confined to few hours, and to a small parcel of ground, as to the *suffering*, yet being everlasting, infinite, and still the same *as to the sufficiency and virtue of it*, co-extends itself most perfectly to all both times and places when and where those scattered members will ever come to offer up themselves to God with their Head.[22]

On a number of occasions, Brevint draws attention to the inseparable

link between baptism and eucharist, and in the following passage he
sets this in the context of God's covenant, a theme which we shall
encounter in Taylor, and to an even greater extent in Thorndike and
Patrick:

> ... because Christ offers Himself for us at the holy Communion
> in a more solemn and public sacramental way ... we are then
> obliged, in a more special manner, to renew all our Sacrifices, all
> the vows of our baptism, all the first fruits of our conversion, and
> all the particular promises which, it may be, we have made ... [23]

Brevint stands as a link between various traditions. Theologically,
he serves the acknowledged function of having inspired some of the
greatest hymns on the eucharist ever written, for when the Wesley
brothers produced their *Hymns on the Lord's Supper* in 1745, they
prefixed them with an abbreviated version of Brevint's work.[24] Moreover, they adopted a similar division of their hymns according to *genre*,
as memorial, as a means of grace, as a pledge of heaven, as a sacrifice,
and as self-oblation. Epworth rectory, where the Wesley brothers were
brought up, is not far from Lincoln, and piety can be very local in the
way it travels.

In terms of the kind of book he has written, Brevint is nearer the
works of Taylor and Patrick than Andrewes or Cosin. He is writing in
a devotional style, distilling his theology into the language of prayer:
it is often hard to see exactly when his discourse ends and his praying
begins, though the prayers are clearly so-marked at the end of each
chapter. In the next two chapters, we shall be looking at Taylor's
Worthy Communicant and Patrick's *Mensa Mystica*, both of which were
published in 1660. Although much longer than Brevint's *Christian
Sacrament and Sacrifice*, we seem to be reading works written in a
different style, which are more concerned with building up lay piety
with theological instruction, exposition, and prayer. We are, in Brevint
in particular, nearer to Hooker, but he also has much in common with
Taylor in some of his language, and in his vision of heaven and earth
united in Christ's eternal offering and intercession.

But there is another link which Brevint makes. In the last chapter,
we saw how Forbes used his extensive travelling and width of reading
to approach the eucharist from perhaps a wider perspective than any
of the writers we have so far seen. Now, in Brevint, we have a Channel-
Islander, with a French education, supplemented by an English one,

who is ordained both as a French Reformed pastor and as an Anglican, coming to England in triumph to a prebendal stall in Durham Cathedral at the Restoration. It was quite a pilgrimage, which involved a fair degree of change in worship. The Channel Islander Calvinists adopted the early French Reformed custom of baptising in basins, not fonts, and their chalices were low wide bowls in their shape. The grand and sumptuous plate at Durham Cathedral and the sumptuous decor inherited from Cosin in Brancepeth church must have seemed a far cry from his youth. Nonetheless, are there any special influences that can be discerned from his French Calvinist formation?

The answer probably lies at Saumur, where he would have known Philippe du Plessis-Mornay, who published in 1598 his *De l'institution, usage et doctrine du sainct sacrement de l'eucharistie en l'église Ancienne* ('On the institution, use and doctrine of the holy sacrament of the eucharist in the ancient church'), a work of considerable scholarship, which appeared just five years after the foundation of the university there.[25] It is a vast and detailed book, and it sets out to fulfil the double purpose of investigating the origins of the eucharist and how these came to be distorted into the mass. Brevint, by contrast, reserved his polemical writings for works like *Missale Romanum*, to which we have already referred. In the section dealing with sacrifice, du Plessis-Mornay defines the sacrament as a sacrifice in so far as it is a commemoration of the propitiatory sacrifice of Christ – which is the sense of the title of Brevint's work. He goes on to state that in the eucharist, Christ is represented as crucified before our very eyes; that faith applies this sacrifice and makes it particular and special to us now; and that in the eucharist there is a peace-offering between God and his people, a sacrifice of praise and thanksgiving for all God's goodness, and a sacrifice of ourselves, to live and die in the Christian faith. One can see in much of this an approach similar in style to Brevint himself, in the insistence on the vivid character of the memorial, the centrality of the cross, and the biblical language of sacrifice that makes an integral connection between ourselves and Christ.

As Frère Pierre-Yves Emery of Taizé has shown,[26] du Plessis-Mornay was the leader of a group of French Calvinist scholars who were able to develop Calvin's theology of the eucharist in the light of increasing studies on the early sources. It could envisage the eucharist as a sacrifice in so far as it was focused on the commemoration of the cross, the sacrifice of thanksgiving and intercession, the offering of the gifts, and the sacrifice of the worshippers – all of them themes covered in different ways by Brevint. Such a step bears strong comparison to the one we have seen slowly emerging in previous chapters in the British Isles, with Andrewes and Forbes in particular. This development comes to a head with writers like Taylor and Baxter, and also Thorndike and Patrick. Sacrifice is no longer a cul-de-sac but part of the main road. One can use the tradition, starting with the Old Testament, and take the early Fathers as helpers, in the development of that tradition. For Brevint, this meant taking precisely that road; following Calvin's example, he ensures that Christ was at the centre. The result is a striking devotional scene, in which the worshipper walks round and round Calvary, finally seeing it – and humanity with Christ – in heaven.

What Brevint succeeded in doing was to open up the road to sacrifice to precisely those who needed it but who were fearful of where it might lead and perhaps distrustful of those – like Andrewes – who appeared to be going there also. With his love of the Old Testament, Brevint all but calls the eucharist an 'unbloody' sacrifice in remembrance of Christ's one eternal sacrifice. If disadvantage there be, perhaps it lies in the fact that Brevint's approach is so cross-centred, and perhaps the incarnational element which we saw in Andrewes, and, to a lesser extent, in Hooker, appears diminished. And, apart from mentioning him a couple of times in his prayers, the Holy Spirit does not make much of an appearance in the over-all picture. But theologies of the eucharist are a little like long eucharistic prayers and endless sermons – they try to take on too much and say too much and too often. As a bridge with the French High Calvinists (on the one hand) and the Wesleys (on the other), Brevint shows – above all else – what it is to be truly evangelical and abundantly sacrificial.

Brevint's reputation is attested by the seriousness with which he was taken in the controversies over the eucharist in the next century. When Daniel Waterland wrote his *The Christian Sacrifice Explained* in 1738 for the clergy in his archdeaconry, he remarked that Brevint 'was well read in the eucharistic sacrifice: no man understood it better'[27] and he wished that it would be reprinted.

Brevint ends his treatise with a prayer:

> I dare appear before the Lord *with all my sins and my sorrows; it is very just also, that I should appear with these few blessings, which are*

mine; they are mine by thy favour, and having them of thy hand, now do I offer them to thee. Forgive, I beseech thee, my sins, deliver me from my sorrows, and accept of this small blessing. Accept of this my Sacrifice, as thou didst of that of Abel, of Abraham and of Noah; or rather look, in my behalf, on that only true Sacrifice whereof he is the Sacrament; the Sacrifice of the only unspotted Lamb, the Sacrifice of thine own Son, thine only-begotten Son, of thy Son proceeding from thee, to die for me. O let Him again come from thee to me; let Him come now as the only begotten of the father, full of grace and of truth, to bless me. Amen, Amen.[28]

NOTES

1 See P. H. Osmund, *A Life of John Cosin, Bishop of Durham, 1660–1672* (London: Mowbrays, 1913). See also Geoffrey Cuming, 'The Anglicanism of John Cosin', in *The Godly Order* (Alcuin Club Collections 65) (London: SPCK, 1983), pp. 123–41, and nn. pp. 193–4, and also his *The Durham Book, being the First Draft of the Revision of the Book of Common Prayer in 1661* (London: Oxford University Press, 1961). On Sir Thomas Browne, see H. R. McAdoo, *Anglican Heritage: Theology and Spirituality* (Norwich: Canterbury Press, 1991) pp. 20–5.

2 See Robert Bosher, *The Making of the Restoration Settlement: The Influence of the Laudians, 1649–1662* (Westminster: Dacre, 1951) esp. pp. 54ff, on the exile.

3 See Vernon Staley, *Hierurgia Anglicana*, Part 1, pp. 93ff.

4 See Kenneth Stevenson, 'The Liturgical Work of John Cosin – some remarks on method', paper delivered at 'John Cosin (1594–1672) Priest to Prince-Bishop', Durham City, 2nd–4th July, 1993. I am also grateful to the other contributors to this conference, in particular to Margot Johnson, Nicholas Hepple, Brian Cosby, and Daniel O'Connor.

5 See Oman, *English Church Plate*, pp. 182f.

6 See *John Cosin: A Collection of Private Devotions* (edited by P. G. Stanwood and Daniel O'Connor) (Oxford: Clarendon Press, 1967), pp. 227–34, for text of prayers, and pp. 352–4, for notes. It is interesting to observe the form of private confession which immediately follows the eucharistic devotions.

7 On the origin of this book, see Gordon Donaldson, *The Making of the Scottish Prayer Book of 1637* (Edinburgh: University Press, 1954).

8 See *The Works of John Cosin* (Volume IV) (Library of Anglo-Catholic Theology) (Oxford: Parker, 1845).

9 Contained in the same volume; for quotations, see pp. 16, 46.

10 See *The Works of John Cosin* (Volume V) p. 23.

11 For a discussion of this issue, see Kenneth Stevenson, ' "The Unbloody Sacrifice": The Origins and Development of a description of the eucharist' in *Fountain of Life: In Memory of Niels K. Rasmussen*, OP, pp. 103–30.

12 On 'labels', see chapter 1, and, for this instance, n. 6.

13 See *Works* (Volume V), pp. 351f.

14 See Daniel Brevint, *The Christian Sacrament and Sacrifice, and Missale Romanum* (Oxford: Vincent, 1847), pp. 155–6. He cites Augustine *Ep* 23 to Boniface Facundus Hermianus and *Ep* 118 to Januarius.

15 See the discussion by Bernard Capelle, 'les oraisons de la messe du saint sacrament', in *Travaux Liturgiques* (Volume III) (Louvain: Centre Liturgique, 1967), pp. 242–51, where Capelle looks at the collect, offertory, and post-communion prayers for the feast of Corpus Christi as memorial, food, and pledge, and compares them with Aquinas' *Summa*.

16 *Christian Sacrament and Sacrifice*, p. 3 (Section I.1).

17 ibid., p. 11 (Section II.7).

18 ibid., p. 28 (Section IV.1, compare Sections V.6 and VII.12). Compare also 'the dignity of standing for the *means* and *instruments*, which may convey to us those graces . . . there is the finger of God indeed, and there is a fitter matter for men's admiration than men's knowledge', ibid., p. 34 (Section IV.7).

19 ibid., pp. 37f (Section IV.11); compare 'For Jesus Christ and his Church so concur together in one oblation, that the blessed Saviour contributes all that can go up to heaven to please and appease God; and we, on our part, do contribute but what deserves to be removed out of the way, the corruption and smell of sin', pp. 66f (Section VII. 9).

20 ibid., p. 48 (Section V.8). Compare William Temple, *Christus Veritas – An Essay* (London: Macmillan, 1925), p. 240, where the notion of value is identified as an improvement on substance. I am indebted to Henry McAdoo for drawing my attention to this parallel.

21 ibid., p. 58 (Section VI.4).

22 ibid., p. 69 (Section VII.12).

23 ibid., p. 85 (Section VIII.7); compare p. 11 (Section II.6) and p. 36 (Section IV.9).

24 See this worked out in J. Ernest Rattenbury, *The Eucharistic Hymns of John and Charles Wesley* (London: Epworth, 1948).

25 *De l'institution, usage, et doctrine du sainct sacrement de l'eucharistie, en l'Eglise Ancienne; Ensemble, Comment, Quand, et par quels Degres la messe s'est introduite en sa place; Par Messire Philippe de Mornay, Seigneur du Plessis-Marli; Conseilleur du Roy en son Conseil d'Estat, Capitaine de cinquante hommes d'armes de ses Ordonnances: Governeur de la Ville et Chasteau de Saumeur: Surintendant de ses Maison et Couronne de Navarre* (La Rochelle:

[no publisher indicated], 1599) pp. 313–15. The copy consulted is in Sion College Library.

26 See Pierre-Yves Emery, *Le Sacrifice Eucharistique selon les théologiens réformés français du XVIIe siècle* (Taizé: Presses de Taizé, 1959) for a discussion of the development of this nuanced form of High Calvinism. On this matter, compare with a similar development in Scotland later on in the essay, Bryan D. Spinks, 'The Ascension and the Vicarious Humanity of Christ: The Christology and Soteriology Behind the Church of Scotland's Anamnesis and Epiklesis', in J. Neil Alexander (ed.), *Time and Community: In Honor of Thomas Julian Talley* (Washington: Pastoral Press, 1990), pp. 185–201.

27 See *A Review of the Doctrine of the Eucharist with Four Charges to the Clergy of Middlesex connected with the same subject* (edited by Bishop Van Mildert) (Oxford: Clarendon, 1898) p. 477. *The Christian Sacrifice Explained* was the second of these 'charges' to his clergy.

28 *Christian Sacrament and Sacrifice*, p. 97 (Section VIII. prayer at end). Since the time of writing, Henry McAdoo's important article, 'A Theology of the Eucharist: Brevint and the Wesleys', forthcoming in *Theology* (1994).

CHAPTER SIX

Prolific Complements

Jeremy Taylor (1613–1667) and

Richard Baxter (1615–1691)

In August 1993, a German U-boat was raised from the depths of the Kattegat off the coast of Jutland. It had been sunk right at the very end of the Second World War. Apart from the intrinsic interest that is understandable on such an occasion – rumours of treasure and secret documents – from the human point of view the most significant feature of the operation was the presence on the scene of members of the crews both of the U-boat itself and of the RAF Liberator which sank it.

Many are the tales of former opponents meeting after the conflict. In this chapter, we shall be trying to effect such an encounter for two of the most prolific religious writers of the seventeenth century, Jeremy Taylor and Richard Baxter. History placed them on opposite sides of what became a sharp and decisive divide, for when the Civil War began, these two clerics found themselves as army chaplains, Taylor serving with the King's forces and Baxter with the Parliamentary forces. As it happens, neither remained a chaplain for the duration of the war, and while each was one hundred per cent loyal to his side, there is none the less something inherently untypical about them. For both Taylor and Baxter are difficult to label. Each is very much his own man. Moreover, in their vast literary output, we encounter a new style of writing; no longer is it the Latin text for international consumption and credibility that we met in Andrewes' *Responsio* to Cardinal Bellarmine, or Forbes' *Considerationes Modestae*, or Cosin's *Historia* of Transubstantiation. Taylor and Baxter write exclusively in English, and they write much more consciously for the lay audience. As we saw in the last chapter with Brevint's *Christian Sacrament and Sacrifice* (which first appeared in English after Taylor's death), we are moving back to Hooker's concern to write for a wider market. This is not to suggest that the works just mentioned by Andrewes, Forbes, and Cosin were only read by what we would nowadays call 'theologians', for that would be to distort the picture. But Taylor and Baxter are probably best remembered by their contemporaries for helping laity to understand the Christian eucharist and to grow in its faith and devotion.

JEREMY TAYLOR

Life

In his biography of Taylor, Hugh Ross Williamson writes that 'there can be few great figures about whom so little, factually, is known.'[1] But enough is known to form a clear picture of this don, pastor, writer, and bishop. Jeremy Taylor was born in Cambridge in 1615, and was baptised in Holy Trinity where his father was a churchwarden. After attending the Perse School, he went on to Gonville and Caius College, where on graduating he was appointed to a fellowship, and he was ordained in the usual way. Although Cambridge was at the time strong in Puritans, Taylor seems to have been inclined in other theological directions. Attracting the attention of Archbishop Laud, probably after a sermon in St Paul's Cathedral, in 1635 he was awarded a Fellowship at All Souls College, Oxford – a move which marked him out for the future. It is at Oxford that we see the two strands in Taylor's thought emerging which are to be so important for the future. He wrote a pamphlet entitled *On the Reverence due to the Altar*, and he met William Chillingworth and other members of what was called the 'Great Tew Circle'.

Such a publication associated him directly with the liturgical aims of Laud and King Charles, and it could hardly have endeared him to the Puritans. Bowing to the altar was not even common practice among what might be called mainstream members of the Church of England at the time. To Taylor and others, it was not just an outward gesture, but it expressed the importance of the human body in worship. On the other hand, the Great Tew Circle brought him into contact with a group of people who met regularly at the home of Lord Falkland. This group included both prominent laymen, like Edward Hyde, later Lord Clarendon, a barrister, a member of Parliament, and keen supporter of the King, as well as other clerics, such as Gilbert Sheldon, who became Archbishop of Canterbury at the Restoration. The Great Tew Circle stood essentially for both reason and tradition in the life and thought of the Church. They were in no way opposed to Laud, who, in any case (as we have seen), was a more incisive and less typecast theologian than he has often been represented. But they were part of a new generation which saw the need to reinterpret the Christian faith in the light of reason. But this 'reason' was no arid, cerebral capacity. As we shall see when we come to discuss his eucharistic theology, his view of reason was very much influenced by the group of theologians whom we call the 'Platonists', who came to be strong at Cambridge, and who left an abiding mark upon Simon Patrick. For Taylor – as for Plato and Plotinus of old – reason has a transcendent quality about it, which is the key to the unity between heaven and earth. It comes quite near what the Romantic Age two centuries later came to call the imagination.

Taylor's career took a new turn when he became a parish priest in 1638. He was made Rector of Uppingham, where he ensured that the services were conducted with appropriate decorum. Under his influence, the sanctuary was furnished in the manner which we would associate with Andrewes and Laud: vessels, an altar cloth, a cushion for the service-book, and a surplice for the priest. These were items Taylor had to introduce on his own initiative and we know that his successor had little use for them, nor was he a great enthusiast for frequent eucharists. He also wrote a treatise on *The Sacred Order of Episcopacy* which attracted attention from King Charles, for which he was given an Oxford DD by order of the monarch. The Civil War now intervened and it is a little difficult to tell exactly where Taylor was at certain times. He was with the King at Oxford in 1642, but rector of Overstone in 1643. Then as an army chaplain, he was taken prisoner by the Puritans and in 1646 we hear of him teaching in a school at Carmarthenshire. But he kept up contact with the King, and on meeting him for the last time, the King gave him his watch and some jewels – which is an indication of the close relationship that had grown up between them. That position is also reflected in Taylor's desire to be involved in the theological controversies of the time. Parliament had banned both bishops and the Prayer Book, which were replaced by *The Westminster Directory* and *The Westminster Confession of Faith* in 1645. It was needful for people like Taylor, who were now not allowed to use the Book of Common Prayer in public worship, to state their case. He was not alone in this, as we shall see in the next chapter when we look at the work of Herbert Thorndike. But in 1647, Taylor published his *Liberty of Prophesying*, and this was followed up in 1649 by his *Apology for Authorised and Set Forms of Liturgy*. Some thought that he was not fierce enough in his condemnation of the Puritan position. Taylor's unconventional characteristic surfaced again, this time because he was prepared to tolerate a certain degree of variety in theological approach within the same Church.

It was at the home of the Earl of Carbery, the Golden Grove, in a particularly beautiful part of Wales, that he spent much of his time, and it provided him with the atmosphere and leisure for an enormous amount of writing. Two of these works deserve special mention. The first is *The Life and Death of the ever blessed Jesus Christ the Saviour of the World with Considerations and Discourses upon the several parts and Prayers fitted to the several Mysteries (1649)*. Generally referred to as *The Great Exemplar*, it was the first 'life of Christ' of its kind, and as the title suggests, it is really two books: a devotional narrative of Christ's life based on all four Gospels, and a series of reflections on how these events apply to the Christian faith today. The second consists of the inseparable pair, *The Rules and Exercises of Holy Living* (1650) and *The Rules and Exercises of Holy Dying* (1651). *The Great Exemplar* is dedicated to Christopher Hatton, Lord Kirby, who had been comptroller of the King's household, whereas the latter two are dedicated to his host of so many years, Richard Vaughan, Earl of Carbery.

Taylor kept in touch with congregations who were loyal to the Prayer Book. It is hard to envisage exactly how such proscription worked out in practice. In effect, much of the Church year officially disappeared. Evelyn's diary, for example, has many entries that bewail the absence of services on Christmas Day. On the other hand, Cromwell did allow one or two places to use the Prayer Book, for example St Gregory's Church in London, where Taylor preached from time to time, which gave Evelyn the opportunity to hear him on several occasions, and to use him as his 'ghostly father'. Royalists with private chaplains, like the Earl of Carbery, were not always safe, and in 1655, Cromwell brought pressures against them. Taylor's theological reputation was not of the highest with people whom we might associate with him, for he published his *Unum Necessarium* ('The One Thing

Needful') in 1655, which argued against the traditional interpretation of St Augustine on original sin, backing it up with a sequel in the following year called *Deus Justificatus* ('God justified'). These books are important for two reasons. First, he challenged the theological fashion of the day because he refused to believe that Adam 'had any more strengths than we have': God must be love, therefore he cannot be so cruel as to inflict suffering deliberately on the human race. Secondly, many of the Reformers exaggerated the effect of Adam's 'fall' and spoke about the 'total depravity' of man, which was much further than Augustine was prepared to go. Taylor refused to accept that the unbaptised are damned – which lost him many friends and potential allies.

It was not, however, for these reasons that Taylor found himself for a short spell in the Tower of London, after which he was invited to go to Ireland by Lord Edward Conway. Cromwell himself signed the passport. He went to work at Lisburne and then Portmore, south-west of Belfast, in 1658, where his liturgical practices outraged some of the local populace. He was arrested on one occasion for making the sign of the cross at baptism – one of the Puritan objections to the Prayer Book which Hooker addressed in the *Laws*. When the Restoration came, Taylor could be forgiven for thinking that he might be in line for a diocese, but it was an Irish bishopric that he was given, not an English one. On 21st January, 1661, he himself preached at his own consecration service, at which he and eleven others were made bishop by the new Archbishop of Armagh, John Bramhall. At first he was Bishop of Down and Connor, and later that year he took over Dromore as well. It was a rural area, in which presbyterian colonists from Scotland were strong, and Taylor was faced, too, with a formidable rebuilding programme, starting with Dromore Cathedral, which had been destroyed during the Irish Rebellion in 1641. Taylor set about the tasks of enforcing the Prayer Book polity on his clergy and people and of repairing existing churches. It was not an easy time, and he longed to return to England. But he and Archbishop Sheldon were not the best of friends. It may be that the combination of Taylor's theological unsoundness on original sin, and the sometimes quite sharp perception that is to be found, for example, in *Holy Living* and *Holy Dying*, made him seem to those with influence in high places an uncomfortable and unpredictable potential colleague.

Work

Taylor's life is reflected in his works. They are very much of a piece, for his complex edifice has a consistency about it that enables one to see the different parts fitting together. His views on original sin, for example, produce a greater optimism about the human race than one sees, for example, in Brevint. Moreover, when one reads what he has to say about the eucharist in his various books,[2] there is an integrity and unity of thought which shows that he holds the same kind of position throughout, even though there may be a shift of emphasis here and there.

Five works include important discussion of the eucharist. These are, first, *Great Exemplar* (1649), second, *Holy Living* (1650), third, *Clerus Domini* (1651), and then in two other more specific works that we have not mentioned so far, *The Real Presence and Spiritual of Christ in the Blessed Sacrament proved against the doctrine of Transubstantiation: A Dissuasive from Popery* (1654) and *The Worthy Communicant or a Discourse of the Nature, Effects, and Blessings consequent to the Worthy Receiving of The Lord's Supper* (1660). As far as content and layout are concerned, the first, second, and fifth have a unity about them that makes them easy to compare with each other. *Real Presence*,[3] however, is a more focused and obviously controversial work, and for convenience's sake, we shall discuss it first of all.

It was always important for theologians of the Prayer Book school like Taylor to make their position on the eucharist as clear as possible, not least when there were enough opponents accusing them of popery. What we have here is a carefully stated medial line, which laments the climate of dissension ('the tree of life is now become an apple of contention'), but affirms a strong presence that walks the same tightrope that we have seen before, dealing with the same tension that we encountered in Hooker: 'not only in type and figure, but in blessing and effect'. There is in this work, for all its anti-Roman Catholic context, a strong spiritual flavour that stresses both the mysteriousness of the sacrament and its sacramental reality. The elements of bread and wine 'remain in substance what they were; but in relation to Him are more' and 'they are what they were, but they are more than what they were before'. It may well be that in these and other statements, Taylor has been influenced by his old friend, William Nicholson;[4] at any rate, the two fellow-casualties of the Commonwealth (Nicholson had been Archdeacon of Brecon) are both addressing the same agenda in similar ways. When explaining the change in the elements, Taylor speaks of 'a change of condition, of sanctification, and usage', as an act of God himself, in all his glory, mystery, and activity.

We now turn to the three works, *Great Exemplar*, *Holy Living*, and *Worthy Communicant*.[5] The first two deal with the eucharist in the context of other concerns. *Great Exemplar* appropriately includes its treatment of the eucharist as one of the 'Discourses', this one immediately following the discussion of the Last Supper (the discussion of baptism follows the baptism of Christ). *Holy Living*, on the other hand, ends with the eucharist, arriving there as a climax to the whole book; it comes in four chapters, the 'general instruments serving to a Holy life' (including a very near-the-bone section on the use of time!), 'Christian Charity', 'Christian Justice', and 'Christian Religion'. Taylor is what Henry McAdoo calls a 'moral-ascetic theologian', one of a class of writers primarily concerned with how Christians pray and how they act, and how the link can be made between the two. He therefore deliberately builds up to the eucharist, as if it were what Christianity is all about. Indeed, he says as much, time and again, for example: 'The celebration of the holy sacrament is the great mysteriousness of the Christian religion.'[6]

Worthy Communicant, on the other hand, is specifically about the eucharist. But all three works take the reader through a sequence of the same kind. First, there is an explanation of the origin and meaning of the eucharist, and then there is a (longer) discussion of how to prepare for the eucharist, ending up with prayer, one in the case of *Great Exemplar*, because it is the shortest of the three, but more prayers appear in the other two works. It is in the preparation that Taylor demonstrates his acute understanding of what might be called the human predicament, not least when he deals with the question of frequency, which was obviously an urgent matter at the time. We encountered this in Brevint and we shall encounter it too in Patrick.

Like Hooker and Andrewes, Taylor sets the whole of Christian living in the orbit of the life of the Trinity. The following section from what he has to say about the presence of God near the start of *Holy Living* relates to his discussion of the sacraments:

> God is especially present in the hearts of his people, by his Holy Spirit: and indeed the hearts of holy men are temples in the truth of things, and, in type and shadow, they are heaven itself. For

God reigns in the hearts of his servants: there is his kingdom. The power of grace hath subdued all his enemies: there is his power. They serve him night and day, and give him thanks and praise; that is his glory. This is the religion and worship of God in the temple. The temple itself is the heart of man; Christ is the high-priest, who from thence sends up the incense of prayers, and joins them to his own intercession, and presents all together to his Father; and the Holy Ghost by his dwelling there, hath also consecrated it into a temple; and God dwells in our hearts by faith, and Christ by his Spirit, and the Spirit by his purities; so that we are also cabinets [= inner chambers] of the mysterious Trinity; and what is this short of heaven itself, but as infancy is short of manhood, and letters of words? The same state of life it is, but not the same age. It is heaven in a looking-glass, dark, but yet true, representing the beauties of the soul, and the graces of God, and the images of his eternal glory, by the reality of a special presence.[7]

If Taylor's basic theology could be summed up in one paragraph, it is surely here. For here we have the emphases that recur again and again throughout his books: humanity placed in history, which is part of eternity; the Trinity participating in that life, and sharing it with the creature; above all doing this last function through Christ's prayer to the Father, and in the power of the Spirit; and all skilfully woven into a scene that speaks volumes about the reality of what we experience now and the promise of what is to come. 'Heaven in a looking-glass' is one of Taylor's more memorable phrases, without doubt intended to convey sacramental innuendos. It is within such a wide context that the eucharist must be set. It is so easy to come straight to the altar, and indeed it is true that Taylor did write *Real Presence* and *Worthy Communicant* specifically for the Lord's Supper. But though his heart goes out to the eucharist, it only does so because the eucharist is fundamentally about *God* and *humanity* and is no mere cultic act. Of particular prominence is one feature we have seen already, the mysteriousness of the presence, and another which we shall come across again, the place of the intercession of Christ with the offering of the eucharist. It is interesting to compare these two emphases which are equally powerful, but differently expressed, in Brevint's *Christian Sacrament and Sacrifice*.

Because it is the fullest statement of his eucharistic theology, we shall concentrate on *Worthy Communicant*. But first, Taylor's opening words in the 'Discourse' in *Great Exemplar* can set the scene:

> As the sun among the stars, and man among the sublunary crea-
> tures, is the most eminent and noble, the prince of the inferiors,
> and their measure, or their guide; so is this action among all the
> instances of religion; it is the most perfect and consummate, it is
> an union of mysteries, and a consolidation of duties; it joins God
> and man, and confederates all the societies of men in mutual
> complexions, and the entertainments of an excellent charity, it
> actually performs all that could be necessary for man, and
> it presents to man as great a thing as God could give; for it is
> impossible any thing should be greater than Himself.
>
> And when God gave His Son to the world, it could not be but
> He should give us all things else; and therefore this blessed sacra-
> ment is a consigning us to all felicities, because after a mysterious
> and ineffable manner we receive Him who is light and life, the
> fountain of grace, and the sanctifier of our secular comforts, and
> the author of holiness and glory.[8]

Taylor here shows certain of his characteristics. Like Baxter, Thorndike, and Patrick, he can hardly be accused of succinctness – and in that respect he and his aforementioned comrades differ from Hooker and Forbes, who usually do not waste a word. He likes certain expressions, to do with feasting ('entertainments' and 'felicities'), imparting ('joins' and 'a consigning'), and community ('union' and 'confederates'). Some of these we shall come across in Patrick, too. And they all have doctrinal overtones, for in Taylor the eucharist *is* a feast, it *is* an imparting of divine graces, and it *is* the means whereby we are joined to one another and to God.

Of all those words, the most significant from an historical point of view is 'confederates'. It will be remembered that Hooker used the word 'covenant' of baptism, and Andrewes went further and spoke of the eucharist as a 'renewal of the covenant'. In all four of our remaining writers, the theology of covenant is a key element in their understand-ing not only of the sacraments and the Church, but of the nature of what it is to be a Christian. They do not express what is called 'federal theology' in the same way – Baxter takes a more exclusive and traditionally Puritan line. But that in itself shows why it was so important to adopt the language of covenant and expand it into a more mainstream direction. 'Covenant' is a dynamic and biblical image for the way in which human beings express their relationships with each other and with God. For Taylor, with his less rigorous understanding of original sin, and his powerful understanding of how God communicates himself in the sacraments, his view of covenant emerges like a block of wood which has been carefully carved by an expert craftsman. He makes it his own; the covenant is not closed. Like Hooker, he does not want to apply too many tests to people before communion. He can be incisive and penetrating in the way that he examines human motives, such as feelings of anger and jealousy (in *Holy Living* we read 'prayer is the greatest remedy against anger' and 'covetousness makes a man miserable'). Yet he does not want the Church to become a narrow group for the religiously like-minded.

Worthy Communicant was published in 1660 and is dedicated to Princess Mary of Orange, the future Queen. It has a fuller share of footnotes than either *Great Exemplar* or *Holy Living*; these are mainly to ancient or medieval authors and authorities, including two to Thomas à Kempis. There are none from the Reformation era. And, just as *Holy Living* charmingly has a discreet but not obtrusive interlacing of references to 'holy living', so we encounter a gentle sprinkling of 'worthy communicant' in its pages. The style is as fluent as ever. Occasionally there are homely examples that reflect life at the time, for example his reference to 'cupping-glasses', which were gradually replacing pewter (or more precious) goblets for secular drinking purposes about the period of the Restoration. This was the time when communion vessels parted company with their secular counterparts, for up until now the two had walked hand in hand since the Reformation – with the exception of the 'Gothic' chalices of the Andrewes' enthusiasm. There are occasional references to how the service should be performed: he is most keen on 'Amen' said by all after the consecration prayer; this was only inserted in 1662. (He is also keen in *Holy Living* on 'Amen' said by each communicant at the words of distribution of the elements at the altar-rail; Andrewes had directed this for his chapel, and it was a primitive practice.)

The book comes in seven chapters. Only the first is specifically about 'the nature, excellencies, uses, and intentions' of the sacrament; the other six are to do with preparation beforehand: preparation itself, faith as a preparation, charity, and repentance; the actual preparation

on the day; and what to do during the service. In this respect, it
parallels closely the shape of things in *Holy Living* including the relative
distribution of material in the discussion. We shall concentrate on the
first chapter. But in the introduction are a few nuggets:

> For as God descended and came into the tabernacle invested with
> a cloud, so Christ comes to meet us clothed with a mystery: He
> hath a house below as well as above; here is His dwelling and
> here are His provisions, here is His fire and here His meat; hither
> God sends His Son, and here His Son manifests Himself: the
> church and the holy table of the Lord, the assemblies of the saints,
> and the devotions of His people, the word and the sacrament,
> the oblation of bread and wine and the offering of ourselves, the
> consecration and the communion, are the things of God and of
> Jesus Christ, and he that is employed in these is there where God
> loves to be, and where Christ is to be found; in the employments
> in which God delights, in the ministries of His own choice, in
> the work of the gospel and the methods of grace, in the economy
> of heaven and the dispensations of eternal happiness.[9]

That statement of mystery with its allusions to the liturgy draws
from him two truths. First, we must search ourselves – 'whoever will
partake of God's secrets must first look into his own'. And, secondly,
we must not expect to understand too much at once in this 'cloud' –
a favourite theme repeated in Taylor, a notable example of which is
in *Great Exemplar* when he meditates on Mary and Joseph losing sight
of Jesus when he is in the temple. The eucharist is, first and foremost,
'His passion in representment' – another favourite Taylor word, which
recurs in *Worthy Communicant*.[10]

The opening chapter begins by making the essential link between
baptism and eucharist which we met in Hooker – 'that Christians may
first wash and then eat'.[11] And he goes on to speak of the eucharist
producing 'all its effects by virtue of the sacrament itself so appointed'.
Later he affirms: 'it is truly Christ's body both in the sacrament and
out of it: but in the sacrament it is not the natural truth, but the
spiritual and the mystical.' For 'thus are sensible things the sacrament
and representation of the spiritual and eternal; and spiritual things are
the fulfillings of the sensible.' We are here seeing an intricate fusion
of Hooker's and Andrewes' affirmative but cautious treatment of the
presence of Christ with the mystical view of 'reason', with its contrasts

between the higher and the lower worlds. This runs the risk of driving a wedge between 'spiritual eating' and actually eating the bread and wine of the eucharist. But he is rescued by a strong doctrine of the Holy Spirit: 'For here being (as in baptism) a double significatory of the Spirit, a word, and a sign of His own appointment, it is certain He will join in this ministration.'

We saw how Hooker draws the Spirit into the communicant, how Andrewes goes a little further in praying for the Spirit to 'hallow' the gifts, and how Forbes knew of the Greek emphasis on the Holy Spirit's blessing in the eucharistic prayer. (As we shall see, Taylor has such a prayer in his 1658 liturgy.) Taylor reproduces a similar view, using it as an opportunity to warn against any 'automatic' effects or cheap grace: 'Neither the external act nor the internal grace and morality does effect our pardon and salvation; but the Spirit of God who blesses the symbols, and assists the duty; makes them holy, and thus acceptable.'

And, in words that have a remarkably contemporary flavour:

> God does nothing in vain; the sacraments do something in the hand of God; at least they are God's proper and accustomed times of grace; they are His seasons, and our opportunity; when the angel stirs the pool, when the Spirit moves, upon the waters, then there is a ministry of healing.

He blends the 'two righteousnesses' that we saw in Hooker (and since) with human experience of regular worship, and basks in the abundance of God's generosity when he states:

> ... justification and sanctification are continued acts: they are like the issues of a fountain into its receptacles; God is always giving, and we are always receiving; and the signal effects of God's Holy Spirit sometimes give great indications, but most commonly come without observation.

Like Hooker and Andrewes, too, he brings out the purpose of the eucharist to make us like God:

> ... they are instruments in the hand of God, and by these His Holy Spirit changes our hearts and translates us into a divine nature; therefore the whole work is attributed to them by a synecdoche; that is, they do in their manner the work for which God

ordained them, and they are placed there for our sakes, and speak God's language in our accent, and they appear in the outside; we receive the benefit of their ministry, and God receives the glory.

But what of the sacrifice? Taylor has already alluded to the placing of the gifts on the altar, and the self-oblation of the communicants. In the passage quoted earlier from *Holy Living* we saw the picture of Christ in heaven interceding for humanity. Taylor brings all this, and much more, together, by linking the One Sacrifice continually presented by Christ in heaven, and represented commemoratively by the priest in the eucharist, and the sacramental presence in the elements. There is a strong sense of *coherence* and *unity* in such an approach:

> He intercedes for us, and represents an eternal sacrifice in the heavens on our behalf . . . Christ in heaven perpetually offers and represents that sacrifice to His heavenly Father, and in virtue of that obtains all good things for His church . . . the holy table being a copy of the celestial altar, and the eternal sacrifice of the lamb slain from the beginning of the world being always the same; it bleeds no more after the finishing of it on the cross; but it is wonderfully represented in heaven, and graciously represented here; by Christ's action there, by His commandment here. And the event of it is plainly this; that as Christ in virtue of his sacrifice on the cross intercedes for us with His Father, so does the minister of Christ's priesthood here, that the virtue of the eternal sacrifice may be salutary and effectual to all the needs of the church, both for things temporal and eternal. And therefore it was not without great mystery and clear signification that our blessed Lord was pleased to command the representation of His death and sacrifice on the cross should be made by breaking bread and effusion of wine; to signify to us the nature and sacredness of the liturgy we are about . . .

Taylor sees the Church's offering as part of Christ's offering of himself, with prayer and supplication before the Father in heaven – his sacrifice is *eternal*, not confined to history, as ours must be without Him. Moreover, that intercession with which we are linked is not just for consecrating bread and wine, but for all the concerns of the Church as it gathers to celebrate that sacrifice: in this respect, Taylor is near Forbes' parting shot to the effect that the eucharist benefits the whole

Church, living and departed, as well as Cosin's insistence that 'we and all thy whole Church may obtain remission of our sins' refers to the past, the present, and the future. We see, too, a special focus on the distinctive role of the priest, the ordained minister, in relation to that intercessory work of Christ. All our writers would be at one in restricting presidency of the eucharist to the ordained, but they would vary slightly over how this restriction alters *in kind* what the priest is there to do. Laud made the distinction between the kind of sacrifice the priest offers (commemorative), what the people offer (praise and thanksgiving) and what individuals offer on their own (themselves as a living sacrifice). Taylor perhaps goes further along this road than the others, but not as specifically as Laud, and by tying his view to the intercession of Christ may well bring to light something hidden and deep about the essentially pastoral character of ordained priesthood in terms of representative prayer.

Taylor is eloquent about the *effects* of communicating. They are intangible, yet real: 'thou art the same thou wert, and yet very much another person in the progression of faith.' This thought inspired one of Taylor's greatest images of the eucharist and the future, in *Great Exemplar*, in which he likens Christ in the sacrament to being like the tree of life in paradise.[12]

He goes on to deal with the various aspects of preparation, along similar lines to the discussion of virtues and justice in *Holy Living*. He seldom seems lost for words. Assuredly one of the most innovative of the theologians we have so far looked at, we can discern the different influences at work: the tradition going back to Hooker, the mystical view of reason in the Platonists, and his own reading of the early Fathers. Henry McAdoo thinks that his view of the eucharistic presence 'skims the cream off virtualism'.[13] In other words, he takes the very best from that view of the eucharist which wants to affirm the moral and spiritual power which the elements have by virtue of being consecrated. If that is so, I would suggest that this may well be the abiding pattern in all the theologians we have seen so far. In an age in which transubstantiation – or anything like it – was regarded as a sign of popery, it was important to work within the confines of seeing the eucharist as *personal* and *Christ-centred*, rather than 'mechanical' or 'objective'.

There are other important aspects of his writing: the stress on mystery ('secret'), the collective images of feasting and covenant, as well as the essential link between eucharist and baptism. It is, however, his vision of the Christ in wounded but triumphant glory in heaven that marks off his theology as most distinctive. Here, surely, was the result of much meditation, both on Christ and on the human condition, from a man who was widowed, lost his children, and was deprived of his proper work. These tender areas lie carefully concealed in the pages of *Holy Living* and they witness to the fact that the best theology arises out of a special union of meditation and experience within the tradition itself and its living heart. Not for nothing does he write: 'Let reason, and experience, and religion, and hope relying upon the divine promises, be the measure of our judgement,' and:

> The consideration of God's goodness and bounty, the experience of these profitable and excellent emanations from him, may be, and most commonly are, the first motive of our love; but when we are once entered, and have tasted the goodness of God, we love the spring of its own excellency, passing from passion to reason, from thanking to adoring, from sense to spirit, from considering ourselves to an union with God: and this is the image and little representation of heaven: it is the beatitude in picture, or rather the infancy and beginning of glory.[14]

Before we leave Taylor, a word must be said about his *Collection of Offices* which appeared in 1658. At the time, the Prayer Book was officially outlawed and there were various ways in which the Prayer Book language and style could be used but in a form of service that reflected the looser directions of the *Westminster Directory* of 1645. The liturgy contained in it on the one hand reflects Prayer Book language but on the other hand branches off into other paths.[15] A prayer of preparation refers to 'a holy, venerable, and unbloody sacrifice'. This is the same idea of Brevint's when he compared the eucharist with the cereal-offering placed over the animal and it recurs in the Fathers, as Andrewes and his colleagues knew well.[16] But it is the first time that the word appears in an Anglican liturgy. The Beatitudes follow, occupying a position similar to the Byzantine eucharist. The priest then offers a prayer that echoes Taylor's sense of the mystery of the eucharist and the union of the heavenly and the earthly: 'a sweetsmelling odour in the union of that eternal sacrifice'. At the consecration, there is an invocation of the Holy Spirit 'upon these gifts' before the words of Christ at the Supper, and a prayer remembering the work of Christ afterwards that looks forward to the end of the world. Taylor, always sensitive to the needs of private devotion, also provides two prayers which may be said silently during the distribution of communion, both of which are taken from the Byzantine rite; the second begins with the same scriptural allusion that is found in this position in the Roman rite, 'Lord, I am not worthy that thou shouldest come under my roof' (Matthew 8:8; Luke 7:6). This liturgy is a classic case of a theology that is pressed into service as a form of prayer.[17] For those familiar with Taylor's rolling sentences, its style and tenor come as no surprise.

Jeremy Taylor emerges, therefore, as a curiously prophetic figure. He has a novel understanding of eucharistic sacrifice in terms of the union of earthly and heavenly which has much to commend it. We shall see a more 'earthy' version of this view in Simon Patrick, where he fuses 'covenant' and 'sacrifice' into yet one more variant, the sacrifice of the Church in its offering of herself to her Lord in worship and service. Thomas Carroll offers a perceptive analysis of Taylor's eucharistic theology that has much in common with McAdoo's, and has all the more significance in that it comes from an Irish Roman Catholic priest:

> Taylor's eucharistic theology opened up from the Patristic past a new or renewed understanding of the Mystery that is ever ancient and ever new. By celebrating the Sacrifice of Christ within the sacramental framework he restored to the eucharistic rite the commemorative, demonstrative and prophetic dimensions of the signs, which the ancients felt as a unity and which Taylor's contemporaries and reforming predecessors, both Catholics and Protestants, had fragmented in time and space.[18]

Meanwhile, we leave Taylor in Ireland, where he built up a strong following, not only with his theological gifts, but also in his enthusiasm for the practice of the liturgy according to the norms we have already seen in Andrewes.[19] For Taylor's lengthy spell at the Golden Grove may have had a tragic cause (the Commonwealth) but it also had astonishing results in his literary output, with all the reflectiveness that is embedded therein. Right at the end of *Holy Living*, there is a prayer for use immediately after receiving 'the cup of blessing' at communion which expresses much of what we have so far glimpsed at:

It is finished. Blessed be the mercies of God revealed to us in

Jesus Christ. O blessed and eternal High-priest, let the sacrifice of the cross, which thou didst once offer for the sins of the whole world, and which thou dost now and always represent in heaven to thy Father by thy never-ceasing intercession, and which this day hath been exhibited on thy holy table sacramentally, obtain mercy and peace, faith and charity, safety and establishment to thy holy church, which thou hast founded upon a rock, the rock of a holy faith; and let not the gates of hell prevail against her, nor the enemy of mankind take any soul out of thy hand, whom thou hast purchased with thy blood, and sanctified by thy spirit. Preserve all thy people from heresy and division of Spirit, from scandal and the spirit of delusion, from sacrilege and hurtful persecutions. Thou, O blessed Jesus, didst die for us; keep me for ever in holy living, from sin and sinful shame, in the communion of thy church, and thy church in safety and grace, in truth and peace, unto thy second coming. Amen.[20]

RICHARD BAXTER

Life

The contrast between Taylor's roots and Baxter's could not be more different. Baxter was born in Rowton, Shropshire, and all his life he retained a strong affection for this part of the country. He went to Ludlow school, and was by all accounts a serious young man. He read the poems of George Herbert and had what appears to have been a moderate Puritan upbringing within the Church of England. He describes his confirmation by Thomas Morton, then Bishop of Lichfield, and soon to go to be Bishop of Durham in 1632. The rite took place 'in a Churchyard and in the Path-way, as the Bishop past by, we kneeled down, and laying his Hands on every Boy's Head, he said a few words.'[21]

He refers to the service as being 'Bishop't', probably an old nickname for confirmation. But the context and content did not make much impact on him. Bishop Morton was merely following old precedent whereby confirmations frequently took place out of doors. Indeed in medieval times bishops were known to confirm from horseback. By one of those ironies, it was John Cosin, whom Baxter was to meet in

1661 at the 'Savoy' Conference, who ensured that the revision of the confirmation service stipulated that it must take place in church. And we probably owe it to Cosin too that it begins with a renewal of baptismal vows – a conscious affirmation of faith of the like Baxter himself would have approved.

Baxter's education after school appears not to have been a formal one, but he was ordained deacon at the end of 1638. We have no exact record of his being ordained priest, but it seems certain that he was. He went to Bridgnorth to serve as an assistant. Here, he disliked the open character of the Lord's Supper, preferring a more rigorous examination of communicants beforehand. And his position on liturgical matters shows his definite, but not extreme, Puritan leanings. He did not use the sign of the cross at baptism, nor did he wear the surplice, but he did kneel at communion (something he refused to condemn later in his life after leaving the Church of England) and he used the ring at marriage.

The call soon came to Kidderminster to serve as 'lecturer', one of those posts which was often available in the larger parishes. William Travers had been lecturer at the Temple Church when Hooker arrived there as Master. The bishops were not enamoured of these appointments, since they were funded by local congregations and they were therefore denied control over them. Baxter enjoyed preaching more than pastoral work. In 1642 he was ejected by Royalists and went to work as a chaplain with the Parliamentary forces. He also preached in the rather different liturgical environment of Holy Trinity, Coventry. In 1645 he became a proper army chaplain, though he had to give this up in 1647 because of poor health. He returned to Kidderminster, by then under the control of the Parliamentarians, and replaced the vicar, George Dance, who though deposed, was allowed to remain in the vicarage. It was at Kidderminster that Baxter was remembered for his ministry for a long time after his death: his chair is still in the parish church, the communion table he used is in the United Reformed Church, whereas the pulpit is in the hands of the Unitarians. That particular ecumenical spread somehow expresses the character of the man.

He was against set forms of liturgy, he enjoyed hymn-singing (at that time not a norm in Prayer Book worship) and he always prayed aloud before he preached. We have already taken note of his dislike of Andrewes' sermons, which would have been in circulation while he was a young pastor. 'I felt no life in it,' he remarked. He did not keep Christmas Day, but he celebrated Easter with a eucharist. His sacramental policy was to be open about baptism but tough about who should be admitted to the Lord's Supper.

At Kidderminster he helped to form a 'Worcestershire Association', which showed his concern for the unity of the Church and his solicitude over new religious movements moving into the area, including 'Anabaptists' (the name given to those who insisted on believers' baptism and who therefore 'baptised again' those who were already baptised as infants). Baxter had a strong understanding of the corporate nature of the Church, even though he was little attracted to the system of bishops and Prayer Book that were the main religious points at issue in the Civil War and Commonwealth. His views are summed up in part of a letter written to Peter Ince, a fellow-cleric from Wiltshire: 'Bottom on Christ the great fundamentals. Unite in those with men of holiness and righteousness. Prosecute that union affectionately and unweariedly and keep your eye upon that glory where all shall be one.'[22]

At the Restoration, Baxter's position was a potentially difficult one. He was far too candid and forthright in controversy throughout his ministry and his theological views, though soundly Puritan, were sufficiently eclectic (the result of wide reading) as to mark him off as a man with an unusual mind. He had been in touch with James Ussher, former Archbishop of Armagh, who on being deprived had moved to England where he worked for a reconciliation between the three mainstream groups, episcopalians (who wanted bishops), presbyterians and independents. Ussher had died in 1656 but there were still people like him who wanted to use the Restoration as an opportunity not to *revert* to the system of church government and worship expressed in the Prayer Book, but to *reform* the pattern along primitive lines. (We shall be encountering one example of this kind in Herbert Thorndike, who wanted to reform episcopacy.) On the other hand, when he had come to Kidderminster for the second time, the vicar there was deposed, and one of the first acts of the new Parliament was to rule that all clergy who were in livings where such forcible ejection had happened should themselves be deprived. Accordingly, Bishop Morley, then Bishop of Worcester, deposed Baxter. When Baxter subsequently refused the see of Hereford, he was on his own.

However, he was chosen to represent the Puritan group at the

'Savoy' Conference for the revision of the Prayer Book, where he met Cosin and Thorndike, and also Morley, and others. 'I perceive that they intended no abatements', was his verdict on the real character of this meeting. It was at the Savoy Conference that he produced his liturgy, which we shall shortly look at. The rest of his life, however, was spent as a kind of free-lance preacher in London, preaching sometimes at home, sometimes in chapels, but always with the threat of imprisonment or confiscation of property over his head. He died in 1691.

Work

Baxter was a self-taught theologian who was an omnivorous reader of books. He also wrote vast quantities: it is estimated that he published about two hundred works. His style is lengthy but direct. It has little of the polish of Taylor, and certainly none of the tight discipline of Hooker. The classic for which he is most remembered is *The Saint's Everlasting Rest*, which was published in 1650. The following passage is typical of the controlled fervour and earthed humanity of his writing, which is reflected in his poetical works such as the hymns 'He wants not friends that hath thy love' and 'Ye holy angels bright':

> As thou makest conscience of praying daily, so do thou of the acting of thy graces in meditation; and more especially in meditating on the joys of heaven. To this end, set apart one hour or half hour every day wherein thou mayst lay aside all worldly thoughts, and with all possible seriousness and reverence, as if thou wert going to speak with God Himself or to have a sight of Christ or of that blessed place, so do thou withdraw thyself into some secret place, and set thyself wholly to the following work. If thou canst, take Isaac's time and place who went forth into the field in the evening to meditate; but if thou be a servant, or poor man, that cannot have that leisure, take the fittest time and place that thou canst, though it be when thou art private about thy labours.[23]

The other classic is *The Reformed Pastor* (1656), which has also been reprinted again and again, and not only provides an inner eye into Baxter's own dedicated, warm, but firm pastorship at Kidderminster, but contains a great deal of lasting insight into the care of souls today.[24]

Baxter is one of the few Puritans to leave behind details of all three aspects of his eucharistic worship, a description of a service at

Kidderminster, a form of service, and his own theological and devotional undergirding. Here is an account of the service, taken from a letter that he wrote in 1657:

> A long table being spread, I first open the nature and use of the ordinance, and the qualification and present duty of the communicants; and then the deacons (3 or 4 grave, pious men chosen and appointed to that office) do set the bread and wine on the table; and in prayer we beseech the Lord to accept of those his own creatures now dedicated and set apart for his service, as sanctified to represent the body and blood of his Son, and after confession of sin, and thanksgiving for redemption, with commemoration of the sufferings of Christ therein, and ransom thereby, we beg the pardon of sin, and the acceptance of our persons and thanksgivings now offered up to God again, and his grace to help our faith, repentance, love &c. and renewal of our covenant with him, &c. And so after the words of institution &c. I break the bread and deliver it in Christ's general terms to all present, first partaking myself, and so by the cup; which is moved down to the end of the table by the people and deacons (who fill the cup when it is emptied); and immediately after it, each one layeth down his alms for the poor, and so arise, and the next tableful succeedeth to the last after which I first proceed to some words of exhortation, and then of praise and prayer, and sing a psalm, and so conclude with the blessing.[25]

This account tells us a great deal in its simple elegance, indeed what we have here may well reflect general Puritan practice over the years. One may even be able to fit its choreography into an adapted form of the Prayer Book eucharist in order to recreate some kind of 'typical' parish Puritan communion in Elizabethan times, with a table only set up when there is need, simple bread and wine used, the service perhaps cut down so that only the basic elements are there. Perhaps at the invitation to confession, those not communicating (or debarred from doing so) withdrew. At Hailes, Gloucestershire,[26] a small medieval parish church that has retained some of its old decoration has late medieval bench-pews in the nave, and a seventeenth-century pulpit. The chancel is divided from the nave by the old screen, a simple parclose affair, which has the effect of gently dividing the church into two. Inside the chancel there are bench-seats around the walls and on the east side of the screen, leaving the central entrance free. But the surprise is the old communion table, a seventeenth-century piece of furniture, which is set length-wise in the centre. In this environment we can sense the solemn simplicity of the Puritan eucharist and place some of Baxter's procedure there.

Next, we have Baxter's liturgy, which was part of *A Petition for Peace with the Reformation of the Liturgy As it was Presented to the Right Reverend Bishops by the Divines*,[27] written anonymously by Baxter himself for the 'Savoy' Conference and intended to be a flexible alternative to the Prayer Book, not a replacement. Here is the libretto that really fits Baxter's stage-directions. There is an instruction, an exhortation, a prayer of confession, after which the bread and wine are brought to the minister. Then follows the blessing of the bread and wine by word and prayer, the breaking of the bread and pouring of the wine, with communion, followed by exhortation and thanksgiving. But Baxter weaves into this procedure, which is very much what we find in the 1645 *Westminster Directory*, what may be his own theological emphasis. There are separate sets of prayers over the bread and the cup, as was the common Puritan custom. But the Trinity is brought into the heart of the eucharist: the Father is addressed for the consecration, the Son in the commemoration of his acts, and the Spirit is prayed to in the prayer for participation in communion. Baxter's prayers are usually only sample texts, but this is how he suggests the minister prays to Christ over the bread:

> Most merciful Saviour, as thou hast loved us to the death and suffered for our sins, the just for the unjust, and hast instituted this holy Sacrament to bee used in remembrance of Thee till thy coming; We beseech Thee, by thine intercession with the Father, through the Sacrifice of thy Body and Blood, give us the pardon of our sins, and thy quickening Spirit, without which the Flesh will profit us nothing. Reconcile us to the Father; Nourish us as thy Members to Everlasting Life.[28]

Bryan Spinks has pointed out that some of the theological ideas which are to be found here and in other parts of his liturgy are also found in Taylor, e.g., the sacrifice, the presence, the intercession of Christ in heaven, the imagery of the lamb, and the covenant.[29] And that is what makes the impasse between the opposing sides at the 'Savoy' Conference such a frustrating business. Theologically, some members of the different groups were not that far apart. But it was not just theology that was at stake, it was church order, and the discipline of a prescribed liturgy. In the century that had passed, different types of church ethos had developed and – as is being rediscovered in our own day – cultural forces within the Church are often stronger than those of doctrine. There is also one important element built into Baxter's 'Savoy' service over and above freedom in the composition of prayers, and that is an area that has become part of Anglican liturgy during this century – variety of shape. One suspects that the options Baxter envisaged, such as whether to consecrate both elements before communicating, or doing it separately, were simply too much for the Prayer Book enthusiasts.

Baxter stuck to this rationale for the eucharist, for we find it described in his *Saint or a Brute*, which was a work of practical piety published in 1662, and in much more detail in his enormous *Christian Directory: or a sum of practical Theology* which appeared in 1673.[30] This work comes in four parts, dealing with ethics, 'economics' (family duties), 'ecclesiastics' (church duties), and 'politics' (duties to our rulers and neighbours). It is in the 'economics' area, in the twenty-fourth chapter, that we come across his 'directions for Families about the Sacrament of the Lord's Supper'. Whereas Taylor speaks to individuals, Baxter with his Puritan piety addresses families. The main difference between the two works is that Baxter includes a series of discussions of the various difficulties that were being encountered by Puritans attending churches where the clergy and congregation were not sound in their doctrine, or where practices like kneeling for communion (which he will not make as an obstacle for receiving) are observed. In these pages are the words of a man who is still trying to keep the Church together. Over preparation and frequency one could say that he stands for the same things as Taylor and – as we shall shortly see – Patrick. The main difference is his restrictive view on who can renew the covenant in the eucharist, and that is an issue about one's understanding of the nature of the Church as much as anything else. His concluding words on devotion after the service is over throb with love:

> . . . remember then what was so lately before your eyes, and upon
> your heart, and what you resolved on, and what a covenant you
> made with God. Yet judge not of the fruit of your receiving, so

much by feeling, as by faith; for more is promised than you yet possess.[31]

NOTES

1 Hugh Ross Williamson, *Jeremy Taylor* (London: Dobson, 1952), p. 11.
2 The classic treatment is H. R. McAdoo, *The Eucharistic Theology of Jeremy Taylor Today* (Norwich: Canterbury Press, 1988).
3 See *The Whole Works of Jeremy Taylor*, edited by Reginald Heber, revised and corrected by Charles Eden (Volume VI) (London: Longmans, 1852), pp. 1–168.
4 See McAdoo, op. cit., pp. 148ff.
5 *Great Exemplar* in *Works* (Volume II); *Holy Living* in *Works* (Volume III); *Worthy Communicant* in *Works* (Volume VIII). See also McAdoo, op. cit., pp. 171ff, and also pp. 93ff for a discussion of *Clerus Domini*.
6 *Holy Living* chapter IV, part x, section 1. Cf. Brevint, 'one of the greatest mysteries of godliness', *Christian Sacrament and Sacrifice*, p. 3 (Section I.1), Chapter 5 n. 16.
7 ibid., chapter I, part iii, section 5. Cf. 'And what can more ennoble our nature, than that by the means of his holy humanity it was taken up into the cabinet of the mysterious Trinity?', and 'This was the greatest meeting that ever was upon earth, where the whole cabinet of the mysterious Trinity was opened and showed;' see *Great Exemplar*, in *Works* (Volume II), Additional Section I and Section IX.
8 See *Works* (Volume II), Discourse XIX, Section I.
9 See *Works* (Volume VIII), p. 6.
10 ibid., pp. 7, 9; see also *Great Exemplar*, in *Works* (Volume II), Additional Section VII, part 4.
11 All the quotations are from Chapter I of *Worthy Communicant*, see *Works* (Volume VIII), pp. 7, 11, 13, 16, 21, 24, 27, 28, 31, 32, 37, 38, 43.
12 See *Works* (Volume II), Discourse XIX, section 9.
13 See McAdoo, op. cit., pp. 143 and 189.
14 *Holy Living*, chapter II, section vi.8, and chapter IV, section iii.
15 See W. J. Grisbrooke, *Anglican Liturgies of the Seventeenth and Eighteenth Centuries* (Alcuin Club Collections 40) (London: SPCK, 1958), pp. 183–99, and Grisbrooke's study of the evolution of the rite, pp. 19ff. See also *Works* (Volume VIII), pp. 616–30. See also the important study by Harry Boone Porter, *Jeremy Taylor Liturgist* (Alcuin Club Collections 61) (London: SPCK, 1979), pp. 61–84.
16 For a discussion of this, see Stevenson, article cited in Chapter 15 n. 13.
17 See Bryan D. Spinks, 'Two Seventeenth-Century Examples of *Lex Credendi*,

Lex Orandi: The Baptismal and Eucharistic Theologies and Liturgies of Jeremy Taylor and Richard Baxter', *Studia Liturgica* 21 (1991) pp. 165–89. It is interesting to note Taylor's stated recognition of the need for liturgical variety, at least in the context of private devotion, see *Holy Living* Chapter IV, section vii, 'remedies against tediousness of spirit', 2.

18 See *Jeremy Taylor, Selected Works,* edited with introduction by Thomas K. Carroll (Classics of Western Spirituality) (New York: Paulist Press, 1990), p. 55. I am indebted to Donald Allchin for drawing my attention to this. On eucharistic sacrifice in Taylor, see Boone Porter, op. cit., p. 81.

19 See F. R. Bolton, *The Caroline Tradition of the Church of Ireland With Particular Reference to Bishop Jeremy Taylor* (Church Historical Society) (London: SPCK, 1959). (Taylor had a similar concern for forms of consecrating churches to Andrewes and Cosin, see pp. 298ff.)

20 Compare the concluding prayer in Andrewes' eucharistic devotions, Chapter 3.

21 From *Confirmation and Restauration. The Necessary Means of Reformation and Reconciliation* in *The Works of Richard Baxter* (edited by W. Orme) (Volume XIV) (London: Duncan, 1838), pp. 315f, quoted from Paul More and Frank Cross (eds.), *Anglicanism: The Thought and Practice of the Church of England, Illustrated from the Religious Literature of the Seventeenth Century* (London: SPCK, 1951), pp. 449f.

22 Quoted in Geoffrey Nuttall, *Richard Baxter* (London: Nelson, 1965), p. 84.

23 From *The Saint's Everlasting Rest* (Part IV, chapter xiii, section 1), in *The Works of Richard Baxter* (Volume XXIII), pp. 406f, quoted in More and Cross, *Anglicanism,* pp. 620f. For the hymns, see *The Poetical Fragments of Richard Baxter* (London: Pickering, 1821), pp. 45ff ('He wants not friends'), pp. 72ff ('Ye holy angels bright' – 16 verses), and pp. 184ff (an even longer version, in two parts, with titles for each verse).

24 Richard Baxter, *The Reformed Pastor* (Puritan Paperbacks) (Edinburgh: Banner of Truth, 1983). See the useful introduction to Baxter's theology by J. I. Packer, pp. 9–19. I have also been helped by Alasdair Pratt's STM thesis, 'Richard Baxter and the Puritans, 1660–1691' (Yale University, 1965).

25 Quoted from Horton Davies, *Worship and Theology in England: From Andrewes to Baxter and Fox,* pp. 432f.

26 See illustrations and details in Chatfield, *Churches the Victorians Forgot,* pp. 38ff. Though some Puritans *did* kneel round the table, I wonder if this was in fact the practice in this church.

27 A *Petition for Peace with the reformation of the Liturgy* (London [no printing house indicated] 1661), pp. 46–58. Baxter's prayers are lengthy and laden with copious quotations or allusions to scripture, carefully annotated in the margins. See also E. C. Ratcliff, 'Puritan Alternatives to the Prayer Book', in E. C. Ratcliff, *Liturgical Studies* (London: SPCK, 1976), pp. 233ff.

28 ibid., p. 53.

29 See Spinks, art. cit., pp. 184–8.
30 See *The Practical Works of Richard Baxter* (Volume X) (London: Duncan, 1830), pp. 316–23; and *The Practical Works of Richard Baxter* (Volume IV), pp. 312–42.
31 Quoted from *The Practical Works of Richard Baxter* (Volume IV), p. 342.

CHAPTER SEVEN

Survivors of Adversity

Herbert Thorndike (1598–1672) and

Simon Patrick (1626–1707)

> In the year 1653 when all things Sacred were throughout ye nation Either demolisht or profaned Sir Robert Shirley, Baronet, Founded this church; Whose singular praise it is, to have done the best thing in ye worst times, and hoped them in the most callamitous. The righteous shall be had in everlasting remembrance.

So runs the inscription above the west door of Staunton Harold church, in Leicestershire, perhaps the most defiant witness to the spirit of protest under the Commonwealth. It was built as a private chapel by Robert Shirley next to his private house. Begun in 1653, it was completed two years later. The style is uncompromisingly Gothic, but in a very seventeenth-century manner. An organ stands in a west gallery, the box-pews in the nave have candle-holders, the pulpit and reading-desk do not dominate, but are set at an angle across the nave. The chancel with its painted ceiling and black and white marble floor eloquently sets off the altar, which has a rich purple 'carpet of silk' thrown over it. 'No other pre-Victorian church in England reflects so felicitously one man's beliefs and philosophy, nor rivals it as the consummation of Laud's ideals'.[1] Just for good measure, the chalice is not of the conventional kind of the time, but is in the elaborate 'Gothic' style, with a Good Shepherd engraved on the bowl. The building stands to this day, but Sir Robert Shirley, its enthusiastic founder, did not himself last long. Cromwell heard of the wealth he lavished on this building and asked for money for the army. Shirley refused and was promptly arrested. He died in the Tower of London, aged twenty-seven years.

The building he left behind symbolises the continuity that Andrewes, Laud and many others believed in for their Church, a continuity that was to become one of the characteristics of the Restoration. Yet again we encounter one of those ironies, that at Staunton Harold we do not have a parish church that just happens to be furnished in the architecturally correct manner for a particular fashion in church life. Instead, it is a self-consciously correct building, set up for private use by a local land-owner, as a witness to the enduring spirit of the Prayer Book at a time when it was banned from public, parochial use.

It is easy to exaggerate the Commonwealth's rigours on Prayer Book loyalists. But there is abundant evidence for the force and power of its rule in these matters. While some Puritans, like Baxter, used their freedom under the Commonwealth towards a sacramentally focused ministry, the overall picture is one of eucharistic decay. In some places, there were no celebrations of the Lord's Supper at all, because the local minister deemed no one in the congregation worthy. As we have already noted, John Evelyn's diary from time to time laments the virtual abolition of the church year, and on one occasion alludes to a collection for clergy who had been deprived of their livings. For Christmas Day 1658 he has the following entry:

> I went to London with my wife, to celebrate Christmas-day, Mr Gunning [Peter Gunning – future bishop of Ely] preaching in Exeter Chapel [a private chapel, near the Strand] on 7 Michah 2. Sermon ended, as he was giving us the Holy Sacrament, the chapell was surrounded with soldiers, and all the communicants and assembly surpriz'd and kept prisoners by them, some in the house, others carried away. It fell to my share to be confin'd to a roome in the house, where yet I was permitted to dine with the master of it, the Countesse of Dorset, Lady Hatton, and some others of quality who invited me.
>
> In the afternoone came Col. Whaly, Goffe and others, from White-hall, to examine us one by one; some they committed to the Marshall, some to prison. When I came before them they tooke my name and abode, examin'd me why, contrarie to an ordinance made that none should any longer observe the

superstitious time of the Nativity (so esteem'd by them), I durst
offend, and particularly be at Common Prayers, which they told
me was but the masse in English, and particularly pray for Charles
Steuart, for which we had no Scripture. I told them we did not
pray for Ch. Stewart, but for all Christian Kings, Princes and
Governors. They replied, in so doing we praid for the K. of Spaine
too, who was their enemie and a papist, with other frivolous and
insnaring questions and much threatning; and finding no colour
to detaine me, they dismiss'd me with much pitty of my ignorance.

These were men of high flight and above ordinances, and spake
spiteful things of our Lord's Nativity. As we went up to receive
the Sacrament the miscreants held their muskets against us as if
they would have shot us at the altar, but yet suffering us to finish
the office of Communion, as perhaps not having instructions what
to do in case they found us in that action. So I got home late the
next day, blessed be God.

A well-known private chapel in London may well have been an
easy target for a surprise raid on persons of suspect views. And one
may hazard a guess that others were luckier. But Evelyn's account, like
his description of the ordination in Paris seven years previously, gives
a flavour of the atmosphere of the occasion. There is something slightly
eerie about the way he himself defended prayer for all Christian Kings,
Princes and Governors, as if he were a potential early Christian martyr
protesting that it is perfectly possible to be a committed Christian and
a loyal subject of the emperor.

So far, the only one of our characters who had to live through the
Commonwealth in this country has been Jeremy Taylor, who came to
be a great friend of John Evelyn's. In this chapter, we take a look at
two others. Herbert Thorndike and Simon Patrick both suffered
adversity during that time but they somehow survived. Both had
important parts to play in the future life of the Church, and both used
for the good the experience of having had to survive. In the case of
Thorndike, it was his enthusiasm for restructuring the Church along
primitive but Catholic lines. In Patrick's case, it was his readiness to
revise parts of the Prayer Book at a time when there were attempts
to make the Church of England more 'comprehensive' for Dissenters
after the arrival of William and Mary in 1689. As we shall see, neither
plan saw the light of day. But their positive attitude showed that they

were not prepared simply to go along with the high-talking and at times oppressive line taken by many against what were to become 'nonconformists' in the Cavalier Parliament.

HERBERT THORNDIKE

Life and Main Works

Little is known for certain of the precise whereabouts of Thorndike's birthplace but it is thought to have been somewhere in Suffolk. He went to Trinity College, Cambridge and graduated in 1620, becoming thereafter a major Fellow. He specialised in theology, oriental languages, and rabbinic literature – that is to say the literature of the Jewish rabbis from the time of the end of the Old Testament onwards. The combination of these three strands in theological study was to give him an enduring commitment to the study of the origins of Christianity. He was a friend of George Herbert, and by one of those fortunate coincidences, was given Herbert's prebendal stall in Lincoln Cathedral in 1636. But when he was made vicar of Claybrook, Leicester, in 1639, he resigned his prebend, for he had strong views that clergy should only hold one church office at a time – which was hardly the case with many other clergy of that period (or later), as we shall see in the case of Simon Patrick. In 1642 he moved to be vicar of Barley, then in the London diocese, but only fifteen miles from Cambridge, where he continued his academic work, having been made Hebrew lecturer and senior bursar at Trinity College.

In 1641 and 1642, two important works of his appeared which tried to address issues of controversy within the Church. As Parliament's authority increased and the Civil War broke out, they could hardly have been more timely. *Of the Government of Churches: A Discourse pointing at the Primitive Form* argued for a Church modelled on antiquity. People have often argued for what they want after reading what they can in the documents of the ancient Church. 'He that aimeth at the primitive form and that which cometh nearest the institution of our Lord and his Apostles must not think of destroying Bishops, but of restoring their presbyteries.'[2] In other words, bring the bishop back to work closely with the presbyterate in the running and the worship of the Church and many problems will be solved. What Thorndike managed to do in this way was to tackle the Puritan conception of a

Church reformed along primitive lines, and argue for the office of bishop from the earliest times. It was an influential book, for it helped to persuade a number of young men who were ordained under the (presbyterian) form of the *Westminster Directory* of 1645 that they should be ordained again, by bishops – among them Simon Patrick.[3]

His other work at this time was *Of Religious Assemblies, and the Public Service of God: A Discourse according to Apostolicall Rule and Practice.* As the title suggests, its purpose was to defend a set form of liturgy and the polity behind it on the basis of antiquity. Arguing for a Prayer Book, he states bluntly, 'the form which we use deserves this commendation, that it is possible to alter it for the better, but easy to alter it for the worse.'[4] He went further, against what he saw to be the excesses of some Puritans, when he affirmed that liturgical prayers were more important than sermons. Vestments and ceremonial served the important psychological function of adding dignity and awe to the conduct of worship. Among his comments on contemporary practice was that everyone should join in the singing of the *sanctus.* A book of this nature was bound to find a ready readership, both among those who wanted to have a basis on which to set their case as well as those who disagreed with Thorndike's position altogether.

It comes as no surprise, therefore, that when clergy were being deprived of their posts by Parliament, Thorndike should be among the victims. In 1643, only a year after moving there, Thorndike was ejected from Barley. But it was not until 1646 that he was deprived of his fellowship. In the years which followed he lived in poverty, but he was not entirely without work. Not one for hiding his light under a bushel, in 1649 – the year of Charles I's execution – he published his *Discourse of the Right of the Church in a Christian State,* a significant theme for a significant time. As long as the previous works combined, it shows, like them, all the characteristics of Thorndike's style. As Lacey not unharshly puts it: 'He remained always discursive, unloading his erudition as the drift of an argument called forth. He saw clearly enough, but he saw too many things at once.'[5]

In the years that followed, he was a member of the group of scholars that worked from 1653–1657 on the 'Polyglot Bible' under the chairmanship of Brian Walton. 'Polyglot Bibles' are versions of the Bible in ancient languages and they were a feature of sixteenth- and seventeenth-century scholarship. This particular edition was the most ambitious so far, as it used no fewer than nine different languages, including Hebrew, Greek, Latin, Syriac, Ethiopic, Arabic and Persian, together with many different types of back-up literature from Jewish and early Christian sources. It was the first book in this country to have been published by public subscription. The project obviously brought out Thorndike's earlier academic training and his enthusiasm for ancient sources.

In 1658 he was working on his greatest masterpiece of all, which appeared in the following year. It is long even by Thorndike's standards, and has a title equally expressive of its effusive author:

> An Epilogue to the Tragedy of the Church of England, being a necessary Consideration and brief Resolution of the chief Controversies in Religion that divide the Western Church; occasioned by the present calamity of the Church of England: in three books: viz. of
> I *The Principles of Christian Truth*
> II *The Covenant of Grace*
> III *The Laws of the Church.*

Because of its length and scope, it has been described as a '*Summa de ecclesia*' (a '*summa*' – a definitive work – on the Church). It has all the marks of the exploratory persuasive, which is a far cry from the devotional spirit of Jeremy Taylor or Richard Baxter.

At the Restoration it was inevitable that Thorndike's fortunes should take a turn for the better. In 1661 he was reinstated at Barley and Cambridge, but was also made a prebendary of Westminster in that year, to join the distinguished team under John Earle, the new Dean. It was an era that Jocelyn Perkins has aptly described as 'the rebuilding of the waste places': new copes were made for the coronation of Charles II, and among the new items of furniture in the Abbey featured a font, designed by Joseph Nollekens, a leading sculptor. In this font were baptised two young adult men on 18th April, 1663, one of whom was Paul Thorndike, nephew to Herbert.[6] As we shall see, Thorndike set great store by baptism, so it is right to note this particular Eastertide celebration. Thorndike had taken part in the 'Savoy' Conference as a deputy for one of the bishops. Charles II had him made a DD in 1663, and he died in 1672.

The Epilogue: I and II

Thorndike is the most thorough and self-critical scholar of the primitive Church that we have so far seen. We know that Hooker, Andrewes,

Laud, Forbes, and Cosin read the Fathers, just as it is certain that Brevint and Baxter did also. But by 'self-critical' I mean someone who is prepared to let his own Church be judged by the standards of antiquity. Our other characters have done so to a greater or lesser extent, Taylor perhaps most of all, yet Thorndike takes the process a stage further. He will certainly use the Prayer Book to illustrate some of his insights. But one senses that he wants to get behind both the Prayer Book Church that he knows and loves, and the Church of the various forms of Puritanism, in order to let antiquity judge both, and create a better, stronger, and more authentic form of church polity and worship than either of these can offer. With all his rolling periods, his sentences that sometimes never seem to end, and his almost Thucydidean prolixity, (what John Spurr calls 'his contorted writings'[7]), he is searching and grasping after something new and innovative in the Church of the Fathers, and he is equally ready to judge those of his contemporaries whom he thought misguided. Being a cleric, like being a teacher, is part of the talking business. As a clergy-don, Thorndike was no exception to this, for one gains the impression from his writings of a compulsive talker. It is not always clear exactly what he means in practical terms, for example, by his notion of a bishop with the 'presbytery' around him, the two roles checking each other in creative collaboration, as one can see in the early centuries. These may supply the reasons why he was a controversial figure then.

But the effort of persisting with him is rewarded. We shall concentrate on *The Laws of the Church*. But it is important to note how that work fits into the scheme of things. It is the third of three volumes. In the first, *The Principles of Christian Truth*,[8] he asks the basic question, 'what have Christians in common?' and he goes on to establish his case, founded on the Catholic principle of the 'consensus' of peoples and races. Thorndike is using the argument of history and tradition to produce what we might call a common core of ways of being a Christian in an ordered community. This enables him to discuss the teaching office of the Church. There is much in this volume which the more traditionally minded of his day would have found challenging because of his use of the 'collegial' model of bishop and clergy, a view that would have read strangely to those familiar with a rather different conception of how bishops operate. It stands in contrast to the collegiality almost universal in Anglicanism today.

In the second, *The Covenant of Grace*,[9] Thorndike places the spot-light on baptism, and this is really the part of the book where he answers the Puritan model of the Church. We have encountered the notion of covenant before. Hooker tried to deal with the question of godparents, and insisted that the covenant was one in which both sides had a responsibility, over against the Puritan view, whereby God takes the initiative and decides. Charles Miller has shown how this baptismal view of the nature of the Church is strong and vibrant, allowing the Church both to be a human institution, but also one filled with the divine life. Indeed, the comparison with Hooker is more than apt, it is very close indeed. As Miller points out: 'Just as the ecclesiology of the *Laws* is erected around Hooker's exposition of the doctrine of the incarnation and the Trinity, so the centre of Thorndike's *Epilogue* is its second book [i.e., *The Covenant of Grace*] where Thorndike expounds the doctrine of Christ and the Trinity.'[10]

But since the time of Hooker's *Laws of Ecclesiastical Polity*, the strong ('double') predestinarian view of the purpose of God in creation that had developed under rigorous Calvinism meant that Thorndike needed to paint a more dynamic view of the Church, in which human response is given its necessary freedom, yet making the Holy Spirit the agent who seals that covenant. Thorndike's doctrine of the Spirit is a power-ful one. He disagrees with Taylor over original sin, thereby re-establish-ing the doctrine of justification by Christ. But life in the Spirit, the baptismal life of the Christian, is the means for that covenant in Christ being made – and being renewed. To put it at its sharpest, if 'conditionality' is inherent in the living of the covenant with God, if human beings are to be given the full consequences of their freedom, then the Church becomes necessary as the stage on which that con-ditionality is played out in history. In short, we need an institution like the Church, which exists not for its own sake, but because it *has* to exist.

The Epilogue III: The Laws of the Church

Only on the basis of the foregoing brief and inadequate summary of the first two volumes of the *Epilogue* is it possible to move on to *The Laws of the Church*.[11] This book is twice as long as the other two. In no fewer than thirty-three chapters, Thorndike goes through the worship and ordering of the Church, placing it under a microscope, comparing it with the wider tradition about which he is so knowledgeable, and making comments as he proceeds. For example, the bishop is *the* minister of baptism, and therefore all other clergy act under him. Penance should be revived, as should unction of the sick. Marriage is, primarily, about the blessing of the couple, as in the East,[12] and it would be a good idea to revive the monastic life.

It is, however, in the first five chapters that he deals with the eucharist, which is significant in itself, since he sees the eucharist as embodying the heart of Christian worship. The five chapters deal, first, with the general issues of the eucharist as that embodiment, then with the more specific areas of discussion, such as the natural substance of the elements, the nature of consecration, the words of institution and the elements, and, finally, the sacrifice of the eucharist. He begins his short opening chapter in ironic style in a way that would seem to be aimed at Puritans, and perhaps also Prayer Book traditionalists more anxious to preserve rather than to innovate:

> If God had only appointed the profession of Christianity to be the condition qualifying for the world to come, leaving to every man's judgement to determine, what that Christianity is, and wherein it consists, which it is necessary to salvation he profess, and what that conversation is which his salvation requireth; there had been no cause, why I should go any further in this dispute.[13]

And this leads him to target certain views of the eucharist that he intends to reject, which include Catholics, Zwinglians, Calvinists and Lutherans. In the second chapter, he outlines his view of the presence of Christ, which does not depend on the faith of the receiver, and which is a feasting on the sacrifice of Christ. (We shall meet both these themes in a different form when it comes to Simon Patrick.) Thus: 'Those that communicate in the eucharist do feast upon the sacrifice of our Lord Christ on the cross, which God is so well pleased with as to grant the covenant of grace, and the publication thereof, in consideration of it.'[14]

Thorndike likes to use the expression 'common sense' a great deal in assessing an argument, as in the statement that the 'substance of the eucharist is not distinguishable by common sense from their accidents'.[15]

Just as the Holy Spirit came upon Christ at baptism and the apostles at Pentecost, so he does on the eucharist, which prepares Thorndike for the assertion near the start of his third chapter: 'But this change consisting in the assistance of the Holy Ghost, Which makes the elements, in which It dwells, the Body and Blood of Christ; it is not necessary, that we acknowledge the bodily substance of them to be any way abolished.' And: 'the consecration . . . makes it a sacrament, not . . . the faith of him that receives.'[16]

But strong as is his view of the role of the Spirit, his faith is none the less founded upon the ascended Christ, in words that are reminiscent of Brevint and Taylor, in their different ways: 'The sitting of Christ at the right hand of God . . . the Apostle makes an argument of Divine power and authority, dwelling in our flesh in the person of Christ.'[17]

But how is consecration performed? In the fourth chapter, Thorndike is likewise innovative in the face of his contemporaries, but traditional in so far as he has looked at the early evidence. To focus that conse-cration on the words of Christ 'offereth violence to common sense', as well as to the facts as he sees them. Instead he insists that conse-cration is effected through *thanksgiving*, not by reciting the words of Christ, because that is how the early liturgies developed. And it is not only his acquaintance with Christian texts; it is his knowledge, too, of Jewish liturgical practice, such as the blessings contained in the *Talmud*. Thorndike was one of the first people engaged in theological and liturgical discussion in his country to apply this kind of research to the events of his day. He was far ahead of his time, in an area that has become increasingly technical in recent years.[18] As in the other chapters, he goes into a catalogue of ancient sources and quotations. It is the fullest collection of this kind of evidence that we have seen since Forbes' *Considerationes Modestae*.

In his final chapter, Thorndike almost ties himself in knots in his discussion of sacrifice. We have already seen how his starting-point is the sacrifice of Christ, on which Christians feast. It is by analogy that the eucharist came to be called sacrificial. In the face of the Protestant polemic that this is an impossibility, he states:

> It is not nor can be any disparagement to the sacrifice of our Lord Jesus Christ upon the cross, to the full and perfect satisfaction and propitiation for the sins of the world which it hath made, that the eucharist should be counted the sacrifice of Christ crucified, mystically, and as in a sacrament, represented to, and feasted upon by, His people.

This leads into a careful description of the various categories of sacrifice to different parts of the Prayer Book rite, but he begins this with the statement that links *Laws* with the previous volume: 'The celebration of the eucharist is the renewal of the covenant of grace.'[19]

Then he works out four stages and applies them to different aspects of the sacrifice. The offertory is the 'commemorative and representative' sacrifice; the intercession, which immediately follows in the Prayer Book rite, is 'propitiatory and impetratory'. The consecration is 'typical and representative'. The fourth stage is the self-offering of the people after communion. Were he to have left this alone, the reader would be reasonably satisfied, but the summary which ensues is a little confusing, because he uses some of these descriptions of sacrifice in slightly different ways from his main discussion. (One of the motivations for such a recapitulation is because he then weaves baptism – yet again – into the scheme of things.)

What are we to make of all this? Thorndike works on a broad canvas but he does at least attempt to bring the discussion back to familiar ground in the Prayer Book service. In his concern to shift perspectives of sacrifice on to a wider framework, he concentrates on four moments in the service which he regards as having particularly strong sacrificial resonances. The first is the placing of the bread and wine on the altar. The second is the intercession. The third is the consecration – but he insists that it is the unconsecrated bread and wine, not the Body and Blood of Christ, that is offered. And the fourth and last is the self-offering of the congregation. Such a scheme has its strengths, one of which is the width and depth of possible meanings. Another is the specific character of these associations. Unlike Laud, moreover, Thorndike does not delineate between the offerings of different kinds of sacrifice in terms of priest, congregation, and every individual on their own. Neither is Thorndike's a scheme of abstract views culled here and there from history. They are words and actions in the rite which the reader knows well: placing gifts on the altar, pleading for the needs of Church and world, the act of consecration itself, and finally the self-offering of all in all in Christ. This is the first time we have seen such a discussion.[20]

Thorndike covers other matters connected with the eucharist in *The Laws of the Church*, such as private masses (which he is obviously against), the question of frequency (which he claims the Reformers, against their original pretensions, made worse rather than better), and the need for prayer for the departed. He knew that the 1549 Prayer

Book had a commemoration of this kind, and in 1552 this was deleted, leaving the prayer of intercession to conclude with the sick and the suffering. (This was made up for in 1662: Patrick felt in the same way on this question.) He also refutes the idea, voiced at the Council of Trent, and present in certain medieval theologians, that the priest somehow acts in the person of Christ at the eucharist: no, says Thorndike, it is the whole congregation that does so together. This was made up for in 1662: Patrick felt in the same way on this question. Throughout, his style never loses its directness, hitting at popery here, and Puritans there, constantly aiming his remarks at those who are neither, but have 'common sense', that great virtue of the bluff and the impatient and the visionary.

Other Works[21]

There is an overall coherence in Thorndike's thought of such a kind that one recognises his favourite themes returning again and again. In an unpublished treatise, he begins:

> The necessity of the Sacrament of Baptism and of the Eucharist unto Salvation consisteth in the Covenant of Grace, in which our Saviour consisteth; and which the one of them setteth and enacteth, the other reneweth and re-establisheth.

And he continues:

> As for the offering of our selves, our souls and bodies, to be an holy and lively sacrifice to God [here he is quoting from the prayer of oblation], at the commemoration and representation of Christ's sacrifice upon the cross; it is nothing else, but the formal and express reprising of the Covenant of Baptism on our part.

Moreover, his views on unity and prayer with the departed are more Eastern than Western in their insistence on such prayer being about 'remembering': 'Now, if the Communion of Saints oblige the Church to remember the dead, can it be doubted that it obligeth the dead to remember the living?'

In an unpublished sermon on the eucharist, whose text is 1 Corinthians 10:16 ('The cup of blessing which we bless . . .'), he adopts a strongly liturgical approach. He begins by referring to the invitation to share in 'God's blessings', where he quotes 'Lord, I am not worthy that thou shouldest come under my roof' (Matthew 8:8; Luke 7:6);

this is a pre-communion devotion in both the Roman and Byzantine rites, which, as we have seen, also appears in Jeremy Taylor's *Book of Offices* (1658). He expounds his eucharistic theology by using the Corinthian context – the danger of apostasy through disunity. And he asserts the reality and effectiveness of the prayers over the bread and cup, where he equates blessing with thanksgiving, thanksgiving with consecration, through which we participate in 'the fulness of the Godhead', a feeding that is not to be spiritualised out of all reality, since Jesus himself speaks of abstaining from the fruit of the vine (Luke 22:18). Towards the end, he affirms that 'God's covenant, or will, his word is his act and deed, by which he initiates us in it', which leads into a rhetorical section where the word 'conveyance' is exploited for all its legal and sacramental imagery, in order to provide a picture of God always taking the initiative, and we having the opportunity – by grace – to respond, to be fed, to be renewed.

What kind of theology was Thorndike's? His learning was vast, for he refers to many sources, ancient and contemporary. Of the more recent among the latter, we may surmise that he was familiar with Forbes, whose historical method is so near his own, and Ralph Cudworth, who (as we shall see when we deal with Patrick's thought) was an early enthusiast for a covenant theology of the eucharist, and the eucharist as a feast upon a sacrifice. But what Thorndike is to be most remembered for are the three main features of his main argument as expounded principally in the *Epilogue*.

First, baptism is the basis on which the Church can exist at all, which means that – in the steps of Hooker – baptism is the sacrament of incorporation into the life of the Trinity by the cross of Christ, in the power of the Spirit. That is the personal inauguration of the covenant for believers, continually renewing their 'living faith' (another Thorndike favourite), this covenant of grace being renewed every time the eucharist is celebrated. Secondly, Thorndike's stress on the work of the Spirit in the consecration, doubtless backed up by his knowledge of the ancient liturgies, builds on some of the hints that we have seen in our other characters: Hooker's vision of the Spirit in the communicant; Andrewes' prayer for the Spirit in his devotions; Cosin's enthusiasm for the 'Holy Spirit and Word' prayer in the 1549 consecration as in the Scottish 1637 liturgy, which was turned down for the 1662 revision; to say nothing of Taylor and Baxter, with their insistence on the place of the Spirit at the heart of the eucharist.

Moreover, he was ahead of his time in seeing consecration in Jewish terms, as essentially blessing God over bread and cup. Thirdly, and finally, Thorndike works out a sophisticated concept of offering and sacrifice, culled from history and applied to the Prayer Book. On the basis of these insights, Thorndike emerges as an innovative thinker, who built on the thinking of his immediate predecessors, but who used antiquity rather more thoroughly than they did. That leaves the question of how to use any new or recovered knowledge of antiquity, a question that has not gone away in the time since.

SIMON PATRICK

Life

Simon Patrick spans the definitive arrival of Charles II and the Prayer Book of 1662 in a way that none of our other characters do, if only because he was a younger man, with a long ministry ahead of him. Unlike Thorndike, the prophetic don, much of whose life centred around Cambridge, Patrick moved around more, and he became a senior and influential bishop. Of all the people looked at so far, next to Forbes and Brevint he is one of the most neglected, even though there was an edition of his works in the middle of the last century. He stands unique in one significant respect – he wrote an autobiography. He emerges from it as an attractive personality; like the portraits of him which exist, there is a warm firmness about the man. During the Commonwealth he managed to find a way of surviving in parochial life.[22]

He was born in Gainsborough not far from Lincoln, in 1626, the son of a landowner. His early reminiscences of sermons indicate that he did not like Puritan preaching very much, and when he went to Queens' College, Cambridge, in 1644, he came under the influence of John Smith, who had that year arrived as a Fellow on leaving the Puritan stronghold of Emmanuel College. Smith was one of the group to which we have referred before, called the Cambridge Platonists, who formed part of a reaction against Puritanism in favour of using a more historical perspective in the way Christianity should be thought out. In some ways the forerunners of the 'age of reason' of the following century, they laid great stress on reason in religious enquiry. They were critical of the Puritan tenets of faith, such as predestination, which they found to be impossible to believe. Patrick and Smith developed a close friendship, and Patrick preached at the latter's funeral in 1652. Some years before this, Patrick was ordained as a presbyterian, there being no public alternative. However, on reading Thorndike's *Primitive Government of the Church* and the works of Henry Hammond, like a number of other young men of his time he decided that he should be ordained by a bishop. Joseph Hall, now deprived Bishop of Norwich, accordingly ordained him in his front parlour on 5th April, 1654. He served for a year as Dean of Queens' Chapel, but we then find him moved to London, where he became domestic chaplain to Sir Walter St John, at Battersea Manor. It is not clear why this move was necessary, but we may conclude that he was unacceptable as an academic to the authorities because of his anti-Puritan views. He became vicar of St Mary's Battersea, however, in 1657, being presented to that living by Sir Walter as patron. The church there had survived the ravages of the Commonwealth. It still had its peal of bells, which were renovated in 1653, although the altar-rails had been sold off, because of the practice of sitting for communion which had become customary in many places during the Commonwealth.

How Patrick took services at this time we do not know, but he seems to have prepared his congregation with some skill for the reintroduction of the Prayer Book. On 22nd July, 1660 he notes that he 'read Common Prayer publicly in Church'. When the Presidency of Queens' was vacant soon after, Patrick was elected by the Fellows, but King Charles II forced Anthony Sparrow (later Bishop of Norwich) upon the College. Patrick tried to take the matter up with the King in law, but without success. In September 1662, Patrick was made rector of St Paul's Covent Garden, a prestigious church building designed thirty years before by Inigo Jones. He held this post in conjunction with Battersea, plurality being a common practice at the time. In 1671, he was made a Chaplain to the King and the following year – the year of Thorndike's death – he was made a prebendary of Westminster. Additional responsibilities followed in 1675 when he was made Canon-Treasurer, he and his wife moving into 1, Little Cloister, as the first occupants of a dwelling that has housed a liturgist or two in its time. At the same time he relinquished the living of Battersea. In 1679 he became Dean of Peterborough, which he held in conjunction with the Abbey and Covent Garden. His involvement in the central affairs of the Church increased. He noted James II's demeanour at the coronation in 1685 as that of a Roman Catholic who did not seem to take an Anglican service seriously. He was drawn into theological discussions between the new King and his advisers. But he was one of the group of London clergy who refused to read James's Declaration of Indulgence, not because of the recognition which it would afford other Churches, but because of its possibly harmful effect on the Church of England. It was almost universally ignored and was among the events that led to the Revolution whereby James fled the country in 1688.

When William of Orange and Queen Mary arrived as joint monarchs, Patrick was one of their supporters. King William was anxious to enable the Church of England to embrace and 'comprehend' as many dissenters as possible and a group of bishops and senior churchmen was set up to revise and adapt the Prayer Book in certain ways. Patrick had the responsibility of rewriting some of the collects. As a ready writer, and in the spirit of the age, his draft productions were certainly lengthy. In the event, while there was some support for this move, it was not even discussed by the clergy in the Lower House of Convocation in the Canterbury Province. Patrick was made Bishop of Chichester late in 1689, and two years later he was translated to Ely, succeeding Francis Turner. Turner had resigned because he could not accept the new monarch; by taking over from him, Patrick was siding with the new regime in an unambiguous manner. Patrick continued as Bishop of Ely until his death in 1707. His autobiography tells of much diocesan work, as well as the higher echelons of power in the Church, since he was made part of a group of senior clerics charged with making recommendations about appointments.

Work

Two strands emerge from Patrick's works. One is what might be called the 'traditional', and the other is the 'Platonist'. We came across a similar fusion of these in the case of Taylor. He shares with Taylor a capacity to write fluently, though whereas Taylor's style is at times passionate, Patrick's is enthusiastic. He has a cooler tone than Taylor, though the two have some remarkable resemblances. However, no one would want to place Patrick in the highest grade of theologians. He belongs rather to the 'scholar-pastor' league. Alexander Taylor, his nineteenth-century editor, has this to say about him:

> Patrick must in fairness be judged not so much by the brilliance

or originality of his writings, as by their solidity, accuracy, and breadth of range; by the comprehensiveness, vigour, and fecundity, rather than the boldness or novelty of his mental gifts. Not a line that he has written but is marked by practical good sense, earnestness of purpose and total unconsciousness of display.[23]

Before we look at his sacramental writings, it is appropriate in an author of such width to mention some of his other works. In 1664, *The Parable of the Pilgrim* appeared. In many respects, this anticipates John Bunyan's classic *Pilgrim's Progress* for its scope and vision.[24] In 1668 his *Friendly Debate between a Conformist and a Non-Conformist* was published, which covers similar ground to what we have met in some of Thorndike's writings. Then there are the volumes of notes on books of the Bible over which he laboured, which were too many to be accommodated in the nine-volume collection of his works. Perhaps the following two quotations most succinctly sum up the man and his theological stance. The first comes from a sermon he preached in 1678: 'God hath given us the use of reason, which, if we will blindly resign to any pretended authority, what is it but to shut our eyes when we should open them.' And the second comes from his *Discourse about Tradition* (1683):

> The sense of the whole Church . . . must be acknowledged also to be of greater or lesser authority, as it was nearer or further off from the times of the apostles. What was delivered by their immediate followers ought to weigh so much with us, as to have the greatest humane authority, and to be looked upon as little less than divine.[25]

Here are the two sides of Patrick: the man of reason and the man of tradition. How they combine together may perhaps be seen from the following works.

In 1658, Patrick brought out his first book, entitled *Aqua Genitalis: A Discourse Concerning Baptism.*[26] It had begun life as a sermon at the baptism of the son of a fellow-cleric. Patrick makes great use of the theme of covenant in relation to baptism. It is a short work, which stands in the same kind of tradition as we saw in Thorndike, though *Covenant of Grace* did not appear until 1659. When sermons are adapted for publication, they are usually expanded, and it is interesting to note that there is an extra section 'to persuade to a confirmation of the baptismal vow' – the most important addition made to the Confirmation service in the 1662 revision. Patrick's old friend, John Worthington, another of the Cambridge Platonists, encouraged Patrick to go further and write on the eucharist, and accordingly his *Mensa Mystica: or a Discourse concerning the Sacrament of the Lord's Supper*[27] appeared in 1660. Alexander Taylor, the editor, has this to say about it:

> It is both longer and more systematic than its sister treatise, entering fully and deeply into every aspect of its sacred subject, both dogmatic and practical, and supplying under every head those devotional aids which a careful pastor would wish to see in familiar use among the members of his flock but which were scantily provided in the religious manuals of the time. Its reception was such that a second edition was issued in 1667, in company with a reprint of *Aqua Genitalis*, followed by others in rapid succession. The fifth of these appeared in 1684, the sixth and last during the author's lifetime in 1702, the seventh in 1717, and the demand has never discontinued down to the present time [1858].[28]

The work may well be regarded as Patrick's most significant and most substantial, and from it flowed other works on the eucharist, each with a distinct purpose, but each entirely consistent with the parent-book. *Mensa Mystica* is the theological 'tour de force'. In 1670, he published *Christian Sacrifice*,[29] a devotional guide to the eucharist, consisting mainly of prayers for the use of the worshipper, many of them rich and verbose by modern standards. (He added yet more prayers in the second edition of this work in 1672.) Then in 1679 appeared *A Book for Beginners, or An Help to Young Communicants* in their growth in the eucharistic life.[30] His last book on the eucharist consisted of a course of sermons that he preached in Peterborough Cathedral in order to inaugurate a weekly eucharist there which started at Pentecost 1683; this was being encouraged by the Archbishop for cathedral worship. It was called *A Treatise of the Necessity and Frequency of Receiving the Holy Communion* and was published in 1684.[31] Patrick took the opportunity of inserting to the reprint of *Mensa Mystica* that year a series of prayers in order to express some of the aspirations of his narrative.

The cumulative effect of these works is to make a bold statement about Patrick's eucharistic enthusiasm. This is only heightened by the Latin titles (which have biblical and early Christian overtones) given to his two original works, the 'Water of Birth' and the 'Mystic Table'. He was part of a movement that wanted to heighten the profile of the eucharist in the hearts and minds of post-Restoration congregations, a movement that finds particular expression, for example, in St James's, Piccadilly, which was designed by Sir Christopher Wren and consecrated in 1684. The wide nave looks at once straight ahead to the altar, which has marble rails round it and a pelican over it, carved by Grinling Gibbons, the craftsman whom John Evelyn discovered and whose introduction to the King and to Wren he himself effected. The pelican, according to legend, is a bird who feeds her young with her own blood, which makes her into a special eucharistic symbol of sacrifice in this context. Moreover, the lavish communion-plate given by Sir Robert Gayre (d. 1702) consisted of four chalices, four patens, three flagons, and a large alms dish, twenty-three-and-a-half inches in diameter, depicting the Last Supper in the centre, and with the annunciation, nativity, and resurrection on the rim. To this set were soon added three smaller chalices for use in taking communion to the sick at home. A provision of such a kind in art and communion-ware shows what a central place the eucharist was intended to hold for this new church and congregation.

Patrick is very much part of this change in church life. But the fact that he first writes a treatise, then a devotional manual, then a work for young people, followed by a set of sermons about frequency (a theme covered by Taylor, and alluded to by Brevint) is an indication that he was doing more than following a fashion. At the end of *Mensa Mystica* Patrick perhaps gives vent to his true feelings about one of the reasons for the neglect of the eucharist, namely the influence of Puritans and others during the Commonwealth:

> The way to have reformed us would not have been to leave off Communions, but to make them more frequent. Nor, secondly, to unite and consolidate parishes, but to make more pastors in greater parishes, that by more personal instruction men might be better fitted for frequent Communion. But so it is, that zeal oft-times hath too much passion in it, and too little knowledge. The good Lord pardon us, and be gracious unto us. Amen.[32]

In terms of medium and message, Patrick's works on the eucharist have a uniqueness about them in that, apart from *Mensa Mystica*, each one has an oral origin or focus. *Christian Sacrifice* is for personal prayer.

A *Book for Beginners* reads like a man speaking directly to a young person, even if the style seems somewhat quaint and old-fashioned today. (Bishop Thomas Wilson, of Sodor and Man, was to try the same kind of exercise in 1734.[33]) The *Treatise*, of course, has a directly oral origin, being the text of a series of sermons. Nor is there discernible theological change of mind. He defines principles and practice in *Mensa Mystica* in 1660. He prescribes devotional prayers in 1670. He exhorts the young to come to communion in 1679. (Penelope Patrick bore a son in 1678, who died in his first year, but a second son was born in 1680 and grew to adulthood.) He preaches about frequent communion in 1683, establishing a weekly eucharist, and publishes the sermons in 1684, together with supplementary prayers for the edition of *Mensa Mystica* of that year.

And this consistency of thought is reflected in his liturgical practice. At St Paul's, Covent Garden, there were such large and frequent communions that Patrick and his churchwardens had to decide how to spend the money that accumulated from the collections. In the Church, money comes at the top of the list of topics for discussion in many contexts. It would seem that the good Dr Patrick had to prevail on his churchwardens for the money to be invested in a property to pay for the services of a curate to preach in Patrick's absence. Then as Bishop of Chichester his first act was to celebrate the eucharist and preach in the cathedral. In both his dioceses, he asked specifically about frequency of eucharists in the parishes. And when he died, he left his communion-plate to Dalham parish church, in Suffolk, where he had acquired a house for Penelope, his wife, to live in after his death. The plate is characteristic of the style of the period, the chalice having a large long bowl on a low foot. Penelope added a flagon to the set, which in addition to the chalice includes an alms dish, and two patens, one small and one large.[34] Such a set would be typical of the grander provisions of the time.

What, then, of the content of *Mensa Mystica*? Like Taylor and Brevint, there is a lay dedication, to Sir Walter St John and Lady St John, in whose house the work was written. Like Taylor's *Worthy Communicant*, with whom it has other points in common, it starts with a theological introduction (Section I); moves on to Preparation (Section II); through 'Deportment of soul at Holy Communion service' (Section III); 'post-coenium' – after the service (Section IV); with some discussion of the benefits of Communion (Section V).

Whereas Taylor begins *Holy Living* with the Trinity, Patrick begins *Mensa Mystica* with the incarnation:

> God, who is simple and removed far from all sense, considering the weakness of man's soul, and how unable he is to conceive of things spiritual purely and nakedly in themselves; and yet having a mind to be better known unto us, and to make himself more manifest than ever, was pleased in his infinite goodness to dwell in flesh, and appear here in the person of his Son, who was made like to man, to shew what God is in our nature.[35]

No great gnomic flights of language like Taylor here, just a statement of God stooping down to humanity – what is sometimes referred to as 'kenotic christology', the self-emptying God. From that starting-point, divine nature, rather than the sin of humanity, he constructs his theology of the eucharist. 'We profess ourselves federates of God' – covenant-theology stated boldly. He is firm about the solemn and transcendent character of the Lord's Supper: ' . . . let all Protestants take heed how they do irreverently behave themselves in participation of these holy mysteries, lest we give them occasion to say that we have nothing but common bread and wine empty of all sacrament.'[36]

The main part of the treatise is in the first section, as we found with Taylor's *Worthy Communicant*. We have already mentioned his 'common mean' definition of truth.[37] This is his style and method when he tackles the main issues. He summarises these under seven main headings and it is to these that he attached most of the prayers that he inserted to the 1684 edition.[38] The first heading is remembrance of Christ. Here he states that:

> . . . *anamnesis* doth not signify barely '*recordatio*', recording or registering of his favours in our mind; but '*commemoratio*', . . . a solemn declaration . . . We keep it, as it were, in his memory, and plead before him the sacrifice of his Son, which we show unto him, humbly requiring that grace and pardon, with all other benefits of it, may be bestowed on us.

And again: 'Such an unbloody sacrifice, which is only rememorative, and in representation, we all acknowledge.'[39]

Right at the start, Patrick uses a fresh word, 'plead', of the eucharistic memorial, because he knows that he needs to go beyond 'remember'. He has to find a word that will resonate and look forward. It is a word that has appeared in the time since, and is therefore of some interest. Secondly, by using the expression 'unbloody' of the sacrifice, he demonstrates his knowledge of antiquity. Taylor uses it in his liturgy, with which Patrick was bound to have been familiar. It lies behind much of the writing on sacrifice that we have so far encountered.[40]

The second main heading is the remembrance with thanksgiving. Like Thorndike, but in much less detail, he discusses the Jewish background to the eucharist. His main purpose is to point to the objective character of this thanksgiving: 'I would not be so mistaken, as if I thought the Christian thanksgiving consisted only in inward thoughts and outward words. For there are eucharistical actions also whereby we perform a most delightful sacrifice unto God.' And: ' . . . the spiritual sacrifice of ourselves, and the corporal sacrifice of our goods to him, may teach the papists that we are sacrificers as well as they, and are "made kings and priests unto God." '[41]

Between these lines we may well read a growing self-confidence in the tradition represented by this new generation, in whom the past has been absorbed and adapted into the present, and a fresh 'Catholicism' deliberately sought after. As far as the detail in his ideas are concerned, he links the offering of alms and bread and wine to the self-offering of the people. In 1662, at the start of the prayer of intercessions, 'oblations' were added after the reference to 'alms'. Whatever the intentions of the revisers, it is clear that Patrick was the first known writer to interpret these 'oblations' as referring to the bread and wine.[42] Patrick espouses a notion of offering that is reflected in many of the early liturgies: we hand over bread and wine to God in order to receive it again as the body and blood of Christ.

Patrick's third end for Communion is to enter into covenant with God. 'This eating and drinking is a federal rite', a 'feast upon a sacrifice', and he compares it with the communion-sacrifices of the Old Testament: 'Our approach to this table is but more strongly to tie the knot, and to bind us in deeper promises to continual friendship with him.' We have encountered such 'federal' language before, and Patrick by his open-ended approach to the weakness of human beings clearly follows the 'two-sided', non-exclusive interpretation, rather than the tight, selective approach of Puritans, present in Baxter, with his strictures on who should come to the table.

Where did he get his ideas from? The federal theology which he uses is taken from Ralph Cudworth (1617–88), another of the Cambridge

Platonists, who taught Patrick when he was a student and was Regius Professor of Hebrew. Cudworth wrote a *Discourse Concerning the True Nature of the Lord's Supper* in 1642 in whose last chapter there is a discussion of the eucharist as a federal rite. Patrick does not cite Cudworth in this particular instance, but he mentions him in his references on other occasions, not least in his understanding of the eucharist as a 'feast upon a sacrifice.'[43]

Cudworth is better known for his monumental *True Intellectual System of the Universe* (1678), in which he argued against atheism and extreme Calvinism in favour of revealed religion and moral values. His much earlier discourse on the eucharist, however, is a short investigation of its biblical background in the Passover. He quotes many Jewish sources, including the twelfth-century writer Maimonides. It is clear that his two principal ideas, covenant and feasting upon the sacrifice, provide the foundation of his work. They have a marked influence on Patrick, who applies them in a much broader context, in terms of history, liturgy, and the pastoral approach to preparing for and receiving communion, and probably also on Thorndike in his more historically focused writings. Covenant, of course, is not a new idea. Tertullian, for example, uses it of the eucharist, and we have come across chance references to this image in the writings of Hooker and Andrewes. But it is now, in Patrick and Thorndike, a framework around which is built a whole theology of the eucharist which provides the means for balancing two important foci – God's initiative in reaching out to us and our response to him in that free gift of sacramental grace.

Patrick's fourth heading is the forgiveness of sins. Here he develops his covenant theology by drawing together his previous discussion: the movement of the liturgy from offertory, through consecration and communion is a feast on a sin-offering, where *all* eat and drink. His two final ends are concerned with union with Christ and each other. One can see Hooker in the background, and he quotes him saying that 'the real presence is not to be sought in the bread and wine, but in those that receive them.' But adapting Hooker slightly, he then proceeds to join presence and sacrifice together in the way that we have already seen in Andrewes, Brevint, Taylor and Baxter: 'We are, though not transubstantiated into another body, yet metamorphosed and transformed into another likeness, by the offering up of our bodies to God, which is a piece of this service, Romans 12:1,2.'

And he puts a mild gloss on Hooker when he adds: 'Other union than this (by Christ's Spirit) I know no use of, though we should believe that which we do not understand.'[44]

Of brotherly love Patrick writes with warmth and feeling. Taking the Farewell discourses from the Fourth Gospel as a starting-point, he mentions ancient practices such as the kiss of peace and taking communion to those unable to be present. There is a strong moral element in his understanding of the eucharist, but there is an equally strong note of joy, as in his use of words like 'entertainment', which we met in Taylor.

Theologically, like all our other nine characters, Patrick is a mixture. He unites presence and sacrifice in order to make sense of them; he insists on the objective fact of the eucharist, that it is not basking in something which happened long ago; for him sacrifice has different resonances and applications; and, above all, he blends the theme of covenant so that, like Taylor but in a different way, the eucharist expresses a very *social* nature. It is never there for itself only.

The remainder of the treatise is as pastoral and practical as Taylor. With a different kind of introspection, he suggests that: 'the better we know ourselves and our own wants, the more hungry we shall be; and the more knowledge we have of our own sincerity, with the greater comfort and sweetness we shall eat.'[45]

He has a strong sense of the transcendental character of the eucharist, not as strong as Taylor's, but pronounced enough in its own right. This makes him refer to the *sanctus* – on one occasion voicing with approval Thorndike's suggestion that the whole congregation should join in singing it at the liturgy.[46]

Writing of the hope of heaven, he relies on Christ's promise, 'Come, you blessed of my Father, (You who have loved me, and kept my commandments, you that did what I bid you in remembrance of me), and inherit the kingdom prepared for you.'[47]

Here is a quotation from the 'Great Assize' (Matthew 25:34), with an allusion to one of the Farewell Discourses (John 14:15), as well as a reference to the command by Christ to repeat the Supper (I Corinthians 11:25). Stripped of the parenthesis about discipleship and the eucharistic action, this is taken almost directly from the end of the intercession in the 1549 liturgy, which appeared in the 1637 Scottish Prayer Book, and which John Cosin would suggest (unsuccessfully, as it turned out) for inclusion in 1662. We have already observed how in 1552 that prayer simply ended with the suffering, without any mention of the saints or the departed. In the event, the rather more prosaic prayer 'that with them we may be partakers of thy heavenly kingdom' is all that gained entrance into the service in the revision of 1662.[48]

Patrick's piety is all-embracing. Not as Trinitarian as Taylor's, it still ends in heaven. But there is nothing 'ordinary' about the eucharist for him. It must be frequent, it should be prepared for, it is no mental activity but an objective action in which something really happens; a covenant, an unbloody sacrifice, the work of Christ pleaded before the Father, the means of union with others, renewal in God, in the communion of saints, looking forward to the end of time. In some respects, his approach is prophetic, not in the brilliance of Thorndike, but in the shape of the better things that were to come, for which the Church should always be ready. But there is also a down-to-earth quality to him that we have not so far met. It is therefore appropriate that this, the last of our characters, the one who brings us into the beginning of the following century, should conclude with one of the 1684 *Mensa Mystica* prayers. Not a spectacular piece of writing, but a perceptive one, which unites those who come to the Mystic Table with those who have gone before.

> O God of all wisdom and grace, who hast promised to guide all meek and humble souls in judgement, and to teach me thy way, preserve my mind, I most humbly beseech thee, from all manner of illusions, and free me from all mistakes, about these holy mysteries of our salvation. That I may neither approach irreverently unto thy altar, nor out of causeless fears omit my duty, and lose the comforts which thou impartest there.
>
> Stir up in my soul also that fervent zeal which brought thy ancient servants so frequently thither. And bestow upon me such a constant relish of heavenly enjoyment, that I may not either through sloth or idleness, or through covetousness and love of this world, neglect any opportunity which is presented to me of attending on thee at thy holy table: but that I may rather hunger and thirst after the divine food which thou there preparest for us; and feel my soul so in love with it, and with all the virtue unto which we are engaged by it, that I may have no doubt of thy gracious acceptance, through thy mercies in Christ Jesus. Amen.[49]

NOTES

1 See Carlton, *Churches the Victorians Forgot*, pp. 72ff (quotation from p. 3). Also Yates, *Buildings, Faith and Worship*, pp. 68f; and Oman, *English Church Plate*, pp. 276f and Plate 83a (the chalice cover is purely ornamental, unlike the 'Gothic' chalices earlier in the century, whose covers served as small patens).

2 See *The Theological Works of Herbert Thorndike* (Volume I) (Library of Anglo-Catholic Theology) (Oxford: 1844), pp. 1–97; quotation from p. 91.

3 See John Spurr, *The Restoration Church of England: 1645–1689* (New Haven: Yale University Press, 1991), pp. 141–3.

4 See *Works* (Volume I), pp. 99–394; quotation from p. 384.

5 T. A. Lacey, *Herbert Thorndike (1598–1672)* (London: SPCK, 1929), p. 29.

6 Jocelyn Perkins, *Westminster Abbey: Its Worship and Ornaments* (Volume III) (Alcuin Club Collections 38) (London: Oxford University Press, 1952), p. 42 (Thorndike baptism) and pp. 112ff (the Restoration Chapter).

7 Spurr, op. cit. p. 395.

8 See *Works* (Volume II). See also Buxton, *Eucharist and Institution Narrative*, pp. 121ff.

9 See *Works* (Volume III).

10 See E. C. Miller, jr, *The Doctrine of the Church in the Thought of Herbert Thorndike* (1598–1672) (Oxford University D.Phil. dissertation, 1990), p. 98. I am indebted to Dr Miller for his assistance and encouragement here. It is a pity that this distinguished thesis has not so far been published.

11 See *Works* (Volume IV parts 1 and 2). The section on the eucharist consists of the first five chapters of the first part.

12 A similar insight is worked out in Kenneth Stevenson, *Nuptial Blessing: A Study of Christian Marriage Rites* (Alcuin Club Collections 64) (London: SPCK, 1982).

13 *Work* (Volume IV parts 1 and 2), p. 1.

14 ibid., pp. 17f.

15 ibid., p. 26.

16 ibid., pp. 34, 36.

17 ibid., pp. 40f and 51ff.

18 See, for example, Paul Bradsaw, *The Search for the Origins of Christian Worship* (London: SPCK, 1992), esp. pp. 1–29, and 130–60.

19 See *Works* (Volume IV, part 1), pp. 102, 103.

20 See Kenneth Stevenson, *Eucharist and Offering* (with foreword by Mark Santer) (New York: Pueblo, 1986), for a comparable approach towards a wider view of sacrifice in relation to the eucharist.

21 See Westminster Abbey Library, Th MS 2/1/4, pp. 1, 26, 37; and the sermon, Th MS 3/085. The catalogue numbering is that of E. C. Miller. The legal image of the eucharist was worked out with almost exhaustive logic twelve years earlier by John Thornborough, Bishop of Worcester, in

The Last Will and Testament of Jesus Christ touching the blessed Sacrament of his body and blood. Signed, Sealed and Delivered, in the presence of many Witnesses, and proved in the prerogative of the Church of Christ, by Reverend Bishops, Learned Doctors, and Ancient Fathers of the same Church (Oxford: Turner, 1630).

22 See Alexander Taylor (ed.), *The Works of Simon Patrick, including his Auto-biography* (IX Volumes) (Oxford: University Press, 1858). Autobiography is to be found in Volume IX, pp. 405ff. See also frequent references to Patrick in Spurr, op. cit.

23 *Works* (Volume I), p. xlix.

24 Spurr, op.cit., p. 373.

25 *Works* (Volume VI), p. 476. See also Paul Avis, *Anglicanism and the Christian Church*, pp. 88, 273, 280.

26 *Works* (Volume I), pp. 1–64.

27 *Works* (Volume I), pp. 67–318.

28 ibid., p. lx. See also Kenneth Stevenson, 'The eucharistic theology of Simon Patrick', in Carsten Bach-Nielsen, Susanne Gregersen, Ninna Jørgensen (eds.), *Ordet, Kirken og Kulturen: Afhandlinger om Kristendomshistorie tilegnet Jakob Balling* (Aarhus: Universitetsforlag, 1993), pp. 363–78. I have in my possession a copy of the 1684 edition of the *Mensa Mystica*.

29 *Works* (Volume I), pp. 319–588.

30 ibid., pp. 589–624. There is even a prayer at the end for use after Confirmation.

31 *Works* (Volume II), pp. 1–92.

32 *Works* (Volume I), pp. 317f. On the movement to introduce more frequent eucharists, see Spurr, op. cit., pp. 361–6.

33 See *The Works of Thomas Wilson, Lord Bishop of Sodor and Man* (Volume IV) (Library of Anglo-Catholic Theology) (Oxford: Parker, 1851), pp. 331–423.

34 I am grateful to the Revd Brian Hayes, vicar of Gazeley with Dalham and Moulton with Kentford, for supplying me with details of Patrick's communion plate.

35 *Works* (Volume I), p. 71.

36 ibid., pp. 77, 85.

37 See Chapter 1. n. 9.

38 See Kenneth Stevenson, 'The *Mensa Mystica* Prayers of Simon Patrick (1626–1707): A Case-Study in Restoration Eucharistic Piety', forthcoming in the Aidan Kavanagh *Festschrift*.

39 *The Works of Simon Patrick* (Volume I), pp. 94, 99ff.

40 On 'pleading', see Spinks article, in chapter 5 n. 20. On the 'unbloody sacrifice', see Stevenson article, in chapter 6 n. 16. Hooker uses the word 'plead' of God's omnipotency in relation to the consecration of the elements, *Laws* Book V 67.10 (see chapter 2 n. 34). 'Pleading' of the sacrifice of Christ reappears in theologians – and some liturgies – in the

period since. One of its more classical manifestations is in *Anglican Orders (English): The Bull of His Holiness Pope Leo XIII and the Answer of the Archbishops of England, March 29, 1897* (Church Historical Society) (London: SPCK, 1932), section XI (p. 35): 'we plead and represent before the Father the sacrifice of the cross.' Such language is reminiscent of Patrick and Taylor. It also appears in Charles Gore, *The Body of Christ* (London: Murray, 1901), pp. 165, 193, 198, 201, 288, 301. McAdoo also uses it to describe Taylor's understanding of the eucharistic memorial, see *The Eucharist theology of Jeremy Taylor Today*, pp. 65f.

41 *The Works of Simon Patrick* (Volume I), pp. 114f.

42 For the passage in *Christian Sacrifice*, see *The Works of Simon Patrick* (Volume I), p. 377. On the meaning of 'oblations', see John Dowden, 'What is the Meaning of "Our Alms and Oblations"? An Historical Study', in *Further Studies in the Prayer Book* (London: Methuen, 1908), p. 178.

43 See *The Works of Simon Patrick* (Volume I), pp. 119, 122f and 126. See R(alph) C(udworth), *A Discourse Concerning the True Notion of the Lord's Supper* (London: Cotes, 1642), pp. 56ff (federal rite) and 70ff (feasting upon a sacrifice). Cudworth's parochial record was not a distinguished one, see Spurr, op. cit., p. 178. For Tertullian, see *de pudicitia* ix, where, speaking of the prodigal son, he writes that 'he receives the ring for the first time when on interrogation he sets the seal to the covenant of faith and so thereafter feeds on the richness of the Lord's body, that is, in the eucharist.' For the nineteenth-century edition of his works, see Thomas Birch (ed.), *The Works of Ralph Cudworth in Four Volumes* (Volume IV) (Oxford: University Press, 1829). There are three references to Cudworth elsewhere in the *Mensa Mystica* (pp. 92, 122, 156); on p. 122, Patrick refers to him as 'an excellent doctor of our own.'

44 See *The Works of Simon Patrick* (Volume I), pp. 151f, 158, 160, 167. The reference to Hooker is *Laws* V 67.6.

45 ibid., pp. 186, 209, 213.

46 ibid., p. 261 (cf. p. 113).

47 ibid., p. 220.

48 See Stevenson, article cited above, n. 37 for a discussion of this issue.

49 See *The Works of Simon Patrick* (Volume I), p. 224.

CHAPTER EIGHT

Drawing the Threads Together

Look in what sense the Son of Man
To be in Heaven whilst yet on earth He stayed
In the same sense we grant His Body, though
In Heaven, may still be said to be below.
He is ascended all agree, that same
Material Flesh and Blood of His that came
From the pure Virgin's womb, Heavens now retain,
And until all things be restored again,
Must still retain it; yet it is confesst
That when the holy Elements are blest
By the Priest's powerful lips, though nothing there
To outward sense but bread and wine appear,
Yet doth there under those dark forms reside
The Body of the Son of Man that died.
This, what bold tongue soever doth deny
Gives in effect even Christ Himself the lie.
Yet this whoe'er too grossly doth maintain
Pulls His ascended Lord from Heaven again.
A middle course 'twixt these two rocks to steer,
Is that becomes the Christian Mariner.
So to believe the Ascension as to grant
His real Presence in the Sacrament;
Yet so His Real Presence there to own
As not to make void His Ascension.[1]

After a colourful but not entirely successful career in North America and elsewhere, Nathaniel Eaton (?1609–74) wrote this poem as rector of Bishops Castle, Shropshire in 1661 as part of a series of devotions for the Christian year. Although this particular example was written specifically for Ascension Day, it expresses in general terms that kind of doctrinal and devotional synthesis that we have seen reappearing throughout our study. The way to Christ's presence – and sacrifice, for that matter – is through his cross *and ascension*.[2] And the quality of that synthesis emerges no longer as a kind of over-reaction to transubstantiation, but as a mature and rich way of expressing what the eucharist is about which can justly claim to be more than a seventeenth-century British phenomenon in isolation from the rest of Christianity. It rightly belongs with the whole Catholic Church across the centuries. This is the central theme of our study, but before we discuss it further, it is worth making some wider observations, first about that century, and then about some of the writers we have not included.

From Queen Elizabeth I to Queen Anne

The eucharist never happens apart from what is going on around it. In the ten characters, we have seen how what later came to be called Anglicanism grew out of various dreams and tensions. From the start, Henry VIII saw his Church as a national body, a vision which persisted through all the monarchs who succeeded him down to Charles II. The dreams were shared by more than those monarchs, but there were just too many of them, and too many resultant tensions, for this single, united Church ever to be a reality. At the political level, there are some significant 'might-have-beens'. Had Mary Tudor not been an ardent Roman Catholic, those able men who returned from exile at the start of her younger sister's reign might not have been so fervent in their Calvinism. Had James I of England realised more fully the need to treat the land where he was still James VI as requiring a different kind of Church, another kind of synthesis could have emerged in Scotland between Genevan Calvinism and the other strands of Protestantism in these islands. By tying bishops to the monarchy, both James and Charles I did not do either themselves or the Church a favour. They are frequently blamed for inventing the 'divine right of kings', but Elizabeth I behaved as if she all but did as well. There is a story recounted of Lancelot Andrewes in company with other senior bishops discussing young Prince Charles's attitude and giving a warning that the man would end up losing his head, his kingdom, and probably also the Church.[3]

There are other possibilities, too. Had the Civil War not broken out, had Charles understood the need to take Parliament seriously, England might have seen a more moderated Puritanism happy to coexist within the established Church. Moreover, had the Commonwealth not happened, there could have been a more accommodating atmosphere towards tender consciences in 1662; instead, the 'Cavalier' Parliament was intent upon settling the Church issue once and for all. It was Parliament, rather than the 'Savoy' Conference, or the meetings of Convocation, that took the final initiative and authority here. The Restoration Settlement, with its Prayer Book, was no conspiracy of clerics. It was the responsibility of the laity in Parliament in the end. Cosin's dream of a Prayer Book more like the Scottish 1637 liturgy was as far from reality under such circumstances as was Baxter's 1661 'Savoy' service-book. Yet the 1637 book embodied much of what many of our divines believed and expressed.[4] In Baxter, too, we see much of the *liturgical* protest against the Prayer Book, though hardly a theological reaction to it when it comes to the eucharist itself.

In both Cosin and Baxter there is a sense of the corporate failure of that dream of the single Church. For in the years to come, it was the two extremes that found themselves having to leave. Nonconformists went in the years after the Restoration and the group of 'Non-Jurors' after 1689 because they could not accept King William and Queen Mary replacing what they thought were dubious measures by Parliament after James II's flight. When Archbishop Sancroft would not crown them, it was a signal that once again the Church was living with tensions – in this case their dream of a Church united to the historic monarchy. In his recent book, John Spurr has drawn out the way in which the Church of England moved from being a 'national' Church in 1662 to being only an 'established' one in 1689, when Nonconformists were at last given the right officially to exist.[5] And that brings in another possibility: had James II (regardless of his Catholicism) learnt from his father's mistakes and seen the importance of working with Parliament, that further schism might not have taken place.

Here, liturgy can assist in the purpose of comparison. Baxter's liturgy was so at odds with the Prayer Book that it was virtually impossible to placate his and some of his colleagues' demands at the 'Savoy' Conference. The Puritans had, after all, developed their own culture surrounding the Lord's Supper, with examination of communicants, followed by the service itself, gathered round a table specially set up for the occasion, and the bread and wine served to the people by their deacons, as they sat to receive the sacramental food. This was all a far cry from a eucharist celebrated after Morning Prayer, with a public exhortation and confession, in which (in nearly all but the most flagrant cases of notorious sin) people decided for themselves whether or not they would communicate. The eucharist itself would follow with intending communicants probably moving into the chancel for this purpose in order to kneel at the altar rails while the priest, in most cases standing at the 'north end' of the table, would recite the words in the book, and not extemporise, or write prayers specially for the occasion. On the other hand, the 'Non-Jurors' – even though they went on to produce their own liturgies[6] – included the kind of leadership at the time of their inception in 1689 that looked wistfully back to the 1637 Prayer Book. But unlike the Puritans in 1662, the Non-Jurors began their life content with the Restoration liturgy.

The question of accommodating Nonconformists, however, reared its head again in 1689, and we have noted how Simon Patrick was involved in that liturgical project – yet another abortive service-book. There were some significant alterations to the eucharist, but they are small ones; for example, 'Amen' is to be said by each communicant after the initial sentence at the distribution ('The Body of our Lord Jesus Christ . . . everlasting life'), and before the second ('Take this . . . thanksgiving').[7] Such a proposal probably reflects the way of popular usage already established. We have already seen how Lancelot Andrewes and Jeremy Taylor wanted communicants to say the 'Amen', and they were not alone in this enthusiasm. However, taking both the eucharistic and the other proposals in the 1689 book together, it is doubtful if these could really have been acceptable to all but a few Nonconformists. It was a brave attempt, but an unsuccessful one, to keep alive the vision of the national Church at precisely the moment when it was about to meet its inevitable fate, namely of becoming an established one. The tracks of history were leading in that direction in any case.

The dream had died because of the tensions that got in the way, and our study of certain characters ended in the reign of Queen Anne with an episcopate that included Patrick himself, and the Churches moving separately into a century that would react against religious conflicts played out on the national stage. The only exception here was the other 'Non-Juring' group, the successors to those bishops, clergy and faithful in Scotland who refused to recognise William and Mary, and who split off in order to form a continuing branch of Anglicanism north of the border. Allying themselves to the Jacobite rebellions of the Hanoverian age in 1715 and 1745, their future was fraught with persecution and difficulty. But out of that suffering and persistence emerged the landmark of eighteenth-century Anglican worship, the Scottish liturgy of 1764.[8] It was Scottish influence on the First American Book of Common Prayer of 1789 that ensured that this tradition was exported – at a time when liturgical revision in England was debated here and there but was a practical impossibility.[9] It is in this wider context that the struggles about the eucharist from Elizabeth to Anne – and from before and after – must in the end be seen.

Other Contemporaries?
But our ten characters did not work in isolation, for the seventeenth century bulged with theologians of various different hues. It would be impossible even to summarise them all. We here make mention of only five.

Richard Field (1561–1616) had a working life which like Andrewes' spanned the reigns of both Elizabeth and James. He served as lecturer of Lincoln's Inn in 1594; and rector of Burghclere and prebendary of Windsor in 1604. He was Dean of Gloucester in 1610 until his death. He was a friend of Hooker, and at Gloucester was succeeded by Laud, who created the storm when he had the altar fixed to the east end and railed off – an indication that Field tolerated wider eucharistic practices. He wrote a four-volume treatise *Of The Church* as a defence of the position of the Church of England. When he discusses the eucharist, he opts for bold language but a careful synthesis. Christ is 'mystically communicated' and the offering is twofold, first of the actual bread and wine, and secondly in the way in which the one sacrifice of Christ is set 'before His [i.e. God's] eyes'. And he speaks of the outward and the inward; outward in bread and wine, inward in the 'faith and devotion of the Church and people so commemorating the death and passion of Christ.'[10] In the general approach, the influence of Hooker can be detected. It is as if Hooker himself were at last handling sacrifice.

George Herbert (1593–1633) was rector of Leighton Bromswold from 1626 to 1630, where he installed twin ambos at the entrance to the chancel to serve as reading-desk and pulpit. He became rector of Bemerton, Salisbury, in 1630, at Laud's instigation. He did not write treatises, but became much more memorable through his poetry. In the poem called 'Holy Communion' he reflects some of the same insights, using different metres to reflect, first, the work of Christ in itself, and, secondly, the consequences in the faithful receiver of that work. Here are two sample stanzas from each of the pairs of four:

> Not in rich furniture, or fine array,
>> Nor in a wedge of gold,
>> Thou, who from me wast sold,
> To me dost now Thyself convey;
> For so Thou should'st without me still have been,
>> Leaving within me sinne:
>
> But by the way of nourishment and strength,
>> Thou creep'st into my breast:
>> Making Thy ways my rest,
> And Thy small quantities my length;
> Which spread their forces into every part,
>> Meeting sinnes force and art.

And then after two further stanzas:

> Give me my captive soul, or take
>> My body also hither,
> Another lift like this will make
>> Them both to be together.
>
> Before that sinne turn'd flesh to stone,
>> And all our lump to leaven;
> A fervent sigh might well have blown
>> Our innocent earth to heaven.[11]

John Bramhall (1594–1663), a friend of Laud, started off in England, but moved to Ireland in 1633 as Archdeacon of Meath. He became Bishop of Derry in the following year, and was Archbishop of Armagh at the Restoration. Of all the theologians of the seventeenth century he is one of the most obviously influenced by Thomas Aquinas, which comes across in what he has to say about the eucharist. He refers to transubstantiation, but has a very strong view of the real presence, and the kind of view on sacrifice suggested by Forbes. As far as the former is concerned, he took care to attack adoration of the consecrated bread and wine and witholding the cup from the laity. As to the latter, he believed the eucharist to be sacrificial in four senses: a memorial of the sacrifice of Christ, a representation of it before God now, an 'impetrative' in the sense of praying through it for the world, and 'applicative' as praying for the benefits in our own lives. This places him between Field and the comparable scheme worked out by Thorndike. He wrote many works, frequently concerned with the Church of Ireland and the Roman Catholic Church.[12]

Thomas Ken (1637–1711) was a parish priest for a number of years and was chaplain to Bishop Morley of Winchester. He was made Bishop of Bath and Wells in 1684 but was deprived in 1691 because he refused to take the oath of allegiance to William of Orange. He is regarded as a 'Non-Juror' but he was opposed to a continued succession of non-juring bishops and would not take part in their consecrations. Queen Anne tried to induce him back to Bath and Wells but he refused. His *Manual of Prayers for the Use of Winchester Scholars* (1674) has a prayerfulness about it, demonstrating the same qualities which made him refuse to receive Nell Gwyn at Winchester and caused him to reprimand William at The Hague for his treatment of Princess Mary while he served for a short time as her chaplain there. One of these short prayers, which repeats the reality and the mystery of Christ's presence is: 'I believe Thy body and blood to be as really present in the Holy Sacrament, as Thy divine power can make it, though the manner of Thy mysterious presence I cannot comprehend.'[13]

George Bull (1634–1710) left Oxford prematurely because he refused to be loyal to Parliament and was ordained, like Patrick, by one of the deprived bishops, in 1655, thanks to his reading of Thorndike. He took Prayer Book services, reciting them by heart, and at the Restoration became a parish priest in Gloucestershire. In 1705 he was made Bishop of St David's, the same see Laud held for a short time many years earlier. In style and approach he closely resembles Patrick, stressing the commemorative character of the sacrifice and the personal quality of the eucharistic presence, but there is less of the Cambridge Platonist mystery. He cites the early Fathers and attacks the Roman Mass, both typical propensities of his time. He was concerned about the tendency to undermine the basic doctrines of the Trinity and the Incarnation that were to leave an imprint on parts of the Church in the eighteenth century.[14]

Each in his own way, these five senior churchmen left his mark. They show a wider degree of participation in the co-operative venture of making theology at the time. They also set the scene for a closer look at the main issues raised by this study.

What Are The Main Issues?

We have seen how our ten characters wrestled with many areas of eucharistic faith and practice as these presented themselves in their time. Not all of them followed the same path. They responded in different ways and they had different backgrounds. But at the front of the picture there are particular areas which they could not avoid.

The first two are eucharistic presence and sacrifice. Far from being tediously detailed, they have emerged as fruitful areas of exploration. Obviously the Reformation sets the agenda: the Roman Catholic understandings of transubstantiation and offering the mass have to be dealt with. But it cannot be emphasised too strongly that it was not just Roman Catholic *theologians* who made these questions central, it was the Roman Catholic *piety* that needed to be altered.[15] This is one of the reasons why the scene is so different today, when it could be said with some credibility that Roman Catholics and many Protestants worship in ways that have more in common with *each other* than they have with their respective predecessors in the sixteenth and seventeenth centuries. Piety is about culture and culture is about liturgy, which is why – for better or worse – it is the constant repetition of the Prayer Book in its evolving forms throughout our period which provides an essential background to the formation of the theology that we have been looking at. We shall return to this question, but it is necessary before that to make some observations on the methods and influences that can be discerned in the way they worked.

In each one of them, there is a discernible grasp of the need to express that presence in terms which are *personal*, *strong* and *objective*, and to avoid driving a wedge between presence and sacrifice as if they were two problems that somehow have to be solved. Each writer, too, communicates the conviction that the personal nature and strength of power in the sacraments in no way diminish – but rather enhance – their objective character, which is one of the reasons why 'receptionism' is wide of the mark as a description of what the eucharist means to them. For Hooker, this comes in the language of participation. For Andrewes, to a certain extent followed by Laud and Cosin, it is expressed in images of force and virtue. This tendency, which repeats itself particularly in Taylor, leads McAdoo into his eloquent affirmation that Taylor 'skims the cream off virtualism'[16] – a verdict which I would share with nearly all our characters. 'Virtualism' as a term is often used of writers influenced by Calvinism, and is meant to describe a tendency to see the presence of Christ in his virtue and power in the elements, while the elements themselves remain bread and wine. In one sense, Calvin's influence is a lasting one, because some of the questions he raises and the way he answers them can be seen behind the writings of many of our characters. But when Andrewes refuses to follow Calvin where he is not in line with the early tradition of the Church he is saying as much as Forbes when, early on in the first chapter on the eucharist in the *Considerationes Modestae*, he states that while admiring Calvin he finds him 'uncertain, and doubtful, and slippery'.[17] Among all our writers, except Baxter, it is not the eucharistic theology of Calvin that is the problem.[18] It is Calvin's view of predestination, church order, and the forms of worship associated with Calvinism itself that stand in the way of any ultimate understanding or even *rapprochement* between Puritans and the Prayer Book tradition.

In order to express this personal, strong and objective presence, a number of roads are taken. The two which appear to the present writer to be the most significant are first, their use of imagery, and second their Trinitarian theology. As to the former, the pathway is rich indeed. Hooker's tight and controlled development of 'participation' covers everything, placing Christ at the centre, 'assisting this heavenly banquet' and with us doing so 'by habitual and real infusion'. Andrewes takes his own road, with 'conduit-pipes' and 'arteries', as well as his refreshing adaptation of biblical images, such as covenant. Brevint, in the confines of a much smaller work, has similar imagery when he uses expressions like 'the true effluxes of that Sacrifice', and 'the effusion of his own blood'. For an age still enjoying the restoration of the cup to the laity as a relatively new practice, such language has a special focus of its own.

Taylor, perhaps the most eloquent of our writers when it comes to mystery, says that 'the sacraments do something in the hand of God', within a context that repeats both the reality of the action and what we might not too anachronistically call the 'cloud of unknowing' that is part of human experience before the things of God. (One of Taylor's repeated warnings concerns new Christians who begin with the excitement of a fresh faith but have to adjust to the ordinariness of day-to-day living.) Thorndike remains more within the orbit of biblical and traditional concepts, like covenant (a theme which he makes his own in a special way) and that almost idiosyncratic term 'common sense'. Baxter and Patrick, in different ways, have a more homely style, but it certainly lacks little in power. Baxter's vision is a more practical one, with families (the only one of our characters to model the euchar-istic assembly in those terms) gathering to participate in the Supper. Patrick, on the other hand, with his elaborate scheme for the meaning of the eucharist, speaks with depth about the union between Christ and the Christian in the eucharistic bread and wine.

When it comes to Trinitarian theology, moreover, we are presented with a similarly varied scene. Hooker cannot start speaking about the eucharist until he has offered the reader a vision of the Trinity that is both totally involved in itself and utterly involved with humanity; and a Christ who is in heaven but also on earth at the Supper. Andrewes uses the church year to dwell on the mysteries of the Trinity, calling the faithful to the crib and the cross, and to be filled with the divine power of the Spirit in the bread and wine. Laud, Cosin and Forbes are less eloquent here, because the specific purposes of their works are directed towards other goals – yet the Trinity and the work of Christ are in the background. Brevint, following the lead given by his High Calvinist mentors at Saumur, approaches the eucharist through the eternal high point of the ascended Christ, bearing the marks of suffering and glory, through whom alone we can dare to gather for sacramental feeding. In Brevint, too, one can discern one of that rare breed of theologians, who take a single theme, as Hooker does with participation, and on it build an elaborate edifice that beckons more than a casual look. For in his Christ-centred vision, with its images of abundance and never-ending power, there is no doubt about the fact that the eucharist is *real*. Unlike Hooker, who places the Spirit both in the background and the foreground, both in heaven and in the Supper with the communicant, Brevint lacks a full perspective on the work of the Holy Spirit, even though, like Patrick, he gives him a strong place in the prayers he specially writes to accompany his explorations.[19]

Taylor and Thorndike, however, make the Spirit central to the life of faith and the working of the sacrament. Taylor concentrates on the human being as the dwelling of God (as do Hooker and Andrewes)[20] in the scene near the start of *Holy Living* where he says that 'the temple itself is the heart of man . . . and the Holy Ghost by his dwelling there, hath also consecrated it into a temple', and from that starting-point constructs a theology in which both Christ and the Spirit have inseparable and intertwined saving activity in human beings, who are 'cabinets of the mysterious Trinity'. There is always an equal stress, for one of the consequences of overplaying the Spirit is to immobilise Christ; on the other hand, to make Christ everything to the exclusion of all else is to reduce the eucharist to gazing on a far-off scene and little else. Thorndike makes the founding and organic building of the Church in *Covenant of Grace* so fundamental that when he speaks of consecration, it is by the prayer of the Church and the power of the Spirit that any 'consecration' of gifts and people is able to take place. One result of this overall Trinitarian focus is to make inevitable the gradual drift towards wanting to introduce the invocation of the Spirit in some way into the eucharistic prayer – something Andrewes makes plain in his eucharistic devotions.

Over the specific question of sacrifice, one sees a gradual shift from Hooker's reluctance to develop the theme to more creative, innovative ideas. (As we saw, the sum-total of the picture offered by Hooker's 'participation' makes sacrifice as an extra ingredient superfluous to his requirements.) It is too easy to dismiss this development as no more than a desire to bring something back because the early Fathers saw no difficulty in viewing the sacrifice in those terms. Not one of our characters will use the past in order to turn the life of faith into something equivalent to a theological 'keeping up with the Joneses' – the Joneses in this particular instance residing in Rome. The reason for this move is at root because of their outworking of the experience of the Supper, their reflection on the work of Christ, and the passing of

time as the Reformation disputes move on. To not one of them does
the action or symbolism of offering the gifts of bread and wine become
problematic. But the real issues lie elsewhere and concern the inner
action of the eucharist in relation to Christ himself. Just as du Plessis-
Mornay and his French school of theologians were able to develop the
Calvinist tradition towards a more constructive attitude in this regard,[21]
so all our characters in their different ways see the eucharist as a
sacrifice in three stages; first through Christ the High Priest, then in
terms of the memorial itself (Cudworth's 'feast upon a sacrifice', taken
up by Patrick), and then as the union of the Church with Christ
in self-offering. Sacrifice, moreover, becomes a central theme at the
Restoration, and it is taken up by artists, as with the pelican-figures in
new altar-pieces, not only at St James's Piccadilly, but around the same
time at All Hallows, Lombard Street.

Apart from Brevint's focus on the intercession of Christ, by far the
most creative development is to be found in the writings of Thorndike
and Patrick. Their lasting contribution is to take the theme of covenant and spread it right across the eucharist as butter over an open
sandwich. In one sense, the ground had been laid. One only has to
consider Hooker's notion of union, and then move through Andrewes,
Laud and Cosin, with their accent on the presence *among* God's people.
The idea takes further root through their basic Protestant desire to
explore a biblical image which was in danger of being taken over by
extreme Puritans. Instead of employing it in exclusive terms, they used
it in order to illustrate the more open meaning of the Prayer Book rite.
And that rite ends with one of the finest compositions of Cranmer's, the
'prayer of oblation', in which the Church offers herself as a 'living
sacrifice' to the eternal God. A 'living sacrifice' (Romans 12:1) is at
face value a contradiction in terms, because when looked at literally,
animal-sacrifices can only be dead. Perhaps it was this very paradoxical
notion – of the Church offering herself as something dead yet alive,
touched by 'the hand of God' (to use a phrase from Taylor) – that
encouraged further reflection. Perhaps the very neglect of this biblical
theme in the theologians of the Middle Ages caused this shift. It
is certainly one that merits greater attention today, like Hooker's
'participation', of which it is in some ways an offshoot.

For what the covenant-theology does in Thorndike and Patrick is
to take hold of the eucharist and see it in terms of what we would
nowadays call 'solidarity' – which perhaps needs to be expanded to

become 'solidarity in Christ'. Thorndike sees that covenant-community as the scene of human history, in which human freedom is celebrated both in its tragedies and its triumphs. Not for nothing does he begin the *Laws of the Church* with the eucharist, having dealt with the Christian religion in the first volume of the *Epilogue* and the nature of the Church in the second. Patrick's is perhaps the more carefully worked out view, in his discussion of that covenant-renewal in terms of deeper union with God, with Christ, and with one another. When Taylor, Thorndike, and Patrick exhort the faithful to more *frequent* communion, they often do so in the firm belief that, were the Church to celebrate the eucharist more often, the world would indeed become a better place. In this connection, one has to see their understanding of the meaning of the eucharist as all of a piece with their understanding of daily living. Taylor and Patrick, after all, repeatedly stress the need for self-examination, not in a morbidly introspective manner, but as a way towards making the eucharist (to use the language of Hooker) an 'instrument of God' – a force to be reckoned with, a celebration of the values of God not written in a book but lived out in the eternal Christ as he is met with in the life of people now.

The use of the term covenant, too, would at that time gain a corporate significance through the political overtones which covenant had earned after the Scottish Presbyterian 'Covenant' inaugurated in 1638 as a national protest against the King. In terms of apologetic, it was important for the coming generation of our characters to make use of that term and give it new meanings that would reflect their wider vision of the Church. Here, one is reminded of what twentieth-century Christians have learned to call 'the cost of discipleship'. There is something very contemporary in the way our writers explored the outworking of 'living sacrifice' – as witness some of the recent writing about the eucharist from Roman Catholic scholars. It may well have been Thorndike's treatment of that self-offering which inspired Charles Gore to bring down the curtain on liturgy and let it spill over into joyful service when he remarked that 'in the self-oblation of the Church is the culmination of the sacrifice.'[22] For sacrifice, as we have seen in several of our writers, particularly Taylor and Thorndike, is inextricably linked with intercession, where there is a heightened dimension of cost when the Church pleads the world's needs, both in specific (and sometimes all too familiar) terms, as well as in general (and perhaps more easily forgotten) contexts. All our characters write in a style that is steeped in prayer – a prayer frequently intercessory in its tone and application. In the suppliant dynamic of the eucharist, the life of the Trinity usually (but not always) figures prominently, and one can see this in both presence and sacrifice, united together. For presence is ultimately the gift of the Father, through the Son, in the Spirit, whereas the offering of the Church is made, in complementary fashion, in the power of the Spirit, through the Son's eternal sacrifice, to the Father in heaven. It is a dynamic of initiative and response – but that response is always part of the initiative of God's grace, dwelling in us eternally.

We have spoken of the Trinity and the Spirit, and the intercession of Christ. But what of the broad picture of Christ that is to be seen in our characters? Hooker taught 'two righteousnesses' – that we are justified by 'imputation' (the work of the cross) and also by 'infusion' (the capacity for good in Christ alone). This was another necessary corrective to the view of humanity as 'totally depraved' which was a popular view among extreme Calvinists at the time. Such language, too, is used by Brevint. We have seen, too, how those 'two righteousnesses' persist in some of the other characters, for example in Forbes and Thorndike. For Thorndike 'justifying faith' provides the key for his approach to offering the eucharist, that it is something the Christian can – indeed must – *do*. Taylor, on the other hand, is perhaps ahead of his time in his rejection of the traditional view of original sin and this has an effect on his own doctrinal and pastoral scheme. It does not prevent him from soul-searching, nor from his placing emphasis on the need for forgiveness. But it results in a different view from the others, though perhaps Patrick shared some of Taylor's instincts here. These differences apart, what we have before us is a definite move from the medieval and the Calvinist view of the work of Christ, to a more symbolic, pictorial and dramatic picture. Nearly all of them, with the exception of Baxter, have so absorbed the writings of the early Fathers that they are able to use those very contemporary images that we have drawn attention to as the means whereby their hearers and readers can see themselves being reconciled to God by absorption rather more than by acquittal.[23]

Patrick can indeed be colourful in the scene he evokes in the worshipper's inner eye of the suffering of Christ, but it is always done with the sense that this is the life of God dynamically displayed before humanity – God reaching out in judgement, yes, but in a covenant which can always be renewed – because there is always another chance. It would be easy to see this approach in superficially optimistic terms, in much the way that one 'drops in' for a eucharist nowadays. But that would be to misunderstand what, for example, Taylor, Thorndike, and Patrick are trying to articulate. With their strong, human-centred view of the Trinity – (Andrewes' 'The Son in the water, the Holy Ghost in the dove, the Father in the voice') – there comes a strong, human-centred view of the significance of the cross, in which the drama of redemption is played out, and conflicts are resolved. It may be no coincidence that the generation which lived through the Civil War had a similar experience to those many areas of Christianity in our own time where there has been acute suffering and persecution. They emerged with a deepened faith in the living Lord who is able to transform suffering and conflict – even, or especially, when that suffering and conflict has had a strongly religious motivation. A young Estonian Lutheran pastor said to me of the attitude of Christians after his country's freedom from Soviet domination, 'You cannot build something new and beautiful if there is bitterness in your heart.'

There is another aspect of the eucharist that comes across in our characters, and that relates to the communion of saints and the vision of heaven. Neither is particularly prominent in the 1552 and 1559 Prayer Books, though All Saints' Day continues to be part of the Kalendar. But these themes return in 1637 and (less expressively) in 1662. For such a (partial) restoration, we can only turn to Hooker, with his 'stars of heaven'; Andrewes' sense of contemporaneity with the Fathers; Forbes' and Thorndike's enthusiasm for the living and departed being united by prayer; Cosin's similar conviction, backed up by his love of painted angels in church buildings; Taylor's obvious love of the vision of God, now revealed, now covered in a cloud; Baxter's powerful faith in the saint's everlasting rest; and Patrick's evocation of Christ calling 'Come, ye blessed of my Father' at the end of time.[24] They are striving for another balance, determined by mystery, between prayer 'doing' something for the departed (as in Roman Catholic piety) and a psychological uplift of some sort that is not founded in any understanding of the Church that goes beyond the here and now. For in the eucharist, there is a true feasting with Christ, in company with the saints, looking forward to the end of all things, in a unity renewed at that table.

So far, we have noted various different types of motivation for these developments, only some of which we have drawn out; and they include using the Bible, being faithful to tradition, and grasping opportunities offered by the onward march of history. In theological terms, these are obviously scripture, tradition, and reason. But one rider needs to be added, concerning the use of reason. All our characters either mention it or assume its importance, starting with Hooker and ending with Patrick. There is a critical discernment going on all the time as the current scene and the distant past are repeatedly scrutinised from different perspectives. And in this venture they are by no means infallible – Hooker is quite capable of using the Fathers to suit his own ends, and the same is true of some of the more obscure footnotes in Thorndike. (Taylor is sparing in this respect, because enforced seclusion at the Golden Grove limited the amount of tomes which he could consult.) Yet the very use of the word 'reason' seems to have varied as time went on.

Hooker sees reason as a God-given critical faculty, and it always retains that quality in our other characters. But by the time we come to Taylor and Patrick, and to a lesser extent Thorndike, 'reason' has the added dimension of revelation, partly mediated through experience. Reason becomes the means whereby the divine and the human worlds are united, through which sense can imaginatively be made of them. But both these uses must be distinguished from the 'age of reason' of the following century. When Taylor writes in *Holy Living* that 'the reason of man is a right judge always when she is truly informed; but in many things she knows nothing but the face of the article,' it is indeed a far cry from what was to come. As Henry McAdoo has observed, 'part of the failure of the succeeding period was its inability to keep natural theology in its place, as the Cambridge Platonists and the naturalists and the scientists had done.'[25]

That third generation which took over during and after the Restoration were doing so at a time when new kinds of knowledge were developing, when there was a need for religion and science to talk to each other. John Evelyn made Taylor his 'ghostly father' – an appropriate choice for a man who was to become Secretary to the Royal Society in 1672. Such a generation, as we have noted in Evelyn's own diary, perhaps found sermons in the Andrewes' style insufficiently practical. Somehow, the balance was found – of maintaining an orthodox Christian faith and applying it to everyday living, of looking at the Christian faith in the light of reason, but of using that reason in the full knowledge that there are *limits* to what human beings can understand about everything – whether that is the visible world of the created universe or the eucharistic bread and wine. An age that courts the practical and the immediately applicable above all else will soon get bored of sacramental worship. That was a danger in Taylor's time – hence his (and others') frequent calls to celebrate the eucharist more often, but to do so with greater devotion.

What then?

There is an inevitable gap between our own age and theirs. This is partly made up of the legacy they gave to the next century. *Isaac Watts* (1674–1748) after a time as an Independent pastor resigned due to ill health. In 1707 his *Hymns and Spiritual Songs* (in three books) appeared. In the third book, there is a section of twenty-five four-line hymns for the Lord's Supper. One of them is so well known that it has been forgotten by many that it was originally written not for Good Friday but for the eucharist. In 'When I survey the wondrous cross'[26] we have a picture of the crucifixion and the place of the worshipper, who respond, in the last verse to this unspeakable gift; 'Were the whole realm of nature mine, that were a present far too small'. The hymn demonstrates how near Nonconformity could come to the theological structure of the Prayer Book, especially in that final stanza, for it is at the end of the Prayer Book rite of communion that the worshipper makes the self-offering in response to the gifts of Christ.

John Johnson (1662–1725) who was vicar of Cranbrook, Kent, from 1707 to his death, wrote a two-volume work on the eucharist with a lengthy title whose first three words are *The Unbloody Sacrifice*, in which he argued strongly for a sacrificial view of the eucharist, developing many of the lines of thought from the seventeenth century.[27] He was read by the 'Non-Jurors' and by John Wesley, so that his influence was a wide one. Then in *Thomas Wilson* (1663–1755) we come across the legendary Bishop of Sodor and Man, an office he held from 1698 until his death – fifty-seven years in all. In 1734, he brought out his *Plain and Short Instruction for the Better Understanding of the Lord's Supper with the Necessary Preparation Required for the Benefit of Young Communicants*. Like Patrick's book for young people, it has a strongly pastoral flavour. It had a wide readership and kept being reprinted. The main innovation was to include the full text of the Prayer Book service, a practice that was to be followed in the nineteenth century by others. Wilson's work helped Charles Simeon at his conversion.[28]

The 'age of reason', however, is perhaps best expressed in Benjamin Hoadly's (anonymous) *Plain Account of the Nature and End of the Sacrament of the Lord's-Supper* (1735), which is both plain and an account. It caused a stir when it appeared and it sets out to make the eucharist accessible to people in a way that makes it a bare memorial, with a strong hint of Zwinglian instincts, the 'vain and empty sign' that Calvin deprecated.[29] Hoadly went on to become Bishop of Winchester. There was an inevitable reaction to this rationalism when *John* (1703–91) and *Charles* (1707–88) *Wesley* issued their *Hymns on the Lord's Supper*. As we have already noted, these were inspired by Brevint's *Christian Sacrament and Sacrifice*, and the hymns are grouped according to divisions partly taken from Brevint's work, an abbreviation of which was published with it. This is one of the most remarkable collections of hymns ever written, and they are sung all over the English-speaking world today. Like Brevint's book, they have a strength and a profundity that is unique and they often encapsulate in poetic form many of the best aspects of the theology of the preceding century. They supply one of the enduring elements in the bridge between our age and the seventeenth century because of Daniel Brevint himself. In the Wesleyan tradition, renewal of the covenant becomes a special, annual occasion, but it is always to take place within the eucharist. Here we have one of the shorter of the Wesley eucharistic hymns, a typical example of their art of writing, where succinctness does not mean brevity of scope:

> O thou who, hanging on the cross,
> Didst buy our pardon with Thy blood,
> Canst Thou not still maintain our cause
> And fill us with the life of God,
> Bless with the blessings of Thy throne,
> And perfect all our souls in One?
>
> Lo, on thy bloody sacrifice,
> For all our graces we depend,
> Supported by Thy cross arise,
> To finish'd holiness ascend,

> And gain on earth the mountain's height,
> And then salute our friends in light.[30]

Many familiar themes are present in this hymn: the eternal sacrifice, the intercession, participation in the life of God by the worshippers, and the joys of heaven in the communion of saints. It is a fitting note on which to move to the present.

What Now?

It is always tempting when writing about the past to turn great men into paragons of perfection. One of the reasons for including biographical sketches in this study was to show that they were all human beings. Indeed, in nearly all of them, there is something unfulfilled, even off-beat about them.

Hooker died young, not having completed all the books of his *Laws*. Andrewes did not go to Canterbury to succeed Bancroft – though that may well have been a blessing in disguise. Laud met his end with the executioner – having lived the latter part of his life with gloomy forebodings. Forbes, like Hooker, died prematurely and left his great *opus* unfinished for an old colleague to prepare for publication. Then Cosin comes along, nailing his colours at an increasingly controversial time to the monarchist mast – and suffering exile in consequence. Brevint like Forbes had an adventurous life but suffered exile like Cosin. Taylor and Baxter were on opposite sides in the Civil War, the latter triumphing during the Commonwealth, whereas Taylor seems to have had a sad episcopate. Posterity looks to those long years of writing during the time of persecution as the most fruitful time. In Thorndike we have a prophetic figure who could see a way out of some of the conflicts of his time – but people were not ready corporately to look so far into the past and apply uncomfortable and administratively awkward lessons to the present. Finally, in Patrick we have an example of the kind of gentle but strong personality who keeps surviving. As personalities, they vary greatly. Not all their attitudes are to be commended. That Laud had a pet tortoise perhaps says something about the loneliness of prelacy in those days.

None the less, there are a number of comments that can be put forward when these characters – and others like them – are considered in the light of today's Church.

First, both individually and cumulatively, we have before us an *ecumenical theology.* Every single one of our characters deserves to be looked at not only in the time and country of their immediate context but as people who strove after a vision of a united Church. There are occasions when they try to speak on behalf of a wider constituency than they perhaps should; and one thinks here of Hooker being amiable or of Laud assuming that every Protestant agrees with the Church of England. Perhaps the most obviously 'ecumenical' is Forbes, for the sheer scope of the writers he sifts and quotes. His approach is summed up in the wry remark (perhaps made with an Aberdonian twinkle in the eye) that if there had been more of the ilk of Cassander and Witzel (of whom few may have heard) there would have been no need for Luther or Calvin (two names all too familiar to everyone). They may not have been successful in the short term, but in the long term, by aspiration as well as net result, all of them deserve to be placed in the wider context of the whole of the Church Catholic. We mean no cheap Anglican triumphalism by making such a suggestion. Henry McAdoo has placed the eucharistic theology of Jeremy Taylor under the searchlight and made comments on how his writings anticipate and even go beyond the official ecumenical statements of our own generation.[31] In so much of their method and scope, not least in the way several of them cut through the conceptual red tape in order to make some sense of the tradition by uniting presence and sacrifice, they looked for new and *unitive* paths, whether it was Patrick's notion of 'pleading' the sacrifice of Christ, or Brevint's picture of Christ in heaven and on earth at one and the same time. Others have since attempted the same brave course, for example the classical Luther scholar of this century, Regin Prenter, when he affirms that 'in this meal-offering are real presence and sacrifice one.'[32] Without depriving them of their very seventeenth-century (or in the case of Hooker, their late sixteenth-century) identities, they can speak to many in the ages to come of a vision of co-operation and unity.

Secondly, there is in their method and style a conscious and unconscious desire to look for a *synthesis of continuity and discontinuity*. We have seen it again and again in their varied use of the tradition, with Hooker, for example, using what he thought was a work of Cyprian's but which has since turned out to be by a friend of Bernard of Clairvaux. It is apparent in the subtle fusion of ideas in Andrewes' preaching, turning the manger into a witness to the meagreness of God's abode among human beings, or in Patrick's ability to adapt yet further the covenant-theology of the eucharist in order to recast a biblical idea to make the eucharist live for the people of his day. Every age has to be a mixture of continuity and discontinuity – and ours is no exception. There are certain parts of the scene which do not alter, one of which is *baptism*, the gateway into the Church, inseparably linked to eucharist, where we are washed before we eat (as Taylor describes it), washed lavishly (Forbes' 'laver'), and without 'superfluous scrupulosity, lets and impediments' (as Hooker put it). Another is the divinisation of humanity, the end result of 'participation' – which is no less than sharing in the life of God. Our characters resolutely refuse either to internalise baptism into a defined spiritual experience, or to delay that participation in the divine nature conveniently to the end of time. It is as if they are consciously heeding the fundamental protests of the Reformation (the triumph of God's grace on the cross) and at the same time heeding the beckoning call of early tradition (God's action visible and sacramentally active among people now). The visible witness to this mixture in the century we have been looking at lies in the architecture and communion plate of the time. As Nigel Yates has recently shown, church-building at the time was not the makeshift and thoughtless process that it has sometimes been regarded, and Charles Oman has made similar claims about the church plate that was being made or adapted.[33] Churches kept being built for praise, prayer, word and sacramental use, such as the little building in Minsterley, Shropshire, which dates from 1689, a charming mixture of Renaissance and Baroque decoration; the pulpit and reading desk used to stand by the south door, facing north to the font directly opposite, the pews in the nave looking towards those two focuses of worship. The sanctuary, however, is reached through an elaborately carved gateway, through which, slightly elevated, the altar is clearly visible. In an age like ours that has seen so much liturgical change, it is sobering to contemplate another so like our own in method – you receive what you are given and then take the risk of turning it into something else by a God-given phenomenon called organic growth.

Thirdly, one has to ask if the *labels* of churchmanship or theological jargon fit. We have tried to avoid using many of them in the six central chapters of this study. It was a deliberate move. There have been times when the temptation to go back on this decision has been great. But the result has been – we hope – that ten individuals have been able to emerge without being fastened to fixed points in a league-table of height or depth, nor yet have attached to them pejorative interpretations of the eucharist such as 'receptionism'. For nearly all of them, I suspect, the only label of which they would be proud is that they were all lovers of dynamic tradition. In practice, nine out of those ten are Anglicans, and the one remaining – Baxter – is living proof of the failure of one generation's dream to be worked out in practice a few generations later. If one really wants to classify them in theological terms, I would suggest 'Reformed Patristic', because they were faithful to their evolving Reformation heritage, but this heritage was always offset by a (not uncritical) reverence for the age of the Fathers. No one section of the Church of England – or world-wide Anglicanism for that matter – today 'possesses' any of these characters simply by virtue of a label, and even though they certainly do not have all the answers, it is time for them – and their ilk – to be looked at and listened to afresh. Each one of them – Baxter included – can justly claim to be theologians who are both 'Catholic' and 'Evangelical'; Catholic because they are looking at the whole tradition that is before them, and Evangelical because in their hearts they have the gospel of free grace which they want to celebrate around that Table. At the risk of turning that universal scope into caricature, I muse that each one has a 'High' tendency, that uses tradition, a 'Low' conviction, that wants to make the mysteries of God accessible through style and vivid language, and a 'Middle' instinct which wants to take seriously a changing world.

Fourthly, each one of them, again including Baxter, *relates theology to prayer*. Time and again we have observed the way in which prayers have been used to illustrate theology, and theology expressed in order to lead into prayer. Hooker cannot finish his tightly-knit discussion of the eucharist without being carried away, as if in some kind of ecstasy, into a long conclusion deliberately placed in quotation marks, parts of which are also in italics, and reaching a climax in the exclamation, 'O my God thou art true, O my soul thou art happy.' There is an integrity between Andrewes' sermons and his devotional prayers that demonstrates a unified picture of reality that he can both explore and wonder at. Brevint and Patrick insert prayers to their writings for the use of his readers, and Taylor does the same, at times leaving them delightfully pondering at what stage the dissertation ends and the praying begins. A method in theology that is both highly traditional and profoundly contemporary, it is the most reliable way of ensuring that theology is rooted in the praying life of the Church itself. A close parallel here is with the classical Lutheran tradition, where the book is not one of prayer but of praises, hymns specifically composed to express the song of the Church before the Lord. In the broadest cultural terms, the Prayer Book tradition comes very close to Lutheranism. But there exists another close parallel with the Byzantine liturgy, where we can see the same insistence that has continually surfaced in our study: the interaction of a carefully nurtured liturgical text, in a carefully wrought context of art and movement, within an equally carefully worked out tradition of mystagogy – liturgical interpretation.[34] Such is no simplistic approach to the doing of theology. It does not mean that anything goes. What it does mean is that reflection on the important aspects of the life of the Church – which includes the eucharist – is fed by worship and at the same time addresses the real issues of the day, even when this involves conflict. The rich eucharistic legacy that we have been viewing is in part the result of conflict within the Church, and its authentic character is further enhanced by the degree of social conflict in the wider world from which it emerged. It is also founded on a profound sense of the communion of saints, for the eucharist stands in relation to past worship and teaching, and moves ever onwards in faith – and risk – towards the end of all things.

Fifthly, there is an integrity, too, between the *critical faculties* and the fact that human beings are not able to understand everything. This is most prominent in Taylor's sense of mystery, but it is a feature of nearly all the other writers in question. Taylor uses the Cambridge Platonist emphasis on reason with its transcendental faculties to give it full expression. But that sense of having to stop short of over-scrutinising before the things of God is apparent again and again. And these things of God are the material of creation, hence the centrality of the human body, the liturgical actions and gestures, and the materially insignificant but spiritually transformed elements of water, and bread and wine. In our own day, there is a need to recover precisely that capacity to develop understanding as a way of opening new perspectives, of using the imagination as a way of dreaming, of capturing visions – and at the same time of matching those perspectives, dreams, and visions to the possible, the down-to-earth, the business of ordinary discipleship. But life as we know, and this includes our eucharistic celebration, needs to be judged by those perspectives, dreams and visions. Andrewes churned out brilliant sermons year by year, and when one reads them one never gets the slightest impression that he wants to say it all, because he so manifestly knows that there will always be more to say, more to wonder at. That sense of wonder, too, is not confined to the liturgical actions, for it is bound up with the way liturgy and life meet, hence Taylor's concern with virtues, Patrick's interest in 'deportment afterward', and Thorndike's conviction that more frequent eucharists would make for better Christians – and a better world. In our own age, we have those more frequent eucharists, something each one of our characters would envy. But we have not 'arrived'. Reverence before mystery – the mystery of the eucharist and the mysteries of the consecrated bread and wine – is part of the life of God, the life he wants to share with us.

Sixthly, there is an integrity between *piety and tradition*. In our own age, there have been – and continue to be – heated debates about liturgical revision and change, just as there were in the seventeenth century. When the cover is removed from the debates that went on then, one can see certain parallels with our time, in the ecclesiastical politics, the way in which certain things can be agreed – or not – because one person is around at a particular time to make a protest or a counter-claim. Liturgy has always had something of this element about it. The main difference today is that within that part of the Church Catholic now called Anglican, the kind of world we inhabit has changed in so many ways that there is pressure for the liturgy to adapt. In this field of concern, the Anglican Communion is by no means alone: all the branches of the traditional Western Churches have had to learn to live with it. And here the parallel is not with the 1662 Prayer Book so much as that very flexible 'alternative' liturgy, with its family piety, which Mr Baxter put forward at the 'Savoy' Conference, complete with its scope for the liturgical president to use the set words or not, as the case may be. (If the tale of Anglican liturgy this century has any message to give in this regard, it is that Baxter's solution finally won.) But when such a dislocation as this takes place, it is all the more important for norms to be agreed, and for theology itself, the collective consciousness of the worshipping congregations – including those who would never receive communion – to be allowed to find a proper climate and level. Perhaps as Churches we are collectively bringing to birth a new synthesis of authority and freedom.[35] Addressing this situation, it is doubtful if Hooker or Andrewes would know what to say, and it would be anachronistic to try to make any speculations. They would, however, be conscious of the need for rhythm, familiarity, memory – and prayer. Cosin's *Devotions* stand out as a successful experiment in building up a piety of integrity for the laity, probably because he – like our other characters – knew full well how important it is not to leave the worshipper in the lurch by the mere provision of the public liturgy, and nothing more.

Seventhly, in several of our characters we noted an *innovative use of language*, whether it was in Andrewes' 'arteries', Brevint's 'effluxes', or Taylor's 'hand of God' – all of them images of divine generosity in the grace-conveying Supper of the Lord. Fresh language could also be fashioned from biblical imagery, such as in Thorndike's assertion that 'the celebration of the eucharist is the renewal of the covenant of grace.'[36] I cannot help feeling that such innovations were a deliberate desire to bring new breath into an area of life that is a never-ending source of vitality itself – the Christian eucharist. The effect is not to invite slavish imitation; one remembers in this connection the preachers John Evelyn heard who attempted to preach as Andrewes did, and it just did not work. But what it does inspire is a conviction that imagery and language are an activity of the life of faith in its imaginative enterprise. Andrewes wanted to be an instrument of God in enabling the eucharist to speak its own strange language in fresh ways. He wanted his hearers, in every sense, to 'participate'. In our own day, with the temptation to internalise religion into the private world of the 'Nicodemus Christian', who is on the side of the angels but cannot face public celebrations of that faith, it is all the more important that we honour this art of imaginative communication, but that we do so without turning the end-product into something instant and glib. Taylor may have been long-winded but he was never superficial, especially when describing his fellow-humans as 'cabinets' of God himself. Thorndike may have been obtuse on occasion, but there is an internal coherence to the way he expresses himself that is rare and far-reaching. Part of the Christian vocation, therefore, is to trust the inherited imagery but not to shrink back from the task each one of our characters enjoyed – reinterpretation.[37]

A Postscript

If there be any that look upon eating and drinking of the bread and wine only as symbols of believing in Jesus Christ, the matter

> draws to the same point: for faith is the condition of the covenant of grace, and comprehends in its signification all that God requires.[38]

So wrote Simon Patrick when working out his understanding of the covenant-relationship that lies at the heart of the eucharist, a mystery so deep, and yet so close, so profound, and yet so simple, so challenging, and yet embracing, so aweful, and yet so intimate. And it is faith which is the key, faith as gift of God and human response, faith as implanted and renewed by God, and as offered back to God in return, faith as the context in which the eucharist enters the world as an embodiment of Christ's presence and power.

Mark Frank (1613–64) was a Cambridge don who was a well-known preacher in his time. Deprived during the Commonwealth, at the Restoration he was made Master of Pembroke Hall, Archdeacon of St Albans, and Prebendary and Treasurer of St Paul's Cathedral; right at the end of his life he succeeded Thorndike as rector of Barley, near Cambridge. Our journey has taken us into many parts of that terrain which is sometimes called the 'living word'. The union of that living word so often finds expression in the joining of the earthly and the heavenly, gloriously depicted in the frontispiece of Charles Wheatly's *Rational Illustration of the Book of Common Prayer*, where the reader views a eucharist being celebrated in a classical church, above which, in a cloud, stands Jesus surrounded by angels at the eternal altar. It is therefore supremely appropriate to end this road with the concluding words of a sermon Frank preached at the eucharist one Candlemas, where this theme of offering is explored with a rare beauty, which, like much of what we have thus far seen, ends in heaven:

> This day was his offering day – is to be ours. Offer we then him, offer we ourselves; take we him; take we him up into our arms, into our hands and hearts; having first lighted a candle and swept our houses to receive and entertain him, and having humbly, and cheerfully, and devoutly, and thankfully received him, we bless God.
>
> God be gracious unto us, and purify our hearts and hands, that we may worthily receive him; strengthen our arms, that we may behold him; open our mouths, that we may bless him for him; accept our offering, and Christ's offering for us, – his perfect sacrifice, for our imperfect offerings; that we may receive all

the benefits of this great sacrifice – the remission of our sins, the cleansing of our souls, the refreshing of our bodies – the fulness of all graces, the protection of our souls and bodies in this kingdom of grace, and the saving them in the kingdom of glory; that as we this day bless him here, so we may bless and praise and glorify him hereafter for evermore.[39]

NOTES

1 Quoted from More and Cross (eds.), *Anglicanism*, pp. 466f (No. 202).

2 See in general Cocksworth, *Evangelical Eucharistic Thought in the Church of England*, esp. pp. 175ff.

3 The story (whose truth is disputed) was apparently recounted years later by Matthew Wren. It is quoted, for example, in Lossky, *Lancelot Andrewes the Preacher*, p. 25.

4 See, for example, Buxton, *Eucharist and Institution Narrative*, pp. 145ff.

5 See this thesis worked out in Spurr, *The Restoration Church of England*.

6 For the 'Non-Jurors' liturgies, see Grisbrooke, *Anglican Liturgies of the Seventeenth and Eighteenth Centuries*, pp. 273–96, and 297–316; see also his discussion of their origin and significance, pp. 71–112, 113–135.

7 See Timothy Fawcett, *The Liturgy of Comprehension 1689* (Alcuin Club Collections 54) (Southend-on-Sea: Mayhew McCrimmon, 1973), pp. 100–115.

8 See Grisbrooke, op. cit., pp. 333–48, and his discussion of its origin and significance, pp. 150–59.

9 See Marion Hatchett, *The Making of the First American Book of Common Prayer: 1776–1789* (New York: Seabury, 1982).

10 Darwell Stone, *A History of the Doctrine of the Holy Eucharist* (Volume 2), pp. 303f.

11 *The Works of George Herbert in Prose and Verse edited by Robert Ayris Willmott* (London: Routledge, 1857). pp. 45ff.

12 Quoted from More and Cross (eds.), *Anglicanism*, p. 496. On the formation of Bramhall's theology, see McAdoo, *The Spirit of Anglicanism*, pp. 368ff.

13 See Darwell Stone, op. cit., p. 456.

14 ibid., pp. 443–50.

15 A revisionist view, however, not shared by the writer, is taken by E. Duffy in 'Cranmer and Popular Religion', in Paul Ayris and David Selwyn (eds.), *Thomas Cranmer: Churchman and Theologian* (Bury St Edmunds: Boydell Press, 1993) pp. 199–215.

16 See chapter 6 n. 13.

17 See Forbes, *Considerationes Modestae*, pp. 386–9.

18 For a discussion of this and other issues, see B. A. Gerrish, *Grace and Gratitude: the Eucharistic Theology of John Calvin* (Edinburgh: T and T Clark, 1993), esp. pp. 21ff, and 124ff. See also, in general, Christopher Cocksworth, 'Eucharistic Theology', in Kenneth Stevenson and Bryan Spinks (eds.), *The Identity of Anglican Worship* (London: Mowbrays, 1991), pp. 49–68.

19 See Stevenson, article cited in chapter 7, n. 38.

20 See Allchin, *Participation in God* for a wider treatment of this inspiring subject.

21 See Emery, work cited in chapter 5. n. 23.

22 Charles Gore, *The Body of Christ*, p. 213. For an example of Roman Catholic writing, see David N. Power, *The Eucharistic Mystery: Revitalizing the Tradition* (New York: Crossroad/Dublin: Gill and Macmillan, 1992).

23 See F. W. Dillistone, *The Christian Understanding of Atonement* (2nd edition) (London: SCM, 1984), where many of the images we have so far seen would fit into a mixture of Dillistone's 'eternal sacrifice' or his 'all-embracing compassion', pp. 29ff, 216ff.

24 Compare the excellent work, Geoffrey Wainwright, *Eucharist and Eschatology* (London: Epworth, 1971).

25 Quoted from McAdoo, *The Spirit of Anglicanism*, p. 82.

26 *The Psalms of David imitated in New Testament Language: Together with Hymns and Spiritual Songs by the Rev. Isaac Watts, D.D.* (London: Haddon, 1862), Book III, pp. 163f.

27 See John Johnson, *The Unbloody Sacrifice* (2 Volumes) (Library of Anglo-Catholic Theology) (Oxford: Parker, 1847).

28 See chapter 7 n. 33. There are a few specific items which reflect Wilson's love of the ancient liturgies which his son, Thomas Wilson junior, removed in some editions, including that of 1755; see pp. 381, 393, 403, 406. Wilson junior, who was rector of St Margaret's Westminster, had a hand in editing his father's works and used to take some of them to Isaac Watts in order to seek 'ecumenical' comment. Wilson had a strong view of sacrifice which was closely associated with forgiveness, a theme stressed in his *Short and Plain Instruction*. It blended with his love of ancient liturgies to produce the following prayer among his own eucharistic devotions, appointed to be said privately after the consecration: 'May I atone unto Thee, O God, by offering to Thee the pure and unbloody sacrifice, which Thou hast ordained by Jesus Christ.' This takes us a little further on from the seventeenth century. See *Works* (Volume V), p. 75.

29 See *A Plain Account of the Nature and End of the Sacrament of the Lord's-Supper* (London: Horsfield, 1772). (This is the eighth edition.) Hoadly included forms of prayer to accompany it, in the traditions of the writers of the previous century.

30 See Rattenbury, *The Eucharistic Hymns of John and Charles Wesley* (London: Epworth, 1948), p. 211. On the origins and development of the covenant service under John Wesley and since, see David H. Tripp, *The Renewal of the Covenant in the Methodist Tradition* (London: Epworth, 1969). See also A. Raymond George, 'The Lord's Supper', in Dow Patrick (ed.), *The Doctrine of the Church* (London: Epworth 1964), pp. 140–60.

31 See Henry McAdoo, *The Eucharistic Theology of Jeremy Taylor Today.*

32 (my translation.) See original Danish, Regin Prenter, *Skabelse og Genløsning-Dogmatik* (= 'Creation and Redemption: Dogmatic theology') (København: Gad, 1962) p. 529: 'I dette offermåltid er realpraesens og offer eet'. This theme is also explored in Stevenson, *Eucharist and Offering.*

33 See Nigel Yates, *Buildings, Faith and Worship*, and Charles Oman, *English Church Plate.*

34 See Geoffrey Wainwright, *Doxology: A Systematic Theology* (London: Epworth, 1980); Aidan Kavanagh, *On Liturgical Theology* (New York: Pueblo, 1984), for discussions on the reciprocal relationship between doctrine, worship and ethics. The issue is taken up from a perspective of his own tradition by Jens-Holger Schjorring, *Grundtvig og Påsken* ('Grundtvig and Easter') (København: Gad, 1987); on Grundtvig, see below n. 37. See also Robert F. Taft, *The Byzantine Rite: A Short History* (American Essays in Liturgy) (Collegeville: Liturgical Press, 1993) p. 18.

35 See, for example, Michael Perham (ed.), *The Renewal of Common Prayer: Unity and Diversity in Church of England Worship: Essays by the Liturgical Commission* (London: Church House Publishing, 1993).

36 Thorndike, *Laws*, in *Works* (Volume IV, Part 1), p. 102; cited above, chapter 6, n. 20.

37 Compare in a different context the work of the nineteenth-century Danish theologian, Nikolai Grundtvig, for whom see 'N. F. S. Grundtvig: the Spirit as Life-Giver', in A. M. Allchin, *The Kingdom of Love and Knowledge* (London: Darton, Longman, and Todd, 1979), pp. 71–9. See also the essays on Grundtvig entitled, *Heritage and Prophecy: Grundtvig and the English-speaking World* (Aarhus: Universitetsforlag, 1993).

38 Patrick, *Mensa Mystica*, in *Works* (Volume I) p. 127.

39 *Fifty-One Sermons Preached by Dr Mark Frank* (Volume I) (Library of Anglo-Catholic Theology) (Oxford: Parker, 1849), p. 359. See also Charles Wheatly, *A Rational Illustration of the Book of Common Prayer* (London: Rivingtons, 1720). I am indebted to Roger Greenacre for drawing my attention to this. The same union of offering in Christ is to be seen in Taylor's Considerations upon the Presentation of Jesus in the Temple: 'And now, besides that we are taught to return to God whatsoever we have received from him, if we unite our offerings and devotions to this holy present, we shall, by the merit and excellency of this oblation, exhibit to God an offertory, in which he cannot but delight, for the

combination's sake and society of his holy Son', *Great Exemplar*, in *Works* (Volume II) 2.

APPENDIX OF SELECT EXTRACTS

1 *Richard Hooker* (? 1554–1600)

LXVII. The grace which we have by the holy Eucharist doth not begin but continue life. No man therefore receiveth this sacrament before Baptism, because no dead thing is capable of nourishment. That which groweth must of necessity first live. If our bodies did not daily waste, food to restore them were a thing superfluous. And it may be that the grace of baptism would serve to eternal life, were it not that the state of our spiritual being is daily so much hindered and impaired after baptism. In that life therefore where neither body nor soul can decay, our souls shall as little require this sacrament as our bodies corporal nourishment. But as long as the days of our warfare last, during the time that we are both subject to diminution and capable of augmentation in grace, the words of our Lord and Saviour Christ will remain forcible, 'Except ye eat the flesh of the Son of man, and drink his blood, ye have no life in you.'[1]

Life being therefore proposed unto all men as their end, they which by baptism have laid the foundation and attained the first beginning of a new life have here their nourishment and food prescribed for *continuance of life* in them. Such as will live the life of God must eat the flesh and drink the blood of the Son of man, because this is a part of that diet which if we want we cannot live. Whereas therefore in our infancy we are incorporated into Christ and by Baptism receive the grace of his Spirit without any sense or feeling of the gift which God bestoweth, in the Eucharist we so receive the gift of God, that we know by grace what the grace is which God giveth us, the degrees of our own increase in holiness and virtue we see and can judge of them, we understand that the strength of our life begun in Christ is Christ, that his flesh is meat and his blood drink, not by surmised imagination but truly, even so truly that through faith we perceive in the body and blood sacramentally presented the very taste of eternal life, the grace of the sacrament is here as the food which we eat and drink.

1. John 6.53.

The Laws of Ecclesiastical Polity, Book V (1597) Chapter 67, section 1.

2 *Lancelot Andrewes* (1555–1626)

This then is the seal. I add further, that it may be rightly called the seal of our redemption, as whereby the means of our redemption is applied unto us; the body and the blood, one broken, the other shed, of Him Whom God 'sealed' to that end, even to redeem us.

And by and with these, there is grace imparted to us; which grace is the very breath of this Holy Spirit, the true and express character of His seal, to the renewing in us the image of God whereunto we are created. And with grace, which serveth properly *pro totâ substantiâ*, to and for the whole substance of the soul, the two streams of it, one into the understanding part, the other into the seat of the affections. Into the understanding part, the assurance of faith and hope; into the part affective, the renewing of charity, the ostensive part of this seal, *in quo cognoscent omnes*, 'by which all men may know,' and *sine quo cognoscet nemo*, without it no man, that we are sealed aright and are truly His. This grace we are thus to receive there; only, that we 'receive it not in vain'; 'be not wanting to it' after; 'neglect it not'; 'quench it not'; 'fall not from it'; but 'stand fast', and 'continue in' it; be careful to 'stir it up'; yea, 'to grow' and increase in it, more and more, even to the consummation of it, which is glory – glory being nothing else but grace consummate, the figure of this stamp in His full perfection.

Resolve then not to send Him away, on His own day, and nothing done, but to receive His seal, and to dispose ourselves, as pliable and fit to receive it. And that shall we but evil do, nay not at all, unless it please Him to take us in hand and to work us ready for it. To pray Him then so to do, to give us hearts of wax that will receive this impression; and having received it, to give us careful minds withal well to look to it, that it take as little harm as our infirmity will permit. That so we may keep ourselves from this unkind sin of grieving Him That hath been, and is, so good to us. Which the God of mercy grant us, for His Son, and by His Spirit, to Whom, &c.

Conclusion to Pentecost Sermon VI (preached on 23rd May, 1613, before King James at Whitehall) From *Ninety-Six Sermons by Lancelot Andrewes*

(Volume III) (Library of Anglo-Catholic Theology) (Oxford: Parker, 1841) pp. 219f).

3 *William Laud* (1573–1645)

'This book' (they say) 'inverts the order of the Communion in the Book of England.' Well, and what then? To invert the order of some prayers, in the Communion, or any other part of the service, doth neither pervert the prayers, nor corrupt the worship of God. For I hope they are not yet grown to be such superstitious cabalists as to think that numbers work anything. For so the prayers be all good (as 'tis most manifest these are), it cannot make them ill to be read in 5, 7, or 3 place, or the like; unless it be in such prayers only, where the order is essential to the service then in hand; as, for example, to read the Absolution first, and the Confession after; and in the Communion, to give the Sacrament to the people first, and read the Prayer of Consecration after. In these cases, to invert the order, is to pervert the service; but in all other ordinary prayers, which have not such a necessary dependance upon order, first, second, or third works no great effect. And though I shall not find fault with the order of the prayers, as they stand in the Communion-book of England, (for, God be thanked, 'tis well;) yet, if a comparison must be made, I do think the order of the prayers, as now they stand in the Scottish Liturgy, to be the better, and more agreeable to use in the primitive Church; and I believe, they which are learned will acknowledge it. And therefore these men do bewray a great deal of will and weakness, to call this a new Communion, only because all the prayers stand not in the same order.

But they say, 'there are divers secret reasons of this change' in the order. Surely there was reason for it, else why a change? But that there was any hidden secret reason for it, (more than that the Scottish prelates thought fit that book should differ in some things from ours in England; and yet that no differences could be more safe than those which were in the order of the prayers; especially since both they and we were of opinion, that of the two this order came nearest to the primitive Church;) truly I neither know nor believe.

As for the only reason given of this change, 'tis in my judgment a strange one. 'Tis, forsooth, 'for no other end,' they say, 'but that the memorial and sacrifice of praise mentioned in it may be understood according to the popish meaning, not of the spiritual sacrifice, but of the oblation of the body of the Lord.' Now ignorance and jealousy, whither will you?' For 'the sacrifice of praise and thanksgiving,' no man doubts but that is to be offered up; nor doth any man of learning question it, that I know, but that according to our Saviour's own command, we are to do whatsoever is done in this office, 'as a memorial of his body and blood offered up and shed for us.' – S. Luc. xxii. Now, 'tis one thing to offer up his body, and another to offer up the memorial of his body, with our praise and thanks for that infinite blessing; so that were that change of order made for this end, (which is more than I know,) I do not yet see how any popish meaning, so much feared, can be fastened upon it. And the words in that prayer are plain, (as they are also in the Book of England,) that 'we offer and present unto God, ourselves, our souls and bodies, to be a reasonable, holy, and lively sacrifice unto Him.' What is there here that can be drawn to a popish meaning, unless it be with the cords of these men's vanity? Yet thus much we have gained from them, that 'this prayer comes in the Book of England pertinently after the Communion.' Any approbation is well of that 'anti-christian Service-book' (as 'tis often called) and I verily believe, we should not have gained this testimony of them for it, but only that they are content to approve that, to make the greater hatred against their own.

Part of Laud's account of his trial, in which he answers criticisms of the Scottish Prayer Book (1637)'s re-ordering of the prayers at Communion to be in line with the First English Book (1549). See *The Works of Archbishop Laud* (Volume III) (Library of Anglo-Catholic Theology) (Oxford: Parker 1853), pp. 343–5.

4 *William Forbes* (1585–1634)

25. And therefore, wrongly do many Protestants teach that this presence and communication is effected by faith because 'faith,' as they say, 'resting upon the word of God, makes things which are promised to be present.' Faith, as is well known, is more properly said to receive and apprehend, than to promise or to bestow. 'It is the word of God and the promise on which our faith rests, and not our faith, that makes present what it promises.' (see Cl. Espencæus concerning the Conference held at Saint Germans between certain Protestants and Romanists in the year 1561 and J. A. Thuanus.[1] The promise of this presence and communication does not indeed work or obtain its effect (which is most especially salutary) save in those who believe with living faith and who worthily communicate, yet the cause and foundation of both is the word of Christ's promise, not our faith.

26. Moreover, it is falsely asserted, that we no otherwise eat the Body of Christ in the Eucharist, than did the Fathers of the Old Testament who believed in Christ. Undoubtedly the ancient believers before the incarnation of Christ, spiritually ate the Flesh of Christ figured in the manna and in other things, and sufficiently for salvation according to the state of that dispensation.

But nevertheless the Catholic Church has always believed that by the communication of the Flesh of Christ in the Eucharist we Christians are incorporated into Christ in a far higher and more solid way than the ancient believers who lived before the incarnation of Christ, who ate the Flesh of Christ only spiritually or by sole faith. 'What the Jews really took in the eating of the Paschal lamb, was nothing but a lamb,' as the Archbishop of Spalatro[2] rightly affirms,' 'food which is of itself consumable. But the Body of Christ although it was spiritually taken by faith yet was not taken in reality but in hope. But truly, our bread exhibits the very real Body of Christ, in reality and not merely in hope. They, therefore, along with the lamb ate Christ by faith of a future and hoped-for thing; but we eat the same Christ, by faith indeed as they did, but by faith of a present thing, which in very deed and not by hope alone is exhibited to us with the bread, yet in a manner which is ineffable, certainly not corporeal; which did not happen to them, and thus they did not eat the Body of Christ in reality &c.' Therefore even if we admit the exposition of the passage, 'Our Fathers did eat the same spiritual meat,' which (as I hinted above) S. Augustine gives, that is, as he says,[3] 'The Hebrew believers ate the same spiritual meat as we do,' (although S. Chrysostom,[4] Theophylact,[5] and others interpret these words much more correctly of the same food being shared among all the Israelites as well good as wicked, but not with us) yet nothing can be concluded therefrom, but that the food of the Jews and Christians is the same, as regards its signification, yet not as regards the presence and exhibition of the thing signified and figured. 'Different is the passover,' says S. Augustine, 'which the Jews celebrate with a sheep, from that which we receive in the Body and Blood of the Lord.' and; 'Their food and drink was the same as ours in mystery; but it was the same in signification not in substance; because the same Christ to them was figured in the rock, to us is manifested in flesh.' It is not absurd, therefore, to say that the paschal lamb, the manna, the rock, &c. were types and figures of the sacrament of the Eucharist, because what they merely signified and figured typically, this not merely signifies and figures, but in very deed exhibits also, but only to the good and the believing, as we shall presently show; although the mystic bread be neither substantially the Body of Christ itself, nor even substantially contains it in itself.

1 *Claude d'Espence* (1511–1571) and *Jacques Auguste de Thou* (1553–1617) at the public colloquium mentioned by Forbes. Whereas d'Espence was Rector of the Sorbonne, de Thou was a statesman who was keen on the French Catholic spirit, and an opponent of unity imposed from elsewhere.

2 *Marco Antonio De Dominis* (1566–1624) was Archbishop of Spalato (not Spalatro, as Forbes' translator indicates) from 1602–1616 (Split, in Croatia). He came to England in 1616 after resigning his office, and was made Dean of Windsor and Master of the Savoy in 1617, though he left England in 1622, and ended his days as a prisoner of the Inquisition. While in England, he took part in the consecration of George Montaigne (1569–1628) as Bishop of Lincoln in 1617; Montaigne went on eventually

to be Archbishop of York in his last year. De Dominis also wrote in England his *De Republica Ecclesiastica*, the first part, which Forbes cites in a note, ch. 6, nn. 49, 51, 97. The fact that Forbes repeatedly refers to him anonymously as the 'Archiepiscopus Spalatensis', and cites this particular work, written after his resignation, suggests that he wants to use a Catholic authority for all its worth. The main thesis of the *De Republica Ecclesiastica* is to argue for independent national Churches.

3 Augustine (354–430) *In Ps 77* and *Tract. 26 in John.*
4 John Chrysostom (c. 347–407), *Homily 23 on 1 Corinthians.*
5 Theophylact, an eleventh-century Byzantine biblical commentator, who modelled himself on Chrysostom.

From *Considerationes Modestae et Pacificae de Controversiarum: De Eucharistia* (Library of Anglo-Catholic Theology) (Oxford: Parker: 846) Book I Of the Real Presence and Participation of Christ in the Holy Eucharist, and the manner of them, Chapter 1, 25–26 (pp. 417–419).

5 *John Cosin* (1594–1672)

True it is, that the Body and Blood of Christ are sacramentally and really (not feignedly) present, when the blessed Bread and Wine are taken by the faithful communicants; and as true is it also, that they are not present, but only when the hallowed elements are so taken, as in another work (the History of the Papal Transubstantiation) I have more at large declared. Therefore whosoever so receiveth them, at that time when he receiveth them, rightly doth he adore and reverence his Saviour there together with the sacramental Bread and Cup, exhibiting His own Body and Blood unto them. Yet because that Body and Blood is neither sensibly present (nor otherwise at all present but only to them that are duly prepared to receive them, and in the very act of receiving them and the consecrated elements together, to which they are sacramentally in that act united) the adoration is then and there given to Christ Himself, neither is nor ought to be directed to any external sensible object, such as are the blessed elements. But our kneeling, and the outward gesture of humility and reverence in our bodies, is ordained only to testify and express the inward reverence and devotion of our souls towards our blessed Saviour, who vouchsafed to sacrifice Himself for us upon the Cross, and now presenteth Himself to be united sacramentally to us, that we may enjoy all the benefits of His mystical Passion, and be nourished with the spiritual food of His blessed Body and Blood unto life eternal.

This our sacrifice of praise and thanksgiving.] That is, this sacrifice of our Eucharist. In which regard, as in divers other besides, the Eucharist may by allusion, analogy, and extrinsecal denomination, be fitly called a sacrifice, and the Lord's table an altar; the one relating to the other; though neither of them can be strictly and properly so termed. It is the custom of Scripture to describe the service of God under the New Testament, be it either internal or external, by the terms that otherwise most properly belonged to the Old, as immolation, offering, sacrifice, and altar. So the evangelical prophet, Esay, foretelling the glory and amplitude of the Christian Church, speaketh of God's altar that shall be there, upon which an acceptable offering shall be made, ch. ii. 4, &c. And the apostle, Rom. xv. 16: 'I labour in the Gospel, that the oblation of the Gentiles may be accepted, being sanctified by the Holy Ghost.' And Phil. ii. 17: 'The service and sacrifice of your faith.' And Heb. xiii. 10: 'We have an altar whereof they (the Jews) are not worthy to eat.' And indeed, the Sacrament of the Eucharist carries the name of a sacrifice, and the table whereon it is celebrated an altar of oblation, in a far higher sense than any of their former services did, which were but the types and figures of those services that are performed in recognition and memory of Christ's own sacrifice, once offered upon the altar of His Cross. The prophecy of Malachy, concerning the Church under the New Testament ('My name is great among the Gentiles, and they shall offer,' or sacrifice, 'unto Me a pure oblation,' Mal. i. 10,) applied by the doctors of the Roman Church to their proper sacrifice (as they call it) of the mass, is interpreted and applied by the ancient fathers sometimes in general to all the acts of our Christian religion, and sometimes in particular to the Eucharist; that is, the act of our praise and thanksgiving for the sacrifice of Christ once made for us upon the Cross, (as here we use in the Church of England.)

Two extracts from the Second Series of Notes on The Book of Common Prayer, first on the consecration prayer, and second on the prayer of oblation; in *The Works of John Cosin* (Volume V) (Library of Anglo-Catholic Theology) (Oxford: Parker, 1855) pp. 345–6 and 346–7.

6 *Daniel Brevint* (1616–1695)

8. Here, then, I come to God's altar with a full persuasion that these words, *This is my body*, promise me more than a figure; that this holy banquet is not a representation made of outward shows without substance; and that it is not so dangerous a mystery, but that the religious use of it may convey to me, (at the least) as many, and as great blessings, as the profane abuse of it may throw on the abuser, plagues and curses. But how these mysteries become in my behalf the supernatural instruments of such blessings, it is enough for me to admire. One thing I know (as said the blind man after he had received his sight, St John ix. 15), *He put clay upon mine eyes, and I washed and do see.* He

hath blessed and given me this bread, and my soul received comfort. I verily believe that clay hath nothing in itself that could have wrought such a miracle as Israel never saw the like; and I know as much of this bread, that it is not such a jewel as may contain in its substance, or impart from itself to others, grace, holiness, and salvation, which is the juice and the substance of Christ's body. Only I am perfectly satisfied, that it is the constant way of God to produce his greatest works at the presence (though not by the virtue) of the most useless instruments. At the very stroke of a rod, He parted once in two the Red Sea. At the blowing some trumpets, He tumbled down massy, strong walls. At some few washings in Jordan, He cured Naaman of a plague which naturally was incurable; and as soon as but a shadow did pass by, or some oil was dropped down, or some clothes were touched, presently virtue went out, not of rods, or trumpets, or shade, or clothes, but of Himself. *Virtue*, says He, *is gone out of me*, – and thus he cured the sick, &c. Since, then, He hath instituted and adopted unto Himself the Sacraments of the Gospel as the representatives of his sacred body and blood: why may he not take the same course for the dispensing of his mercies at the use of his ordinances? and why should not his very body pour out effusions of life, as well when we take in his Sacraments, as when others did touch his clothes, which surely had less privilege?

From *Christian Sacrament and Sacrifice* (Oxford: Vincent, 1847) Section IV, Concerning the Communion, as it is not a representation only, but a means of grace, part 8 (pp. 34f). English edition first published in 1672.

7 *Jeremy Taylor* (1613–1667)

Thirdly the holy sacrament is the pledge of glory and the earnest of immortality; for when we have received him who hath 'overcome death, and henceforth dies no more,' he becomes to us like the tree of life in paradise; and the consecrated symbols are like the seeds of an eternal duration, springing up in us to eternal life, nourishing our spirits with grace, which is but the prologue and the infancy of glory, and differs from it only as a child from a man.[1] But God first raised up his Son to life, and by giving him to us, hath also consigned us to the same state; for 'our life is hid with Christ, in God.'[2] 'When we lay down, and cast aside the impurer robes of flesh, they are then but preparing for glory; and if, by the only touch of Christ, bodies were redintegrate and restored to natural perfections; how shall not we live for ever, who eat his flesh and drink his blood?' It is the discourse of St. Cyril.[3] Whatsoever the Spirit can convey to the body of the church, we may expect from this sacrament; for as the Spirit is the instrument of life and action, so the blood of Christ is the conveyance of his Spirit. And let all the mysterious places of holy Scripture, concerning the effects of Christ communicated in the blessed sacrament, be drawn together in one scheme, we cannot but observe, that, although they are so expressed as that their meaning may seem intricate and involved, yet they cannot be drawn to any meaning at all, but it is as glorious in its sense, as it is mysterious in the expression: and the more intricate they are, the greater is their purpose; no words being apt and proportionate to signify this spiritual secret, and excellent effects of the Spirit. A veil is drawn before all these testimonies, because the people were not able to behold the glory which they cover with their curtain; and 'Christ dwelling in us,' and 'giving us his flesh to eat, and his blood to drink;' and 'the hiding of our life with God,' and 'the communication of the body of Christ,' and 'Christ being our life,' are such secret glories, that, as the fruition of them is the portion of the other world, so also is the full perception and understanding of them: for, therefore, God appears to us in a cloud, and his glories in a veil; that we, understanding more of it by its concealment than we can by its open face, which is too bright for our weak eyes, may, with more piety, also entertain the greatness, by these indefinite and mysterious significations, than we can by plain and direct intuitions; which, like the sun in a direct ray, enlightens the object, but confounds the organ.

1 'medicine of immortality', Ignatius, *ad Ephesos*; 'hope of resurrection', Optatus of Milevis, *Contra Parmenianum* 6; John 6: 54.
2 Col. 3: 3.
3 Cyril of Alexandria, *In Jo.* 14; 'So even our bodies, recieving the Eucharist, are no longer corruptible, having the hope of the resurrection', Irengeus *Contra Haereses* 4: 34.

From *The Great Exemplar* (1649) in *The Whole Works of Jeremy Taylor* (edited by Reginald Heber, revised and corrected by Charles Eden) (Volume II) (London: Longmans, 1852), Discourse XIX, section 9 (pp. 645f).

8 *Richard Baxter* (1615–1691)

When the minister delivereth you the consecrated bread and wine, look upon him as the messenger of Christ, and hear him as if Christ by him said to you, 'Take this my broken body and blood, and feed on it to everlasting life: and take with it my sealed covenant, and therein the sealed testimony of my love, and the sealed pardon of your sins, and a sealed gift of life eternal; so be it, you unfeignedly consent unto my covenant, and give up yourselves to me as my redeemed ones.'

Even as in delivering the possession of house or lands, the deliverer giveth a key, and a twig, and a turf, and saith, 'I deliver you this house, and I deliver you this land;' so doth the minister by Christ's authority deliver you Christ, and pardon, and title to eternal life. Here is an image of a sacrificed Christ of God's own appointing, which you may lawfully use: and more than an image; even as an investing instrument, by which these highest mercies are solemnly delivered to you in the name of Christ.

Let your hearts therefore say with joy and thankfulness, with faith and love, 'O matchless bounty of the eternal God! what a gift this is! and unto what unworthy sinners! And will God stoop so low to man? and come so near him? and thus reconcile his worthless enemies? Will he freely pardon all that I have done? and take me into his family and love and feed me with the flesh and blood of Christ? I believe: Lord, help mine unbelief. I humbly and thankfully accept thy gifts! Open thou my heart, that I may yet more joyfully and thankfully accept them. Seeing God will glorify his love and mercy by such incomprehensible gifts as these, behold, Lord, a wretch that needeth all this mercy! And seeing it is the offer of thy grace and covenant, my soul doth gladly take thee for my God and Father, for my Saviour and my Sanctifier.

'And here I give up myself unto thee, as thy created, redeemed, and (I hope) regenerate one; as thy own, thy subject, and thy child, to be saved and sanctified by thee, to be beloved by thee, and to love thee to everlasting. O seal up this covenant and pardon, by thy Spirit, which thou sealest and deliverest to me in thy sacrament; that without reserve I may be entirely and for ever thine!'

From *A Christian Directory* (1673) Part II, Chapter XXIV, reprinted in *The Practical Works of Richard Baxter* (Volume X) (London: Duncan, 1830) pp. 338–9.

9 *Herbert Thorndike* (1598–1672)

23. And now, I confess, that all they, who do not believe the promises of the Gospel to depend upon any condition to be performed by our free will, qualifying us with a right title to them, may very well say, by consequence, that it is a disparagement to the sacrifice of Christ upon the cross, to make the eucharist a propitiatory and impetratory sacrifice in behalf of the Church, in that sense and to that effect as I have said. But, supposing that condition, I challenge all the world to say, wherein any such disparagement lies. For let not any man think either me, or the doctors of the Church of Rome, so mad, as to ascribe that propitiation, which is once made for the whole world by the sacrifice of Christ upon the cross, to the representation and commemoration of it by the sacrifice of the eucharist. But in regard the Gospel requires a

certain condition at thine hands, which being not performed, to thee Christ is neither born nor crucified nor risen again, as St. Prosper[1] saith; and that the communion of the eucharist professeth the performance thereof, and that truly if it be worthy (so that the propitiation wrought by the cross, thereby becomes effectually thine): in that regard the eucharist becomes to thee a propitiatory sacrifice, by virtue of the consecration indeed (which makes the elements to become the Body and Blood of Christ mystically, as in a sacrament), but yet in order to the participation of it. And is not this the applying of the propitiation wrought by the sacrifice of Christ's cross, whenas by the sacrament of the eucharist a man becomes entitled to the benefit of it? Nor let any man tell me, that this application is wrought by living faith; as if that were evidence enough, that not by the sacrament of the eucharist. For if, notwithstanding this faith, the sacrament of baptism is necessary to estate us in this right, because there is no living faith without being baptized into God's Church; by the same reason (supposing the frequentation of the eucharist commanded for the daily redressing and maintenance of the same title) of necessity it follows, that the application of that propitiation is to be ascribed to the eucharist, which is not applicable without it. Again: if St. Paul enjoin the Church to offer up their prayers, supplications, and intercessions, for all estates in the world, at the celebration of the eucharist, as recommending them in the name of Christ, there mystically present in the commemoration of His death upon the cross; can it seem strange, that the prayers, which are so powerfully presented by alleging an intercession of such esteem, should have a special virtue, and take a special effect, in making God propitious to His Church, and all estates of the same, and obtaining for them those benefits which Christ's passion tenders? And if so, is not the sacrament, by virtue of the consecration, though in order to the oblation and presentation of it by the prayers of the Church for the obtaining of their necessities? What is there in all this, that the tongue of slander can asperse with the imputation of popery; unless they will have popery to be that Christianity which we have received from our Lord Christ and His apostles? But if from hence any man would infer, that, seeing the sacrament of the eucharist (that is to say, the Body and Blood of Christ crucified there present by virtue of the consecration) is a propitiatory and impetratory sacrifice for the congregation there present, for their relations, and for the Church, therefore it is so, whether they proceed to receive the eucharist or not; therefore it is so, whether they proceed to offer up the eucharist present by their prayers for the necessities of the Church, or not: therefore it is so, whether they pray with the Church or not: the consequence will straight appear to fail; because those reasons, which make it such a sacrifice, make it so in order to the receiving, or to the offering of it by the prayers of the Church in behalf of the Church.

1 Prosper of Aquitaine (c. 390–c.463), probably wrote the 'Capitula Coelestini', an

appendix to the letter Pope Celestine I directed to the Bishops in Gaul some time between 435–442, to which Thorndike here refers.

From *The Laws of the Church* (Volume II of the *Epilogue*) in *The Theological Works of Herbert Thorndike* (Volume IV, part 2) (Library of Anglo-Catholic Theology) (Oxford: Parker, 1852) pp. 119–121.

10 *Simon Patrick* (1626–1707)

The distance being taken away between God and us, this sacrament must be considered as a means of our nearer union with our Lord Christ. He doth not only kindly entertain us when we come to his table, but he likewise knits and joins us to himself. He not only ties us with cords of love, and binds us to his service by favours and blessings conferred on us, but in some sort he makes us one with him, and takes us into a nearer conjunction than before we enjoyed. And who would not desire to be enfolded in his arms? Who would not repose himself in his bosom? But who durst have presumed to entertain a thought of being married unto him, and becoming one with him? And yet who would refuse such a favour now that it is offered to us, but they that neither know him nor themselves?

This covenant into which we enter is a marriage-covenant, and our Lord promises to be as a husband to us, and we choose him as the best beloved of our souls. It is none of the common friendships which we contract with him by eating and drinking at his table, but the rarest and highest that can be imagined; and we are to look upon this as a marriage-feast. What this union then with Christ is, it need not be disputed; we may be sure that it is such an one as is between a man and his wife, the vine and the branches, the head and the members, the building and the foundation (as hereafter will more fully appear), yea far beyond all sorts of union, whether moral, natural or artificial, which the world affords example of. That which I am to shew is, that by these sacramental pledges of his love, and this communion with Christ our Lord, we are faster tied unto him, and the ligaments are made more strong and indissoluble between us.

From the *Mensa Mystica: Or, A discourse Concerning the Sacrament of the Lord's Supper* (1660), in *The Works of Simon Patrick, including his Autobiography* (Volume I) (Oxford: University Press, 1858) pp. 143f.

INDEX